ST. MARY'S COLLEGE OF MARYLAND LIBRARY
ST. MARY'S CITY, MARYLAND

W9-AQC-846

MILITARY MEMOIRS

Edited by

Brigadier Peter Young

D.S.O., M.C., M.A., F.S.A., F.R.HIST.S., F.R.G.S.

© *Longman Group Ltd 1971*

This edition first published 1972 by Archon Books,
Hamden, Connecticut

ISBN 0–208–01231–1

Printed in Great Britain

Blaise de Monluc

MILITARY M

Blaise de

The Habsburg-

and the French W

Edite

IAN

ARCHON

Contents

Maps etc.

Note on the Series

by Peter Young

In planning a series of this sort, there is a bewildering variety of factors to be considered. Of these perhaps the chief is the fundamental question: 'Why do people read Military History?' Is it because the truth is more attractive than fiction? Baron de Marbot, although his tales had unquestionably improved in the telling, has an interest which Brigadier Gerard, despite the narrative skill of Conan Doyle, cannot rival. Marbot's memory could play him false in matters of detail, but not as to the sense of period. He brings to life the atmosphere of the Grand Army in which he served. Marbot, regrettably, is too well known, both in French and English, to parade with the veterans of this series. We have endeavoured to present memoirists who for one reason or another are relatively unknown to the English-speaking public.

In modern times, memoir writing seems to have become the prerogative of generals. One is not, however, without hopes of finding a voice or two from the ranks to conjure up the fields of Flanders or the deserts of North Africa. Of course, we have not rejected generals altogether. But on the whole we have tried to rescue 'old swordsmen' from oblivion. The fighting soldier is more attractive than an officer with a distinguished series of staff appointments to his credit; the tented field has an appeal which the dull round of garrison life cannot rival. We have also avoided those veterans who, their Napier at their elbow, submerge their personal recollections in a mass of ill-digested second-hand campaign history. These are the most maddening of all. What details they could have given us had they chosen to!

The trouble is that memoirists take so much for granted. They assume that we know all about the military organization and tactics of their day. And so we must just be thankful for small mercies. You will not get a fight on every page, but gradually a picture is built up. One comes to visualize the manners of a bygone age, to see how people then could endure the privations of a campaign, the rough surgery of the battlefield, or the administrative neglect of their commanders. In the end we come almost to speak their language, and to hear them speak.

Preface

Monluc and his *Commentaries* are reasonably well known in France, hardly at all in England. While the statement of a French historian, that everyone has read the scene in the book where Monluc pleads with his King for permission to bring the enemies of France to battle, should be treated with the same reserve as Macaulay's famous 'every schoolboy knows', it remains true that Monluc is still popularly remembered in his native land. He helped to establish the legend, a century before the existence of D'Artagnan and Cyrano de Bergerac, of the dashing Gascon cavalier, whose sword brings him fame and honour. He has another, less desirable, reputation, as the bloodthirsty avenger of the Religious Wars. The book in which he told the story of his extraordinary career has always been read. The first edition of the *Commentaries*, published in Bordeaux in 1592, circulated widely, and it has been commended to the French reading public for almost four hundred years by a succession of authorities. New editions have appeared in each century.

But this reputation has not crossed the Channel. Although he had a good deal to say about the English, considering his Gascon ancestors half-English and writing of wars in which England was closely involved, Monluc has not reached a wide public in this country. The initial reception seems to have been favourable: his book appeared at a time of great interest, among Englishmen, in things military, and it found its way into the libraries of martial young men such as Henry, Prince of Wales, eldest son of James I. But neglect followed, and succeeding generations of Englishmen have largely ignored the *Commentaries*. There has been only one translation, that of Charles Cotton—a minor Restoration poet, better known as the translator of Montaigne's Essays, which was published in London in 1674 under the title *The Commentaries of Messire Blaize de Montluc*. Neither the French original nor the English translation has been reprinted in England, except for the briefest selections. The misspelling of the author's name has been perpetuated. The references to the *Commentaries* in the principal English authority for Renaissance warfare, Sir Charles Oman's *A History of the Art of War in the Sixteenth Century*, can hardly be said to do justice to it as an important source for the period.

The present edition may be justified on these grounds. It is a selection, of about one quarter of the original, from Cotton's translation. The introduction and footnotes are based largely on the scholarly work of Paul Courteault, whose study of Monluc and his memoirs spanned half a century, and the reader is referred to his editions of the *Commentaries*—in three volumes (Paris, 1911–25), and in one volume in the Bibliothèque de la Pléiade (Paris, 1964)—and to his two books, *Un cadet de Gascogne au XVIe siécle: Blaise de Monluc* (Paris, 1909), and *Blaise de Monluc historien, étude critique sur le texte et la valeur historique des Commentaires* (Paris, 1907). The first scholarly edition of the work, by A. de Ruble, for the Société de l'Histoire de France, in five volumes (1864–72), contains an important selection of Monluc's letters.

My thanks are due, for help and advice generously given, to Peter Young, the general editor of the series, and to Dr N. M. Sutherland, of Bedford College, London. Neither, of course, is responsible for what I have written.

Note. The text used is that of the translation of 1674, but spelling, capitalization and punctuation have been modernized, and some corrections of the translation have been made. Proper names have been given, in the first instance, as in Monluc's original text (ed. P. Courteault, 1964), but in each case followed by their modern form in square brackets, which is used thereafter. Passages or words in Italian, Gascon or Spanish have also been reproduced as in Courteault's edition. Chapter headings and linking passages are supplied by the editor and are in italics throughout. All omissions are indicated by the spacing between paragraphs.

Introduction

The Man and his Career

The date and place of birth of Blaise de Lasseran-Massencome, seigneur de Monluc—to give him his full style and title—are both uncertain. He came of a family of Gascon gentry, long established in an area, roughly midway between Bordeaux and Toulouse, which is drained by the Garonne and its tributaries, the Gers and the Baïse. This region of gently rolling plain, with its sizeable towns, Agen, Nérac and Condom, presents a more prosperous appearance than the harsh mountain landscape traditionally associated with Gascony. It lies on the northern edge of the province, a good hundred miles from the peaks of the Pyrenees and the Spanish border. Gascony in the early sixteenth century, the period we are dealing with, still preserved many traces of its independent character. It had formed part of the dowry Eleanor of Aquitaine had brought to the Plantagenets, and had been ruled by the English crown for over three centuries. Members of the local gentry tended to intermarry and the Monlucs were closely connected to several other landed families of the region, including the noble house of Montesquieu. Their estates had at one time been considerable, but by this date the family were impoverished. It was probably on part of the narrow domain remaining to his father, the castle of St Puy, close to the cathedral city of Condom, that Blaise, one of eleven children, was born, about the year 1501.

He was brought up there, in a castle 'full of children and empty of money',[1] till the age of fifteen or so, when he was apprenticed as a page to the court of Lorraine, in distant Nancy. It was customary for rising sons of the gentry and lesser nobility to gain their education in the houses of the great. Blaise was thus introduced at an impressionable age to the ducal family of which the powerful Guises were a branch; and the connection then made was to prove helpful to him later. At Nancy he gained the groundwork of an education that would enable him, in old age, to cite the classics. He was, however, to show that his interests were not literary but warlike.

It was appropriate that they should be. Gascony enjoyed the reputation of being fertile only in soldiers, its poor upland soil breeding a hardy race, whose sons were forced to seek their fortunes beyond their ancestral walls. The province has provided literature with a type,

[1] Courteault, *Un cadet de Gascogne*, 3.

the poverty-stricken but ambitious young adventurer, brave, proud and boastful, of which the best-known examples are D'Artagnan and Cyrano de Bergerac. Blaise fitted this mould well. His inclinations were to war, and his family circumstances deterred him from remaining long at home. 'We who are come out of the family of Monluc,' he explained later, 'have been constrained to follow the fortunes of the world' [59].[1]

At Nancy he had been dazzled by the brilliant court of the Lorraines, by the tales still told there of the prowess of the old Burgundian chivalry, and by the presence of the knight *sans peur et sans reproche*, the Chevalier Bayard. Monluc served as an archer, that is, light horseman, in the company of which Bayard was Lieutenant. Above all, as a high-spirited young swordsman, his imagination was fired by Italy, then 'the scene of action' [36]. Since Charles VIII had first opened up the rich peninsula to French arms, Italy had been a uniquely attractive goal for the warlike gentry and nobility: it was both an Eldorado and a Wild West, offering in equal abundance, so it was believed, material wealth and all the arts of civilization on the one hand, and adventure and the chance to win 'honour' on the other. As the Valois kings did not hesitate to pawn their thrones to follow war— 'war was the business of kings'—so their subjects thronged the passes into the north Italian plain. Monluc determined to take part in this great adventure and win fame and fortune for himself. He went home, equipped himself as best he could with 'a little money and a Spanish horse' [36], and set out for Milan.

The prime objectives of French strategy were the kingdom of Naples and the duchy of Milan, to both of which the Valois kings laid claim. But the unstable and atomistic character of Italian politics, and the interest of other nations in the fate of Italy, ensured that the French invasions would soon draw in the other great powers of Europe. By the time of Monluc's entry upon his military career Francis I of France and Charles V, uniting in his person Spain and the Empire, were engaged in a series of wars, intermittent rather than continuous, which they and their successors continued until 1559, and which involved the England of Henry VIII, the Papacy and the Ottoman Empire. This general conflict was fought not only in Lombardy, Tuscany and Naples, but on the borders of France with Spain and the Empire, in the Pyrenees, Lorraine and elsewhere.

[1] Page numbers within square brackets, in the Introduction and the Appendixes, refer to the text.

2

Monluc, who came upon this scene about the year 1520, had therefore the promise of long service in arms, in several theatres of war. A young man of gentry family had the choice of serving as a junior officer of foot, or as a gentleman in a troop of horse. An infantry officer in the French armies of the day might expect to lead native foot, such as Gascon or Picard crossbowmen, and fight alongside the great bodies of mercenary Swiss and German pikemen in the pay of France. A cavalryman would serve as a man at arms or one of his lightly armed assistants, an archer. Such was the prestige of the *gendarmerie* that 'in those times', Monluc later wrote, 'several lords and great persons' were prepared to ride as archers [36]. Monluc, a Gascon, with uncles already established in the army to look after him, was quickly preferred to an archer's place in the company of Thomas de Foix, sieur de Lescun, whose forces were drawn largely from Gascony, and he later served as a man at arms. This was an expensive position to uphold, however, and he soon realized his ambition to become an officer of foot. It was with the infantry that he was to make his reputation.

His first forays were in unlucky circumstances. The French commander in Italy, Odet de Foix, Vicomte Lautrec, the brother of Lescun, whom Monluc admired, achieved little in the Milanese, and was defeated at the battle of Bicocca in 1522. Monluc spent a brief interlude on the Spanish frontier with France, then returned to Italy in the forces which Francis I had raised to chase the Imperialists out of south-east France. He was involved in the disastrous defeat of the French army at Pavia (1525), and followed his King into captivity. He was too poor to be worth ransoming, however, and was quickly released. He had no better success when he joined Lautrec for the expedition to the kingdom of Naples two years later. He shared the misfortunes of a campaign in which the army was decimated by plague, lost its chief commanders and was forced to retire with nothing accomplished. Monluc was severely wounded in the arm and leg.

He had totally failed to establish his reputation in the course of these events. His first patron, Lautrec, was dead. In the peace that followed defeat, 1528, he retired to his native Gascony and to the wife he had married two years before. In the next seven years he raised a family, which would eventually consist of four sons, three of whom would follow their father to the wars, and several daughters. Although, as a prudent landlord, he took care to preserve his diminished inheritance, he found civilian life inexpressibly dull and unrewarding: 'the days of peace were whole years to me,' he confesses in his *Commentaries*, 'so impatient I was of lying idle.'[1]

The wars were, however, to break out afresh in 1535. Francis I had reorganized his armies in the year before. In order to improve the quality of the French infantry, the weakest element in his service, the King attempted to create seven legions of foot on a regional basis; and in one of those actually raised Monluc took service as a Lieutenant. He saw action in 1535 as an officer in the forces opposing the Imperialist advance into Provence. More anxious than ever to win honour he volunteered for the hazardous operation of destroying some mills close to the Imperialist positions and which supplied them with flour. He was brilliantly successful, but received no recognition for this feat of arms. Nor was he any more fortunate in 1537, in the campaign in Picardy. The Truce of Nice (1538) brought this phase of the wars to an end.

At the age of forty or so Monluc had seen much of war on the disputed frontiers of France, and in Italy: but he had risen no higher than Captain of foot and had not attracted the attention which he ardently desired and which he felt he deserved. A further interval of peace interposed itself before he once again had the opportunity to prove his ability in action. The scene on this occasion was Piedmont, where both the French and the Imperialists had established strong garrisons. In 1543-44 Monluc undertook a series of daring exploits in and around these fortresses. The ambush laid for the Imperialist governor of Fossano, the destruction of the bridge of Carignano, Monluc's mission to the King to plead for permission to bring the enemy to battle, and the battle itself—the resounding victory of Cérisoles, in which Monluc played a crucial role—all, as recounted by Monluc in the *Commentaries*, read like adventure stories suitable for the *Boy's Own Paper*: and, at last, they transformed his prospects. He was knighted on the battlefield at Cérisoles. In September 1544 he was promoted camp-master—roughly the equivalent of brigadier—while engaged in the siege of Boulogne, recently captured by Henry VIII. He held this command in the forces before Calais, the English foothold in France, and in defence of the French coast against English attack, 1544-45.

Several factors conjoined now to aid Monluc's rapid advancement.

[1] *The Commentaries of Messire Blaize de Montluc, Mareschal of France,* trans. Charles Cotton, (London, 1674), 30. Hereafter cited as *The Commentaries.*

Francis I died in 1547, and the young King, Henry II, had, as Dauphin, observed Monluc's quality on more than one occasion. He was to remain popular with Henry and—equally important for the future—with his Queen, Catherine de Medici. In Picardy also Monluc had caught the eye of François, second Duke of Guise; in this way he resumed acquaintance with the family of Lorraine, at whose house he had been educated, and he attached himself to this rising star at court. His brother Jean, later Bishop of Valence, was also in favour with the King and the Guises; he was well known as a skilled diplomat, having aided in the negotiations which resulted in the celebrated French alliance with the Turks in 1536, and was a persuasive ally of Blaise at court. He needed strong friends near the King, for he had made an enemy of the royal favourite, Anne de Montmorency, Constable of France, and henceforth this influential family was to oppose his every move. But Monluc would flourish so long as Henry was King, the Guise interest prospered, and his brother was well received at court.

He was marked out for early advancement so soon as the wars resumed, and in 1553 won further honours by his skilful siegework in Piedmont. He retired briefly to Gascony—where his fortunes were repaired by the inheritance of the castle of Estillac, near Agen—but was recalled for his greatest charge, the command of Siena, in March 1554. The city of Siena had rebelled against its Imperialist and Florentine overlords in 1552, and had raised the banner of republican liberty and of France, to which it looked for support. A Florentine exile and enemy of Cosimo, the ruler of Florence, Pietro Strozzi, who was also the cousin of the French Queen, was made commander of the French forces in Tuscany; Monluc was to be his deputy in Siena itself. He arrived there in July 1554. Shortly afterwards Strozzi was defeated by the Imperialists, and he and other representatives of France left Siena, entrusting the city, now environed by the enemy, to the care of Monluc. The siege that followed, Monluc's heroic resistance until forced by starvation and sickness among the population to render the city six months later, became the most famous chapter of his memoirs and firmly established his high reputation. He was fêted by the court on his return, made Colonel-General of the infantry and *Chevalier de l'Ordre du Roi*. He consolidated his success by further distinguished services in Piedmont (1555–57), and under Guise, his patron, at the taking of Thionville on the Moselle in the summer of 1558. This was the climax of his military career.

His good fortune was, however, brittle. A financial crisis and mutual exhaustion forced the great powers to make peace at the Treaty of Cateau-Cambrésis, 1559. By its terms the claims of France in Italy were given up, and most of the strongholds in Savoy and Piedmont, fought over for more than twenty years, were abandoned. At a stroke of the pen, Monluc and other military men complained, the means whereby the warlike gentry of France had been supplied with place, enrichment and honour for two generations were much diminished;[1] the peace put an end to lucrative military governorships in occupied territories and a host of other profitable commissions. Worse was to follow. Henry II, Monluc's 'good master', was accidentally killed whilst jousting during the celebrations for the peace; and in the following year Henry's eldest son, the new King, Francis II, died. These disasters, and the prospect of a long minority, weakened the authority of the crown, and encouraged the growth of feuds at court. Many were converted to the Reformed faith.

These events bore heavily on Monluc. He lost his post of Colonel-General of foot—and the considerable patronage which went with it—to d'Andelot, its original possessor, and his own troop was reduced. While Francis II lived the Guises were influential, but on his death they were quickly displaced and throughout 1561 remained in eclipse. In that year Catherine, as Regent, and the Bourbons, were predominant. With the confusion of the present political situation and the uncertainty of the future, the decline of his friends and the loss of his commissions, Monluc's fortunes seemed to have reached their nadir.

For two years he joined the crowd of out-of-work officers who clamoured at court for their pay or drifted close to one or other of the factions which were struggling for supremacy in the kingdom. Huguenotism exacerbated this situation, for, although, as Monluc said, 'the martial sort of men are not very devout', the Protestant churches provided an outlet for their talents; they could profit from the fact that a division on religious grounds was—in that age—almost unbridgeable [230]. Thousands of old soldiers, released from royal service, disobeyed the injunctions of the court to keep to their old faith and their ancient loyalty to the crown; instead they swelled the ranks of one faction or another. For a period in 1560–62 Monluc himself inclined towards the Huguenots of south-west France, who had set up, under the powerful patronage of the Navarre family, 'a

[1] H. Lapeyre, Les Monarchies Européennes du XVIe siècle, 143.

sort of military republic'.[1] He may have hoped, in these troubled years, to attach himself to the Navarre interest and to find a new patron in Jeanne d'Albret, Queen of Navarre. He listened to the attractive offers made him by the Huguenots of the military leadership of their cause, and he attended the Reformed church at Nérac, actually aiding in the service there when Theodore Beza, Calvin's chief emissary and his successor, came to preach and encourage the faithful. This is why Beza, remembering the occasion later, described Monluc as an apostate. His brother, the Bishop of Valence, was sympathetic to the reformers, helping to arrange the Colloquy of Poissy in 1561, which attempted to bring all sides in the religious dispute together. But Monluc fell out with the court of Navarre—Antoine was ineffective and wavered in his allegiance to the Huguenots, but Jeanne d'Albret was a formidable opponent—and came to view the local Huguenots as subversive: with their private armies, incipient democracy and hostility to the crown, their refusal to pay tithes to the established church and rent to their landlords, he saw them as a threat to the old Gascon nobility. In fact he was little attached to religion, and soon abandoned a cause that did not interest him. With this decision he quickly became the champion of the old order from Bordeaux to Toulouse, leading the crusade against the reformers in the first religious war of 1562–63, winning the battle of Vergt and becoming the royal Lieutenant in Guienne.

With the protection of the Queen Mother, Catherine de Medici, who favoured him as her husband had done, Monluc executed royal policy in the south-west. He kept the peace in Guienne for five years, a feat of which he was justifiably proud. But it was not achieved without considerable bloodshed. He made his reputation as a hammer of the Huguenots, believing that 'One hanged man is worth a hundred killed in battle'.[2] From his capital at Agen and his newly rebuilt castle at Estillac close by, his armies terrorized the opposition. He raised the first of the Catholic leagues in France, putting himself at the head of the loyal Gascon nobility; and, like the later Catholic League of the Guises, looked to Philip II of Spain for help. Secret messages ran back and forth between Agen and Madrid.[3] Monluc, it was later alleged, offered Philip the conquest of south-west France if he would aid in the suppression of the Navarres and save the nation from Huguenotism.

[1] N. L. Roelker, *Queen of Navarre*, 163.

[2] Quoted in A. W. Whitehead, *Gaspard de Coligny*, 126.

[3] H. Forneron, *Histoire de Philippe II*, I, 293–302, 342–3.

So long as straightforward suppression of the Huguenots was required Monluc proved a capable and untiring servant of the state. But more subtle shifts in royal policy left him stranded. He found in the renewed conflicts of 1567–68 and 1568–70, and the peacemaking of those years, that it was increasingly difficult to satisfy all parties. He was blamed for allowing the Queen of Navarre to pass through Guienne in 1567, but was then prevented from undertaking the siege of La Rochelle, the Huguenot 'capital' to which she had retired. The Duke of Guise, his old patron, had been assassinated in 1563. Envy of his large appointment in Guienne—such a charge was normally reserved for *les grands*—quickly accumulated. The hostility of the Queen of Navarre to this interloper in 'her' province was unremitting: she was unlikely to forget that he had pressed for an attack on her strongholds in Béarn and had declared his eagerness 'to find out if it was as much fun to sleep with queens as with other women'.[1] His enemies at court, particularly the Montmorencies, raised a clamour against him. They claimed that his campaigns against the Huguenots had been marked by excessive brutality and gross peculation: Monluc —the charges ran—was a *forceur de filles*, and he had enriched himself at the King's expense, diverting fines on Huguenots and profits from their sequestrated estates from the crown to his own pocket. He was accused, with justice, of treasonable dealings with the King of Spain. These divisions culminated in his great quarrel with Marshal Damville, the son of the Constable, who was Governor of Languedoc. Faced with revolt in Agen he had asked Damville for aid, and this had been refused. At the same moment that his enemies gathered for the *coup de grace*, Monluc was severely wounded in the face by an arquebus shot while leading an assault—at the age of seventy or thereabouts— on the small but well fortified Navarre stronghold of Rabastens, in the Pyrenees. In the following month, August 1570, the Peace of St Germain marked the beginning of a period of accommodation with the Huguenots, and the growing influence with the King of those— such as Damville, or those Protestants sympathetic to the Dutch rebels against Spain—who were hostile to the Guises. Monluc was viewed as a Guisard and pro-Spanish, and as an intransigent Catholic who would be unwilling to carry out the terms of the peace. It was natural that the hammer of the Huguenots, now *hors de combat*, should be dropped. He was relieved of his post and disgraced, while a commission was set up to investigate the complaints against him.

[1] Roelker, *Queen of Navarre*, 196.

This train of events had exposed certain weaknesses in Monluc. His many soldierly qualities had not been sufficient to ensure his success in the delicate political climate of his day. He lacked the finesse of his brother, the subtle negotiator, and could not find the suppleness to bend to each new wind that blew. He now paid the penalty for these shortcomings. He found himself with a period of enforced leisure, in which to convalesce and to take stock of his position. He gradually recovered from his wound, though his face was so shattered that he had to wear a mask for the rest of his life. He was a lonely and embittered old man. His remarriage, to the daughter of a prominent local family, and the raising of a new family in his old age—the christening of the first child of this match had taken place, while he still enjoyed royal favour, in the presence of the King and the Queen Mother—scarcely compensated for the loss, already, of two of his soldier sons in battle and the death of a third shortly afterwards. His fall from grace galled him. What would debauch a man from royal service? the French King had asked a Gascon gentleman. 'Nothing sir,' replied the other, 'unless it be a despite.'[1]

But simply to brood on his misfortune would have been out of character for Monluc. He set about clearing his name and recovering his position. He determined to write his memoirs, partly to assuage the bitterness of defeat—consoling himself with the great adventure story of his life, of how 'a poor cadet of Gascony' could arrive 'at the highest dignities of the kingdom' [226]—and partly to draw the attention of the royal family to his many and great services to the crown. In the winter months of 1570-71 the major part of the autobiographical work later published as his *Commentaries* was first drafted.

Monluc's book, though it remained for the time being in manuscript, had the desired effect. Its circulation in the right quarters, and further changes in the political climate, led to his being restored to favour in 1572. He was cleared of the charges against him; and when, in 1574, the Duke of Anjou, to whom he had dedicated his work and at whose court his brother was an important counsellor, became King Henry III, further rewards were heaped upon him. He was created Marshal of France, and honoured everywhere. Three years later he died close to his boyhood home of St Puy, at Condom, where his only surviving son was bishop, and was buried in the cathedral there.

[1] *The Commentaries*, 375.

The Commentaries *and their value*

As we have seen, Monluc's memoirs were written, largely in the period November 1570 to May 1571, in part for his own enjoyment and partly to vindicate himself from the aspersions of his detractors. His work began life as a brief *mémoire justicatif*, which he then expanded into a full chronicle of his career. Although an old man, and recovering from his wound, he kept his secretaries busy during the winter of its composition, rapidly dictating the recollections of his long and extraordinary life. He was not, however, wholly satisfied with the result. As a Gascon, he found that he could express himself easily and well—he had always prided himself on his eloquence, thought necessary to a commander of the period—but he very much regretted that he did not possess the learning and the wit of a Brissac or a Lorraine, or indeed of his own brother, to produce a more finished and scholarly work. So in 1572, having completed the first draft of his book, he began to correct, embellish and enrich his work by borrowings from the 'histories' of other writers, particularly for the first part of his narrative dealing with the Habsburg-Valois Wars, where he had been unable to supply from memory all the details he had wanted. For this earlier period he used and imitated Martin and Guillaume du Bellay, whose *Memoirs*, dealing with the wars of Francis I and Henry II, had appeared in 1569. Monluc borrowed the title 'Commentaries' for his work from du Bellay. For the last ten years of civil war his memory was fresh, and his account of recent events, based on documents, was reasonably complete—or at least as complete as he wished to make it. The final version of his manuscript was published posthumously at Bordeaux in 1592.

He was also influenced by classical examples. In Renaissance France even a soldier's autobiography could not escape the influence of the rediscovery of the ancient world. Monluc took Caesar as his model; he acknowledged him as 'the greatest captain that ever lived' [32], and was sufficiently the Gascon to liken his own work to that of Caesar's *Commentaries*. He displayed a knowledge of Livy, whose history and maxims he freely plundered.

In spite of these additions to his original manuscript Monluc disclaimed any high purpose for his book. 'I pretend not to be an historian', he said;[1] his memoirs were those 'of a soldier, and moreover a Gascon' [32]. They would be read by other soldiers and men of the

[1] *The Commentaries*, 218.

world, like the author, and not by scholars, who, he said, have enough to read already. Monluc's awareness of the audience he was addressing presents us with another reason for the writing of the *Commentaries*. He considered his book as a practical and instructive work on the art of war, a storehouse of military examples which might be of use to 'young soldiers'. This colours his approach to events: he was not writing an impartial chronicle, but a memoir, vivid, fresh and personal. What was significant was an action he had witnessed, however small, if it held lessons for the young soldier; and not an event he had not seen, however important to the historian. Thus he leaves the battle of Pavia to other hands—more skilful historians than he claims to be—and contents himself with a brief relation of his own very minor role in that famous disaster.

For this reason Monluc thought it proper to interrupt his narrative occasionally, to instruct his readers in tactics, strategy, fortification and the principles of leadership in war. He turned aside from the events he was describing to ponder their military significance. His readers might profit from his example: he commends some actions to be followed—'Do the same upon the like occasion.' Others equally reveal the pitfalls to be avoided. This didactic and even moral purpose behind the *Commentaries* is not obtrusive, however; his work is not principally a collection of military and political maxims such as that of the Huguenot captain, François de La Noue, nor is it primarily a treatise comparable with Fourquevaux's *Instructions sur le Faict de la Guerre* on the military world of Francis I. It is not a work of reflection and gathered wisdom. Even with the additions he made to it, Monluc's method of composition would have rendered that impossible. The *Commentaries*, it has been said, are above all concerned with people and events of the sixteenth century, not with ideas.[1]

Monluc set out to praise famous men and signal achievements. He spoke warmly of his masters, from Francis I to the Duke of Anjou, and of the generals under whom he had served. He would not, he said, 'set a mark upon those who behaved ill' [50]. He showed his particular loyalty to and admiration for Lautrec, *ce grand Odet*, with whom he had served his apprenticeship in arms, and whose death was such a blow to his prospects of advancement. He agreed with Fourquevaux, another of the Marshal's admirers, in commending the example of Lautrec to young officers. Win your soldiers' loyalty, advised Monluc, by firm yet friendly discipline; know the names of your men; and

[1] Courteault, *Blaise de Monluc historien*, 610.

note the exploits of your subordinates, to bring them to the notice of your superiors, as Lautrec did for Monluc himself. Over forty years after Lautrec's death Monluc could write, of his own part in a successful battle: 'I have learnt these lessons under the late Monsieur de Lautrec, who was a brave commander.'[1]

At the same time Monluc was critical of the unstinting admiration of some 'official' historians, particularly du Bellay, for the great and powerful, to the exclusion of men of lesser degree. 'Historians', he complained, 'write only of kings and princes.'[2] His concern for the truth as he saw it, for the actions which he himself had witnessed, gave Monluc a rather different perspective. He showed how innumerable and unregarded small actions, and the heroism of minor characters, could influence the outcome of great events. His own exploit as a young and obscure officer, the destruction of the mills of Auriol, was a case in point: great battles and sieges were won by the cumulative effect of such deeds, and Monluc's concern for the particular and the seemingly trivial is often more revealing than the stereotyped accounts of the chroniclers. He championed the cause of the underdog because this was his own cause for most of his life. He cast his quarrel with the powerful Montmorencies, not without justice, as that of the poor cadet of Gascony whose ambitions were frustrated by the jealousy of the great.

How accurate is the story Monluc tells? Monluc was a Gascon, a people famous for their mendacious boastfulness; moreover he admitted to many of the faults of his race, and it is a simple matter to trace in his memoirs the exaggeration of his own part in many actions, the inflation, generally, of his own importance. The purpose of the book, after all, was to show its author in the best possible light; discreditable episodes were omitted, while he enlarged, with invented or borrowed detail, his description of others where he had emerged with credit. It should be remembered also that he was over seventy when he came to write his memoirs, and it may be doubted whether his memory then was as 'good and entire' as he claimed it was [33]. 'I will write nothing by hearsay', he had promised at the beginning of his book [38]: but, as we have seen, he had to borrow from other authors in order to correct and supplement his own recollection of distant events. For the earlier years, particularly, he omitted a good deal, and placed events in the wrong order. His description of

[1] *The Commentaries*, 266.
[2] *Ibid.*, 397. See also [195].

Montmorency fighting on foot at Bicocca, the background for the campaign of 1524-25, and some of the embroidery in his account of the interview with Francis I, he owed to du Bellay. He suppressed completely any account of his activities after 1559 which might be considered doubtfully loyal.

But in spite of these failings, intentional or otherwise, Monluc's writing has great value. His long life encompassed so many developments, political and military, that he is often the best and sometimes the only eyewitness of great events. His skill in constructing his narrative, and his considerable powers of description, outweigh, in most cases, the errors and omissions. His fame as a raconteur, in his own lifetime, which made him welcome at the court of Henry II and his Queen—whose tastes were distinctly masculine—depended on his excellent memory for the telling detail: and this is perhaps the main characteristic of his memoirs. His eye for ground was that of the practised soldier, and his accounts of the 'camisado' of Boulogne, the siege of Siena or the attack on Thionville gain from his ability to remember the terrain exactly, in which these events took place, the particular actions, however small, which occurred, and the obscure and otherwise unregarded individuals who took part. His description of the camisado is marked by its attention to topographical detail, much superior to du Bellay. If there is no documentary support for his account of the meeting with Francis I, there is equally no evidence to disprove it; and his minute description has all the verisimilitude of direct reporting. His narrative of Cérisoles—the prime source for the battle—is detailed and mainly accurate. His long chapter on the siege of Siena is full and evocative, and is naturally dramatic. He muddled many of the incidents of a long siege, and his account often lacks perspective—as a participant he saw more of one part of an action than another—but a comparison with other sources shows how well the former governor of the city told the celebrated story of its defence. Where his accuracy can be tested, as here, we can see that the detailed descriptions he gives, after an interval of up to fifty years in some cases, are remarkably fresh.

Monluc was an observer, over a long period, of changes of great importance in military affairs. He had taken part in five pitched battles, seventeen assaults and eleven sieges. He had begun his career in the same company as the Chevalier Bayard, an exemplar of old-fashioned chivalry; he was till active in the field in the age of Henry of Navarre, the Duke of Alba and William the Silent. Half a century of warfare, the Habsburg-Valois Wars fought in Italy, Piedmont, the Pyrenees and northern France, and the wars of religion in France, are passed in review by Monluc in his *Commentaries*. It is possible to trace in his pages the decisive changes which affected warfare during these years.

The introduction of the earliest form of handgun, the arquebus, is a case in point. In his account of the action at St Jean de Luz, in 1523, he notes that the French forces were without any arquebusiers, and that he had to borrow some Gascon arquebusiers who had deserted from the other side [41]. Spain had pioneered the effective use of the handgun in its wars with the Moors, and had already employed it in Italy under Gonsalvo de Cordoba. Monluc, in the *Commentaries*, made the routine moral condemnation of 'this accursed engine' [41], which allowed an unseen and baseborn assailant to kill at a distance the most splendid knight at arms. How many courageous gentlemen had been slain by this cowardly firestick?[1] But although firearms were not generally adopted in the armies of France until the 1530s, they bulk large in Monluc's pages henceforth. He aspired to command of foot— to set oneself up as a man at arms was an expensive business, and many poor gentlemen preferred to fight on foot—and quickly appreciated the importance of the new weapon. He employed it in the defence of the Maddalena at Naples in 1528; and to protect his men from cavalry attack, in a skirmish with a party of Spanish horse.[2] He soon found how to minimize casualties from volleys of the enemy—getting his men to kneel or to lie flat on the ground—and how to use 'good smart claps of arquebus shot' to halt an advance even by determined horsemen.[3] At Cérisoles he commanded the French arquebusiers, and intermingled some of them with the bodies of pikemen in order to surprise the enemy with a volley of shot—an early instance of the successful combination of these arms [103, 110–11]. His account of the battle is important evidence for the crucial role they played. He knew its effectiveness at first hand: three of his four sons were to die in battle, and all were killed by arquebus shot. He himself bore the marks of seven gunshot wounds: only his right arm remained, providentially, unharmed. His dead sons and his shattered face were testimony to its power.

[1] *The Commentaries*, 118.

[2] *Ibid.*, 19–21, 53–4.

[3] *Ibid.*, 40.

In the same period, and partly in response to the development of infantry firepower, heavy cavalry had to alter its traditional role in battle, to accept new weapons and introduce new tactics. Under the youthful Francis I, as under his predecessors in Italy, the most glorious arm of the French forces had been the *gendarmerie*, the heavily armoured and well-mounted men at arms who were generally considered the arbiter of battles. 'Our *gendarmes* in those days', wrote Monluc of 1543, 'wore great cutting falchions, wherewith to lop off arms of mail, and to cleave morions'.[1] The great nobility of France furnished their splendid accoutrements; they were representative of the most brilliant and courageous gentry in Europe, and they were led by the King himself. They acted, said Fourquevaux, as the 'very shield of the realm'.[2] Their method of attack was simply a frontal assault, in which their great weight, heavy weapons and the fear they inspired, would carry them through all opposition. Nothing, it was believed, could withstand the onward rush and the swordsmanship of the heavy cavalry.

But first the development of the pike, which *en masse* formed an impenetrable barrier to the charging horseman, and then the firearm, which felled him at long range, challenged this supremacy, much as the French knight had been humbled by the English archers in the Hundred Years War. The *gendarmerie* were brought low at Pavia in 1525, when Francis himself and his fellow cavalrymen met the fire of the Imperialist arquebusiers; their slaughter and the King's capture were traumatic experiences for the French nation. The traditional heavy lance, and with it the direct attack on enemy positions, was gradually abandoned. 'We quit them', Monluc was to write of the French lances, 'for the German pistols'.[3] The wheel-lock pistol had been developed in the 1540s—it was the first firearm fully suitable for use on horseback, although mounted arquebusiers were already well known—and was brought into general service by the German reiters; they were successful at St Quentin (1557) against French lancers.[4] Monluc observed some pistoliers—along with mounted arquebusiers —in the Huguenot cavalry six years later. It had the advantage, in his opinion, that the horse could attack in great bodies and not in thin

[1] *The Commentaries*, 44.

[2] *The Instructions sur le Faict de la Guerre of . . . Fourquevaux*, ed. G. Dickinson, xxxv.

[3] *The Commentaries*, 388.

[4] F. Lot, *Recherches sur les Effectifs des Armées Francaises . . . 1494–1562*, 92, 157.

lines. The adoption of the pistol altered the tactics of the horse; charges were no longer pressed home; rather the cavalry discharged their pistols at the lines opposing them, before completing their attack. Cavalry answered firepower with firepower.

Another development whose growing importance can be traced in the *Commentaries* was artillery. Monluc achieved a more balanced judgment on the use of cannon, drawn from his own experience, than did many others. Both siege and field artillery had had a notable impact on the Italian wars from the end of the fifteenth century. But Monluc did not exaggerate their effectiveness. It had seemed to some observers that no town could withstand the battering of the improved heavy cannon, or armies a concentrated bombardment in the field. In the first campaign of the French in Italy towns had surrendered with great rapidity; and by the time of the battle of Ravenna, in 1512, victory could be attributed in part to the use of artillery. But improvements in defence soon kept pace with improvements in cannon. As a young man Monluc had observed with great interest the defensive works constructed by the foremost military engineer of the day, Pedro Navarro; by the 1520s it was possible to defend beleaguered places and to entrench troops in the field successfully. Such works, Monluc found as a commander, could dispel the fears which were still entertained of the power of the cannon. At Cérisoles in 1544 his men were restive under the continual heavy gunfire of the Imperialists and pressed for an attack on the enemy, preferring, as they said, to die in hand to hand combat than to be killed at long range. But Monluc was able to restrain them until the right moment, observing that cannon 'begets more fear than it does harm' [107]. Great terror was struck into the Sienese when Marignano brought up his siege train of large pieces; but again Monluc calmed his followers; they prepared for the bombardment, and the breaches made by the cannon were quickly repaired. Only raw soldiers and amateur strategists could believe that artillery alone could topple towers and win battles.

He applied principles at Siena, in defence, and at Thionville, in attack, which were in advance of their time. He saw the need for defence in depth, as did many others, against the penetrative power of the cannon ball, building a series of earth defences which presented a low profile to the attacker. He had observed, in Piedmont, how the preparation of new works behind the fortifications under attack—retrenchment—could be proof against assault. By continually and unwearyingly spying out the enemy's intentions at Siena he was able to retrench the works Marignano had selected for attack. He developed this tactic to the point where he could ambush an attacker who had penetrated the first lines of defence [152–55].

Monluc displayed to the full his qualities as a commander at the siege of Thionville, where he planned the assault which was to lead to its fall. He spied out the enemy defences and explored its weakest point. He carefully protected his pioneers constructing the approach trenches. Resourceful and cautious, he anticipated a counterattack on the trenches by building 'places of arms', as they came to be called in the next century, to defend them. 'At every twenty paces', Monluc wrote, 'I made a back corner, or return', a space, at right angles to the trench, in which could be concealed a dozen or more arquebusiers and from which they could enfilade the trench [179–80]. These places proved to be the preservation of the works already made when the attack came. They served, as Monluc said, as forts for his own troops [184]. The concept of defence in attack thus introduced was developed in the seventeenth century by Vauban.

On a larger scale Monluc appreciated the strategic importance of fortresses. He well describes, in the *Commentaries*, the difficulty an invader of France encountered in the great number of defensible places, apart from Paris, in which the nation abounded [117]. In describing the abortive siege of La Rochelle, of 1567, he pointed out—as La Noue, its later governor, was also to do—the immensely strong position of the city, with its massive fortifications and its access to the sea. He foresaw its importance to the Huguenots, who made it their capital in 1567 and were to defend it brilliantly under La Noue in wars to come. The failure to take it for the King would have wide repercussions, argued Monluc, particularly if the English, or any other seaborne power should come to their assistance [213]. He clearly stated the problem Richelieu had to face sixty years later, when Buckingham's expeditions to the Isle of Ré and to La Rochelle complicated the minister's plans for the reduction of the city.

The development of increased firepower of one kind or another, and the improvement in defence techniques, made a war of attack dangerous. Generals hesitated to pit their men against an enemy drawn up in good order. The memory of defeat at Bicocca and Pavia made French commanders particularly cautious: before Cérisoles d'Enghien suffered agonies of hesitation [100–2]. These changes can be followed in the *Commentaries*. The resounding battles of the early pages give way gradually to sieges, great and small, and campaigns in which a succession of skirmishes and other minor actions are fought between parties from opposing strongholds. The control of fortified towns, and the area around their walls, the conservation of precious resources, and the regular payment of their troops, become the chief concerns of the generals in the field. For these purposes infantry were more useful than heavy cavalry; the number of the latter decline as the strength and variety of the former increase.

The new importance of foot required that France should have a good supply of reliable infantry. In contrast to her glorious and expensive cavalry, native French infantry were of poor quality. Some areas of France produced hardy soldiers—Monluc's Gascon bowmen performed wonders in Lombardy in 1527—but in general the Valois kings were forced to hire foreign mercenary infantry for their armies. With his long experience of wars where mercenaries were employed by both sides, Monluc was well aware of the drawbacks of non-native troops. The Swiss, who were the main source of pikemen for the service of France, were courageous, but obstinate and wilful; they were good in attack, but of no use for the defence of places; and they were always liable to desert if their pay failed, 'for they are not to be paid with words' [38].

Monluc therefore welcomed the reforms of Francis I, who introduced in 1534 the ordinances setting up seven legions, each of 6,000 men, to be recruited in different areas of the realm. The idea of a native militia appealed to him, as it had done to Fourquevaux, who had made it a main plank of his reform platform, and to Machiavelli, who had recommended the recruitment of such a citizen army, on the Roman republican model, to his native Florence.[1] Monluc echoed these sentiments when he wrote that a native militia, patriotic and virtuous, was 'the true and only way to have always a good army on foot (as the Romans did)' [60]. He recognized the difficulties in the way of achieving this reform: not all Frenchmen were as naturally warlike as his own Gascons [217]; the levies were badly organized, and the officers were corrupt. When, in the 1550s, Monluc was Colonel-General of the infantry, the foot outnumbered the horse by ten to one; yet the bulk of the infantry in French pay remained foreign mercenaries.

Monluc was not so critical of his country's defences as Fourquevaux had been in the 1540s, nor did he set out a considered plan of reform.

[1] *The Instructions sur le Faict de la Guerre of . . . Fourquevaux*, ed. G. Dickinson, Introduction, § III. N. Machiavelli, *Arte della Guerra*, I and VII, and *The Prince*, XII, XIII, XXVI.

But in the 'Remonstrance to the King'—Charles IX—which he incorporated in his work, he indicated the disquiet of 'an old soldier' at the ease with which favourites, promoted at court by 'importunate lords and ladies', could be given high office in the army. He criticized the waste and disorder caused by the increase in the number of officers thought necessary for the command of men, since the days of his youth, and advised the king to select his officers by some form of examination, conducted by old captains of great experience. Once selected, said Monluc, 'advance them according to their quality and desert'.[1]

But was France any worse in these respects than other nations? As occasion served Monluc commented on the quality of the opposition. In general the Spanish and German soldiers had more endurance than the French. 'Our nation', he admitted, 'cannot suffer long' [80]. The Gascons, France's finest soldiers, were notoriously lacking in patience. Even the unwarlike citizens of Italy could endure hardships if the cause was good. He was unstinting in his praise of the Sienese, who, like the proverbially mercurial citizens of Florence in their heroic defence of that city in 1530, showed that their factious and hot-tempered natures—so like his own—could be brought under control and steeled to endurance when the fate of their city was in the balance.

As to France's traditional enemy, England, Monluc set out to unravel an old conundrum, which he called 'the mystery of the English' [129]. Why did they enjoy such a high reputation as fighting men, when, as he believed and was to demonstrate, they were no braver than any other nation? He recognized the superiority of English sea-power, which France found it hard to challenge. But in the course of the campaign before Boulogne and Calais in 1544-45 he concluded that the English were vulnerable and decided to expose them. He prepared an ambush: and when, according to plan, the trap was sprung, they showed a clean pair of heels. Why had they been considered invincible? One explanation was that they still persisted with bill and bow, when the French infantry had modern firearms; and their reputation for courage was based on the fact that, as archers, they were forced to come in close to their enemies before letting fly their arrows. Monluc had himself felt the force of this argument at the camisado of Boulogne, when a party of English had sallied out and had, as he said, 'bestowed some arrows' upon him as they chased him

1 *The Commentaries*, 382–9.

across a river and up a hill in the pouring rain [123-5]. But following the ambush Monluc offered another explanation of the 'mystery', highly characteristic of the author: 'The English who anciently used to beat the French were', he claimed, 'half Gascons', through their possession of the Duchy of Aquitaine, of which Gascony was part. 'But now that race is worn out and they are no more the same men they were' [130]. 'I discovered them', he concluded, 'to be men of very little heart and believe them to be better at sea than by land' [127].

The miseries of war are plainly stated in the *Commentaries*, without sentimentality but not without pity. The peasantry of France bore, like beasts of burden, the vast expense of the gentry's warlike activities. The Italian wars, admitted Monluc, caused untold suffering [37]. He lamented that princes required their soldiers to undertake cruelties and so made the military calling, which he considered glorious, unpopular with the common people [224]. He was a strict disciplinarian and an uncompromising soldier, and in his dealings with the Huguenots in particular he showed himself harsh and unfeeling. But he obeyed the rules of war, which were in this century becoming standardized and widely accepted. He exercised mercy when it was merited, attempting to save life at the taking of Forcha di Penne [54]. Occasionally, as when he and his opponent exchanged Christmas gifts during the siege of Siena, the severity of war could be ameliorated by polite behaviour [138-9]. On the other hand, at Rabastens, the laws of war, if not common humanity, permitted him to take revenge for his dreadful wound on the lives of all within the garrison. It was, however, often a breakdown in the proper conduct of a campaign or a siege which caused the greatest suffering. Non-payment of troops led to plundering, indiscipline to crimes against the civilian population. The destruction of a town taken by assault was usually contrary to the orders of the besieging commander—as at Rome in 1527, or Magdeburg in 1631. There are several indications in the *Commentaries* that its author was moved at times by the plight of the innocent victims of the wars he waged. His account of the driving out of the helpless *bocche inutile* at Siena shows a genuine sympathy for the unfortunate [165-6].

But in spite of this awareness of the horrors of war Monluc celebrated, in the *Commentaries*, the profession of arms, and the qualities of the warlike gentry of France, of whom he was proud to be one. The cadet of Gascony, like the penurious Scottish laird, Irish squireen or Castilian hidalgo, was denied entry into trade and the professions and looked to a military career, to war and foreign conquest, as a means of bettering his prospects. As Monluc said of his own children, who were not content to stay at home: 'Their desire is rather to gain goods and honours, and in the winning of them to hazard their persons and lives, and even serve the Turk rather than remain idle. If they did otherwise, I should not look upon them as mine.'[1] The military calling was one in which the man of talent might rise by his own merits. Monluc had seen 'the sons of poor labouring men . . . through their own virtue' achieve wealth, honour and reputation [226]. He himself had been a poor man and had found war profitable. It was through service in arms that a gentleman could win fame, and for such as Monluc 'a good reputation and renown are immortal as the soul' [232].

Crowned heads should and did honour the profession of arms. The story is told in the *Commentaries* of how the King of France and the King of Spain placed at their table the 'Great Captain' Gonsalvo de Cordoba, and deferred to him. Monluc himself had been honoured by princes, and acclaimed by the people. The Pope and the cardinals at Rome had done homage to the body of his son, Marc Anthony, killed in action. There also the citizens had flocked to see the defender of Siena, as he passed through the city after the siege [226-7].

Though they might serve the Turk if need be, the gentry were principally dependent on the favour of the king for advancement. They were the natural allies of the monarchy and the defence of the realm in time of war; they might even be described, Monluc argued, as the nation's greatest military asset: 'Nobody knows how to fight but the *noblesse*' [219]. They furnished the *gendarmerie* and the leadership of the infantry. If the kingdom were attacked, as in 1557-58, they sprang to arms. In return for this loyalty the crown should not only provide the gentry with the chance to serve, but should actively protect and encourage them, said Monluc.

The devotion of this class to the king was great, but not inexhaustible. They could be alienated if for any reason the crown failed as a patron. For one man it might be a personal 'despite', such as Monluc suffered at times throughout his career, finally and most completely in 1570. He knew the pangs of thwarted ambition of the unsuccessful courtier: in 1547 he had earned the displeasure of the royal mistress, and was forced to retire from court for a year. He had had to struggle hard against the hostility of the Montmorencies and

[1] Quoted in Whitehead, *Gaspard de Coligny*, 334.

his other enemies. His career was damaged, said his first biographer, by that 'mischievous and detestable envy' found in courts.[1]

His *Commentaries*, the counterblast to his critics, and the bitter reflections of a great public servant on his fall from office, were in part a veiled attack on these features of court life. Monluc displayed all the distrust of a rough soldier or a provincial gentleman for the ways of the half-Italian, half-French Valois court. He condemned the idle gossip, particularly of women, which often ruined a good man's reputation and on occasion led to duels. Where so much depended on the goodwill of the king and his principal servants it was unfortunate, in Monluc's view, that the personal influence of factious courtiers, favourites and ambitious royal mistresses held sway.

The disaffection of the gentry could also be general, if the king could no longer find employment for them, and the supply of rewards and favours diminished. In this sense peace had its dangers no less than war. The Treaty of Cateau-Cambrésis, as we have seen, was a reverse for Monluc and his kind. In a famous passage of the *Commentaries* he attacked the peace and its principal authors.[2] An acute critic of the relationship between the gentry and the crown, he was well aware of the incipient lawlessness of the *noblesse*; if one of his brothers was a bishop another was little better than a brigand.[3] Noble banditry was endemic in south-west France even in good years; in bad years social and political unrest could erupt with great ferocity. La Noue deplored the training in licence which the Italian wars provided for the French gentry. No Gascon, once he had tasted blood in Italy, could settle down to a peaceful trade again. Monluc, for his part, advised Charles IX to export war beyond the boundaries of France, to keep the gentry occupied and allow someone else to pay for their wars. In this way the nation could be rid of the ill humours which arise to plague it in time of peace. Similar advice had been given to Francis I by Chancellor Duprat, and was to be repeated to his successors by Coligny, Bodin and Sully.[4]

The unrest following the peace of 1559 was thus predictable. Monluc is a good if partial witness to the divisions in the kingdom,

---

[1] A. Thevet, *Pourtraits et Vies des Hommes Illustres*, II, f. 462.

[2] *The Commentaries*, 214.

[3] His younger brother Joachim, for whose exploits see Courteault, *Un cadet de Gascogne*, 23–4.

[4] Courteault, *Blaise de Monluc historien*, 396–7: L. Romier, *Le Royaume de Catherine de Médicis*, I, 195–7: Whitehead, *Gaspard de Coligny*, 234–5, 335: D. Buisseret, *Sully*, 177.

and the outbreak of the civil wars. They had already cast a long shadow in the earlier pages of the *Commentaries*, Monluc remarking of many of his bravest and most loyal companions in arms during the Italian wars, that they had 'since turned Huguenot'. Although he declared his intention not to meddle with 'the factions and rebellions that have discovered themselves since the death of Francis II',[1] and said nothing of his own temporary attachment to the Huguenots, he gives a reliable impression of the financial crisis, the weakness of the crown, the feuding at court and the plight of the dependent gentry deprived of their careers. His account of the Huguenots in Gascony is harsh and one-sided, but makes clear their attractiveness to disappointed office-seekers and unemployed swordsmen. Their churches were popular, well-organized and rich; their zeal for reform was genuine; and their attack on the king—'a little turdy roylet' [207]—bishops and landlords was a declaration of their independence from the old order. Monluc was not, as we have seen, interested in the religious aspect of the dispute, but he appreciated its significance and depth, correctly forecasting the long continuance of the wars and divisions in France so long as two religions existed side by side [230].

In spite of setbacks, in the earlier part of his career as in the later, Monluc had been in the end fortunate. He had risen to high office in the service of the kings of France, his masters, and he had been, he explained, sufficiently if not liberally rewarded. But exactly how well had he done? Throughout the *Commentaries* Monluc was careful to give the impression that it was honour and reputation, rather than material reward, which he had sought and found; and that, unlike some others whom he could name but did not, he would not disparage the official stipends and gifts he had received, although they were not large and much was still owing him. He was also at pains to emphasize that he had not stooped to dishonest means, as many did, to fill his pockets. As a result he was not a rich man [226]. He had begun life as a poor *hobereau*, and had now retired to his native province after a long career having, as he said, 'acquired but very little wealth' [228].

There is a good deal of special pleading in the *Commentaries*, as we have seen in reference to other matters, and there is no doubt that the author, when discussing his finances, was attempting to rebut his detractors. That his family were poor we may believe. His grandfather had sold threequarters of his patrimony, leaving his many children and

1 *The Commentaries*, 218.

grandchildren unprovided for [34, 59]. The original Monluc estates were not negligible; they did not lie in the most infertile area of Gascony, the barren highlands close to the Pyrenees, but in the more productive valley of the Garonne. Their value before dispersal was nearly 5,000 *livres per annum* [59], enough to have supported a family of minor gentry observing strict primogeniture, giving close and uninterrupted attention to good husbandry, and having available fairly sophisticated credit facilities; but none of these existed for the Monlucs or their kind, as they did for, say, the English gentry in the mid-seventeenth century. Monluc was telling the truth when he said that he had to make his own way in the world.

But all the evidence, apart from the *Commentaries*, is that he accumulated a fortune while doing so. It is true that he obtained relatively little from the crown for several of his commissions, including the governorship of Siena [229]. But he was well paid for many other employments, and enjoyed more than one pension. More importantly, he used his position as military commander, in Italy and in Guienne, to get rich. If he was prepared to bargain away part of France to the King of Spain, Monluc would hardly scruple to defraud the crown, as others did, in the matter of finance, whatever his claim in the *Commentaries*. There can be little doubt that, as was the common practice of the day, he sold commissions, pardons and exemptions, accepted gifts, and falsified musters. As Lieutenant in Guienne he was able to corner the market, in disturbed times, for essential military supplies, which he then resold at great profit. His house in Agen was a kind of bank, for he lent money, at high rates, to intending purchasers. During this period he rebuilt and extended his castle at Estillac, and married his daughters into noble families. He died worth a quarter of a million *livres*.[1]

For a final judgment on Monluc and his book we must first recall the original purpose of his work—the vindication of his past conduct, and the regaining of royal favour. To this end he portrayed himself in simple terms, as the poor cadet of Gascony, who had won, for a time, fame and position, and some, but not much, material reward, but had remained as bluff, honest and simple-hearted at the end of his career as at the beginning. His humble background and his typically Gascon openness of character—'everyone might read my heart in my face', he said[2]—had caused him to fall foul of several great ones in the state; his

[1] Courteault, *Blaise de Monluc historien*, 613.
[2] *The Commentaries*, 289.

memoirs were, therefore, a defence of the underdog, with whom he identified, and a criticism of the court and the atmosphere of intrigue prevailing there. He happily admitted to most of the Gascon vices. His 'scurvy, sour, morose and choleric nature' savoured too much, he said, of his native soil [56]. Like any other Gascon gentleman he was 'proud, heedless and prolific in offspring'.[1] The Duke of Alba judged him intensely vain.[2] His sudden bursts of anger and quickness to take offence are, as we have seen, amply illustrated in the *Commentaries*. These admissions fortified the impression he wished to give. Just as in life—the implication was—he could conceal nothing, so his memoirs were, according to their author, plain, artless and direct [232].

If this was indeed the case, then Monluc's career and his account of it would both be less interesting than in fact they are. Fortunately the reality is different in both cases. The *Commentaries* are certainly 'racy and garrulous' and will continue to be best known for their vivid descriptions; but they are also marked, it has been shown, by intelligent political judgment, acute observation and shrewd assessment of character. They have a distinct value as political history and as a chronicle of military developments. And the reason Monluc did not write a rough soldier's tale, as he intended, is that he was not simply a rough soldier: a comparison of the man and his career with the life story he told in the *Commentaries* has abundantly proved this point. The face he presented to the world, that of a typical Gascon and a representative of the warlike gentry of France, was incomplete and misleading. The nationality of a man is not usually the most important determinant of his character. Monluc's Gascon background was certainly of significance: it made it easy for him in his career as in his book to cast himself in a certain role and to live up to a particular reputation. But we can now see he had other virtues and vices which have little to do with supposed racial characteristics. Some arecontradictory: he pitied the innocent who suffered at the hands of the soldiery, yet there was a strong admixture of the cruel in his nature. He could inflict pain with even less scruple than most soldiers of his age. He was highly superstitious, claiming to have had premonitions of several events in his lifetime, and combined a sort of fatalism—'We cannot frustrate the decrees of fate'—with a strong belief in his own destiny. He was ruthlessly ambitious, determined to seize by main force what destiny had in store for him. And he displayed, in his climb to the

---

[1] Courteault, *Un cadet de Gascogne*, 3.

[2] Whitehead, *Gaspard de Coligny*, 126.

top, not only the well-known hallmarks of a D'Artagnan, swordsmanship hardihood, impetuous courage and audacity, but several less
common qualities. He possessed remarkable ability as a commander.
Like his diplomat brother he had a quick brain, enormous energy and
great fluency of speech in his own and other languages. He was able to
apply these gifts singlemindedly to his trade, concentrating his energy
and his intelligence tirelessly to the solution of military problems.

So it was that he could combine the simpler soldierly virtues, to
which he laid claim, with most of the qualifications for high command.
He could inspire others with his courage and dash, and yet calculate
finely the risks of any enterprise. He had great presence of mind,
thinking and acting decisively and quickly in a dangerous situation;
but at the same time showed himself cautious and circumspect when
need be, and careful in his preparations for any exploit. He was pains-
taking in the mundane but exacting tasks of military administration.
He could tire out an opponent by his indefatigable attention to detail
and his anticipation of the enemy's intentions. He was a good
organiser, in spite of his contempt for paper-work, and cared for the
safety and welfare of his soldiers. He helped to initiate important
changes, as we have seen, in siege and infantry tactics. As Colonel-
General of the French infantry he presided over major developments
in that arm.

If his success is not to be explained in simple terms, neither are his
failures. Monluc would have us believe in a conspiracy against the
poor cadet. But this was true only in part. Some of the disasters that
overtook him are attributable to obvious failings in his own character,
or to the more subtle contradictions within him which are, as it were,
the reverse side of his great qualities. He could throw away advantages
that he had painstakingly acquired by a sudden and rash action. He
could inspire hatred as well as respect. His careful calculation of his
advantage could, in political terms, soon degenerate into secret warfare against his rivals. If he could be patient and watchful in battle, he
could be underhand, devious and calculating, concealing his real
opinions and intentions, when in competition with others. He was an
intriguer as much as those he condemned for their intrigues. He
played for high stakes, believed he could win, and could hardly complain when he lost. His account of his time at Siena or as Lieutenant of
Guienne conceals the plots and counterplots, the secret dealings with
foreign powers and the stratagems at court in which he was deeply
involved. No simple, unpolitical soldier could have led the Sienese for

so long; or, on the other hand, have contemplated an alliance with Philip II and amassed a large private fortune during a time of civil war. His dismissal from office in 1570 was not a sign of political innocence, the impression he fostered in the *Commentaries*, but of temporary political failure.

Monluc has been compared to D'Artagnan and Cyrano de Bergerac, both of whom were the subjects of nineteenth-century romantic fiction. Monluc, however, did not require the aid of a Dumas or a Rostand; he was his own apologist, contributing in his memoirs to the creation of the legend of the 'amusing Gascon braggart', good with his sword and fluent of tongue, who wins fame and fortune in the service of the crown. While he did not sentimentalize warfare, he did attempt to romanticize and simplify his own career, and hoped to free it of all that was awkward or inexplicable within the terms he had laid down. But, as we have seen, his forceful and independent personality could not be constrained in this way: both as a commander and as a man he was a good deal more complex than he cared to make out. He differed as much from the creation of his memoirs as did the real Cyrano—who was not even a Gascon—from Rostand's hero. No doubt because of this his attempt to present himself in a particular role fails, in the end, to carry conviction: his real qualities and defects keep breaking through, and the attentive reader can perceive more than Monluc, the author, intended. In this failure of the memoirist lies, in part, the success of the book.

Chronology

1494   Charles VIII of France invades Italy.

about 1501   Birth of Blaise de Monluc.

1515   Accession of Francis I.
Battle of Marignano, September.
France occupies Milan.

1519   Charles V elected Emperor, June.

1521   Monluc enters upon military service in Italy.

1522   Battle of Bicocca, April.

1523   Spanish invasion of south-west France; skirmish at St Jean de Luz, September.

1524   Boubon and Pescara besiege Marseilles, August.

1525   Battle of Pavia and capture of Francis I, February.

1526   Treaty of Madrid, January.
League of Cognac formed against Charles V, May.

1527   Expedition to Naples under Lautrec.

1528   Death of Lautrec, August.
The treason of Andrea Doria.

1529   Peace of Cambrai, August.

1534   Francis I's Ordinances founding the Legions.

1536   Francis allies with Suleiman II, the Magnificent, February.
French conquest of Savoy and Piedmont, March.
Imperialist invasion of Provence, July.

1538   Truce of Nice, June.

1543   Campaign in Piedmont.

1544   Battle of Cérisoles, April.
Henry VIII's expedition to Picardy; siege of Boulogne, July–September.
Franco–Imperial Peace of Crépy, September.
Camisado of Boulogne, October.

1545   French naval expedition in Channel, July.

1547   Death of Henry VIII, January.
Death of Francis I, March; accession of Henry II.

1552   Rebellion of Siena against Spain and Florence.
French capture of Lorraine bishoprics, March.
Charles V's siege of Metz, October–December.

1554   Monluc Governor of Siena.
        Strozzi defeated at Marciano, August.
        Siege of Siena, October–April 1555.
1555   Capitulation of Siena, April.
        Abdication of Charles V; Philip II King of Spain.
1556   Truce of Vaucelles, February.
1557   Battle of St Quentin, August.
1558   Siege and capitulation of Calais, January.
        Siege of Thionville, and its fall, June.
        Battle of Gravelines, July.
1559   Peace of Cateau-Cambrésis, April.
        Death of Henry II, July; accession of Francis II.
1560   Death of Francis II, December; accession of Charles IX and the
        regency of Catherine de Medici.
1561   Growth of Huguenotism in France.
        Colloquy of Poissy, September.
1562   Massacre of Vassy, March, and beginnings of the civil wars.
        Battle of Vergt (Perigord), October.
1563   Assassination of the Duke of Guise, February.
        Monluc Lieutenant in Guienne.
1567   Second civil war.
1568   Peace of Longjumeau, March.
        Third civil war.
1569   Battles of Jarnac, March, and Moncontour, October.
1570   Monluc wounded at Rabastens, July.
        Peace of St Germain, August.
        Monluc dismissed from Lieutenancy of Guienne; begins his
        memoirs, November.
1572   Massacre of St Bartholomew, August; Fourth civil war.
1574   Death of Charles IX, May; accession of Henry III.
        Monluc created Marshal of France.
1577   Death of Monluc, August.

The Commentaries of Blaise de Monluc, Marshal of France

Part I   From Book I

The Habsburg-Valois Wars, 1521–1544

The author's apology for his own work, and advice to young soldiers

Being at the age of threescore and fifteen[1] retired home to my own house, there to seek some little repose after the infinite pains and labours I had undergone during the space of above fifty years that I bore arms for the several kings my masters, in which service I passed through all the degrees and through all the orders of soldier, ensign, lieutenant, captain, camp-master, governor of places, his Majesty's lieutenant in the provinces of Tuscany and Guienne, and Marshal of France; finding myself maimed in almost all my limbs with arquebus shots, cuts and thrusts with pikes and swords, and by that means rendered almost useless and good for nothing, without strength or hope ever to be cured of that great arquebus shot in my face, and after having resigned my government of Guienne into his Majesty's hands; I thought fit to employ the remainder of my life in a description of the several combats wherein I have been personally engaged in the space of two and fifty years, that I had the honour to command: assuring myself, that the captains who shall take the pains to read my life will therein meet with passages that may be useful to them in the like occasions, and of which some advantage may be made to the acquiring of honour and renown.

And although I have in the several engagements I have undertaken (and some of them perhaps without great reason on my side to justify

---

[1] An indication that Monluc revised this part of his work some years after its original composition in 1570-71.

my proceedings) been exceedingly fortunate and successful beyond all human aim; I would not yet anyone should conceive that I attribute the success or the glory thereof to any other than to God alone; and indeed whoever shall consider the dangers and difficulties I have gone through and overcome cannot but therein acknowledge his Almighty and immediate arm. Neither have I ever failed to implore his assistance in all my undertakings, and that with great confidence in his grace and mercy, and assurance of it; wherein his divine Majesty has been pleased so far to be graciously assisting to me, that I have never been defeated nor surprised in any exploit of war where I have been in command, but on the contrary have ever carried away victory and honour. And it is very necessary and fit that all we who bear arms should ever consider and always confess that we of ourselves can do nothing without his divine bounty, which inspires us with courage and supplies us with strength to attempt and execute those great and hazardous enterprises which present themselves to our under-taking.

And because some of those who shall read these commentaries (for it will be very hard to please all, though some will set a just value upon my book) may perhaps think it strange, and accuse me of vainglory for writing my own actions, and say that I ought in modesty to have transferred that work to another hand: I shall tell such once for all that in writing the truth, and attributing to God the glory thereof, there will be no harm done. Neither (besides that the testimonies of several men of honour yet living will justify the truth of what I shall deliver) can anyone give a better account of the designs, enterprises and execu-tions, and the actions happening thereupon, than myself, who was an eyewitness and an actor in them all; and who also design not herein to deprive anyone of his due and particular honour. The greatest captain that ever lived was Caesar, and he has led me the way, having himself written his own commentaries, and being careful to record by night the actions he performed by day. I would therefore by his example contrive mine, how rude and unpolished soever (as coming from the hand of a soldier, and moreover a Gascon, who has ever been more solicitous to do than to write or to speak well). Wherein shall be comprehended all the exploits of war, in which I have either been personally engaged or that have been performed by my direction; and those beginning from my greener years, when I first came into the world; to signify to such as I shall leave behind me, how restless I (who am at this day the oldest captain in France) have ever been in the search and acquisition of honour, in performing services for the Kings my masters, which was my sole and only end, ever flying all the pleasures and delights which usually divert young men, whom God has endowed with any commendable qualities, and who are upon the point of their advancement, from the paths of true virtue and undisputed greatness. A book not intended however for the learned men of

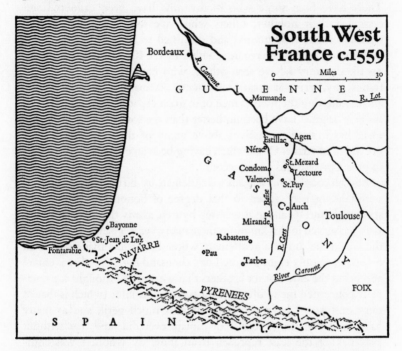

the world, they have historians enough of their own, but for a soldier, and wherein a captain, and perhaps a lieutenant of a province may find something that may be worth his observation. At the least I can affirm that I have written the truth, having my memory as good and entire at this instant as ever, and being as perfect in the names both of men and places as if all things had passed but yesterday, and yet I never committed anything to paper, for I never thought at such an age as this to undertake anything of this kind: which whether I have well or ill performed, I refer myself to such as shall do me the honour to read my book, which is properly an account of my own life.

To you therefore, captains my companions, it is that this treatise does principally address itself, to whom peradventure it may in some measure be useful. And you ought to believe that having so many years been in the same command wherein you now are, and having so long discharged the office of a captain of foot, and thrice that of camp-master and colonel, I must needs have retained something of that condition, and that in a long experience I have seen great honours conferred upon some, and great disgraces befall others of that degree. There have been some who in my time have been cashiered and degraded their nobility, others who have lost their lives upon a scaffold, others dishonoured and dismissed to their houses, without ever having been more regarded either by the King or any other; and on the contrary I have seen others, who have trailed a pike at six francs' pay, arrive at great preferments, performing things so brave, and manifesting themselves men of so great capacity, that several who in their original have been no better than the sons of poor labouring men, have raised themselves above many of the nobility by their prowess and virtue. Of all which having been an eyewitness, I am able to give a precise and a true account.

And although I myself am a gentleman by birth, yet have I not-withstanding been raised to that degree of honour wherein I now stand, as leisurely, and as much step by step, as any the poorest soldier who has served in this kingdom these many years. For being born into the world the son of a gentleman, whose father had made sale of all his estate, to only eight hundred or a thousand *livres*' yearly revenue,[1] and being the eldest of six brothers that we were,[2] I thought it princi-pally concerned me to illustrate the name of Monluc (which is that of our family) as I have also done with as much peril, and as many hazards of my life, as soldier or captain ever did; and that without ever having the least reproach from those by whom I was com-manded, but on the contrary with as much favour and esteem as ever any captain who had borne arms in the armies wherein I had the honour to serve. Insomuch that whenever there happened any enter-prise of importance or danger, the king's lieutenants and colonels would as soon, or sooner, put me upon it as any other captain of the army; of which the ensuing pages will give you sufficient testimony.

From the time therefore that I was first advanced to the degree of an ensign, I made it my business to understand the duty of an officer,

---

[1] The *livre tournois*—the money of account in France until replaced by the *écu* in 1577—contained 20 *sous*; 1 *sou* 12 *deniers*. It is impossible to give an exact English equivalent for Monluc's grandfather's income.

[2] Authorities differ as to whether Blaise or Jean, the later bishop, was the eldest.

and to learn to be wise by the example of such as committed over-sights, or were otherwise negligent in their command. To which purpose I first totally weaned myself from play, drink and avarice, as knowing well that all captains of that complexion are so unfit ever to arrive at anything of great, as to be much more likely to fall into the before-named misfortunes. That knowledge it was that made me positively resolve against all these three things which youth is very prone unto, and which are very prejudicial to the reputation of a chief.

There yet remains a fourth, which if you cannot wholly avoid, yet go to it as seldom and as soberly as you can, and without losing your-selves in the labyrinth, and that is the love of women. Embark not by any means in that affair, for it is utterly an enemy to an heroic spirit.[1] Leave love at home whilst Mars is in the field, you will afterwards have but too much leisure for those delights. I can safely say that never any fond affection or affectionate folly of that kind could ever divert me from undertaking and executing what was given me in command. Such little *amorosos* as these are fitter to handle a distaff than a sword. Love is a great enemy to a soldier, and besides the debauch and the time lost in those little intrigues, it is an occupation that begets a numberless number of quarrels, and sometimes even with your dearest friends. I have known more people fight even upon this account than upon the score of honour. And what a horrid thing it is that a man should forfeit his reputation, and very often lose his life, for the love of a woman!

As for you soldiers, above all things I recommend to you the obedience that you owe to your commanders, to the end that you may one day learn how to command: for it is impossible that soldier should ever know how to command, who has not first learned to obey. And take notice, that the virtues and discretion of a soldier are chiefly manifested in his obedience, and in his disobedience lies the ruin of his life and honour. A restive horse never yet made good proof. The proverb will serve, and you ought not to slight the advice I give you, if but in respect to my experience, who have seen a great deal; and I must needs be a very ignorant and senseless fellow, if in all this time of my life I have made no observation of the successes and misfortunes both of the one and the other. But I have committed some to memory, and that is it which has given me occasion to write this book in the latter end of my days.

[1] An injunction the author does not seem to have wholly obeyed: see below, pp. 149-50.

Monluc's early training at the court of Lorraine, and his departure for Italy in 1521

Having in my greener years been bred up in the family of Anthony Duke of Lorraine,[1] and now grown up towards a man, I was presently preferred to an archer's place in the Duke's own company, Monsieur Bayard[2] being at that time lieutenant to the same. Not long after being inflamed with the report of the noble feats of arms every day performed in Italy, which in those days was the scene of action, I was possessed with a longing desire to visit that country. To this end making a journey into Gascony, I made shift to procure of my father a little money and a Spanish horse, and without further delay began my journey in order to my design, leaving to fortune the hopes of my future advancement and honour. About a day's journey from my father's house, and near unto Leytoure [Lectoure],[3] I turned a little out of my way to visit the Sieur de Castelnau, an ancient gentleman who had long frequented Italy, of him to inform myself at large of the state, condition, manners and customs of that country in order to my future conduct. This gentleman told me so many things, and related to me so many brave exploits which were there every day performed, that without longer abode, or staying anywhere longer than to refresh myself and my horse, I passed over the Alps and took my way directly to Milan. Being come to Milan, I there found two uncles of mine by my mother's side, called the les Stillacs [Seigneurs d'Estillac],[4] both of them men of great reputation and esteem, of whom the one served under Monsieur de Lescun, brother to Monsieur de Lautrec[5] (the same who was afterwards Marshal of France, and then known by the name of the Marshal de Foix), by whom I was presently put into an archer's place in his own company, a place of great repute in those days, there being in those times several lords and great persons who rode in troops, and two or three who were archers in this; but since that discipline is lost and grown degenerate, and all things turned

[1] Antoine, Duke of Lorraine (1489–1544), son of René II, Duke of Lorraine, and uncle of François, Duke of Guise, Monluc's later patron.

[2] Pierre du Terrail, the Chevalier Bayard (1473–1524), was probably the most famous French soldier of his day. He had won particular renown in the Italian wars.

[3] Town on the river Gers, close to St Puy: see map, p. 33.

[4] Estillac, near Agen, was a family estate which Monluc later inherited.

[5] For Lautrec see Appendix I, 'Foix, Odet de'. His brother was Thomas, Sieur de Lescun (died 1525), Marshal of France in 1520 and mortally wounded at Pavia; see below, p. 51.

upside down, without hopes that any man now alive shall ever see them restored to their former estate.

At this time the war betwixt Francis the First and the Emperor Charles the Fifth broke out again with greater fury than before, the latter to drive us out of Italy, and we to maintain our footing there, though it was only to make it a place of sepulture to a world of brave and valiant French. God Almighty raised up these two great princes sworn enemies to one another, and emulous of one another's greatness; an emulation that has cost the lives of two hundred thousand persons, and brought a million of families to utter ruin; when after all neither the one nor the other obtained any other advantage by the dispute than the bare repentance of having been the causers of so many miseries, and of the effusion of so much Christian blood. If God had pleased that these two monarchs might have understood one another, the whole earth had trembled under their arms; and Solyman [Suleiman II, the Magnificent], who was contemporary with them, and who during their contests enlarged his empire on every side, would have had enough to do to defend his own. The Emperor was, it is true, a great and a magnanimous prince, yet in nothing superior to our master, during his life, saving in a little better success, and in that God gave him the grace to bewail his sins in a convent, into which he retired himself two or three years before his death. During the space of two and twenty months that this war continued,[1] I had the good fortune to be an eyewitness of several very brave actions, which were very fit to season a raw soldier; neither did I fail continually to present myself in all places and upon all occasions where I thought honour was to be purchased at what price soever; and it is to be imagined I had my share of fighting, when I had no less than five horses killed under me in the short continuance of that service, and of those two in two days, which Monsieur de Roquelaure, who was cousin german to my mother, was pleased to give me. For in this beginning of my arms I had the good fortune to gain so far upon the affections of the whole company that my horses being lost, everyone was willing to help to remount me, and being moreover taken prisoner in battle, I was soon after delivered by the procurement of my friends.

Let such therefore as intend to acquire honour by feats of arms, resolve to shut their eyes to all hazards and dangers whatever in the first encounter where they shall happen to be present; for that's the

[1] In fact, April 1521 to, at most, July 1522.

time when everyone has his eyes fixed upon them to observe their behaviour, and thence to form a judgment of their future hopes. If in the beginning they shall, by any handsome action, signalize their courage and boldness, it sets a good mark upon them forever, and not only makes them noted and regarded by all; but moreover inspires them themselves with mettle and vigour to perform more and greater things. Now you must know that in this war we lost the duchy of Milan. Of which (though I do not pretend to be any great clerk) I could write the true history, and should his Majesty command me, I would deliver the truth; and I am able to give as good an account (though I was myself very young at that time) as any man whatever in France, I mean of those passages where I had the fortune to be present, and no other; for I will write nothing by hearsay. But I intend not to busy myself with a relation of other men's actions, and less of the faults and oversights by them committed, though they are yet as fresh in my memory as at that moment; and seeing that what I myself performed in that country, at that time, was in the quality of a private soldier only, I being not as yet stepped into command, I shall no longer insist upon this melancholy subject, which has also been writ before by others. Only this I shall make bold to affirm, that Monsieur de Lautrec was by no means to be blamed, he having there performed all the parts of a good and prudent general; and who indeed was in himself one of the greatest men I ever knew. Neither shall I trouble myself to give a narration of the battle of the Bicoque [Bicocca], in which I fought on foot, as also did Monsieur de Montmorency, since Constable of France;[1] a battle that Monsieur de Lautrec was compelled to consent unto through the obstinacy of the Swiss, quite contrary to his own judgment: a nation whose wilfulness I have seen occasion the loss of several places, and cause great inconveniences in his Majesty's affairs. They are, to speak the truth, a very warlike people, and serve as it were for bulwarks to an army. But then they must never want either money or victuals; for they are not to be paid with words.

Spanish forces under Philibert de Chalon, Prince of Orange, invade southwest France, September 1523. The skirmish at St Jean de Luz

After the unfortunate loss of this fair Duchy of Milan, all the forces returned back into France, and with them the company of the said

---

[1] For Montmorency see Appendix I, 'Montmorency, Anne de'. The battle of Bicocca, 29 April 1522, resulted in the complete overthrow of Lautrec. Monluc's claim that he fought on foot at the battle cannot be substantiated.

Marshal de Foix, wherein I then had not only the place of a man at arms, but moreover an assignation of an archer's pay. Sometime after the Emperor set another army on foot to recover Fonterabie [Fontarabie];[1] whereupon our company and several others were ordered to repair to Bayonne to Monsieur de Lautrec, who was his Majesty's Lieutenant in Guienne. The said Sieur de Lautrec, that he might the better make head against the enemy (who made a show of attempting something upon the frontier), made a sudden levy of fourteen or fifteen ensigns of foot; which was the occasion that I (who ever had an inclination for foot service) entreated leave of Captain Sayas (who carried the cornets in the absence of Captain Carbon, his brother) for three months only; that I might accept of an ensign offered to me by Captain La Clotte; who at last very unwillingly granted my suit, although he himself had first sent to Captain Carbon to solicit it in my behalf. Suddenly after this (the enemy being daily reinforced with fresh supplies) La Clotte was commanded away to Bayonne, and a few days after that Captain Carbon took the companies of Monsieur de Lautrec and the Marshal his brother with two companies of foot, to wit that of Megrin de Comenge and La Clotte, to conduct us through the woods straight to Saint Jean de Lus [St Jean de Luz],[2] where the enemy's camp at that time lay. So soon as we were arrived at the top of a little hill about half a quarter of a league distant from Luz (having already passed a little river by a wooden bridge, another half quarter of a league behind this little hill, at the foot whereof, and before us, there ran a rivulet of fifteen or twenty paces broad, and deep to a man's girdle, joining to which there is also a plain which extends itself in an easy descent down to the said rivulet, from whence one may easily discover St Jean de Luz, one of the finest *bourgs* in all France, and seated upon the margin of the ocean sea), Captain Carbon, who commanded the party, leaving two cornets upon this little hill, the one whereof was carried by Captain Sayas, which was ours, and the other by Captain d'Andouins [Andoins], which was that of Monsieur de Lautrec (but both of them only in the absence, the one of Captain Carbon, the other of Captain Artigueloube [Artiguelouve]), and only twenty horse with each, together with our two companies of foot, took the rest of the *gendarmes*, and with them Monsieur Gramont, the same who afterwards died in the

[1] Town on the Atlantic coast of Spain, close to the French border, which had been taken by the French in October 1521. See map, p. 33.

[2] The port on the French side of the border, south of Bayonne.

kingdom of Naples, and who was at this time Lieutenant to the company belonging to Monsieur de Lautrec.

With this party Captain Carbon passed over the little river, and having divided his men into three squadrons (as one might easily discern from the hill where we stood) trotted along the plain directly towards St Jean de Luz. Being come to the middle of the plain, he there made a halt for an hour or more whilst a trumpet went twice, and sounded the fanfare to the enemy, after which being about to retreat, as not believing anyone would stir out of the enemy's camp, the forlorn which he had sent out towards the utmost skirts of the plain returned back upon the spur, to acquaint him that all the enemy's camp began to move; and suddenly after we began to discover three of their squadrons of horse, appearing upon their march, one upon the heels of another, and making directly towards Monsieur de Carbon. Of these the first that came up, presently, and smartly charged the foremost of ours, where there were many lances broken on both sides; but more of ours than theirs, forasmuch as in those times the Spaniards carried but few lances, and those very slender, long and shod with iron at both ends.[1] During this charge Captain Carbon was leisurely drawing off the other two squadrons towards the place where we were, when the second of the enemy's squadrons coming up, and uniting with the first, beat up our first to our second squadron, commanded by Monsieur Gramont,[2] where the skirmish was very hot and a great many men thrown to ground both on the one side and the other, amongst whom were the Seigneurs de Gramont, who had his horse killed under him, de Luppé, Standard-bearer to Monsieur de Lautrec, de Poygreffi [Puygreffier], who is since turned Huguenot, de La Faye, of Saintonge, who is yet living, and divers others. At the same instant we discovered another great party of horse advancing towards us a little on our left hand, at the sight of which the captains who carried our colours came both of them running to me, and saying: 'We are all lost.' Whereupon I told them that it were better, than so to conclude, to hazard fourscore or an hundred foot, to bring off our horse who were engaged. To which La Clotte and Megrin made answer that that venture would only occasion a greater loss, and that moreover they very much doubted the soldiers would

[1] Monluc calls these weapons *arces gayes*, i.e. light lances, in Spanish *azagaya*. 'Assegai' is a modern derivation.

[2] Jean II, Baron de Gramont, served as man at arms and later as lieutenant in the company of Lautrec.

hardly be persuaded to go down, seeing death so manifest before their eyes.

Now you must understand there was no-one present at this discourse, saving the two forementioned captains and myself, our foot standing drawn up fourteen or fifteen paces behind; and it was not amiss; for I make a great question had they heard what we said, and seeing the *gendarmes* in manifest danger to be lost, whether I should have been so cheerfully followed as I was. And it is a good rule, as much as a man can to conceal from the soldier the danger of any enterprise, if you intend to have them go briskly to their work. To this last objection of the two captains I made answer that I would run the hazard to lead them on, and that lost or lost not it was better to hazard and to lose fourscore or an hundred foot, than all our *gendarmes*. And thereupon without further deliberation (for long consultations are often the ruin of brave attempts) I returned back to the soldiers, and the captains with me (for the business required haste), saying to them only these few words: 'Come on, come on, comrades, let us go and relieve our *gendarmes*'; and was thereupon followed by an hundred foot of our own company, who with very great resolution descended with me to the foot of the hill, where at the head of my men I passed over the brook, and there delivered twenty of my men to be led by the Bastard d'Aussan, a gentleman who has nothing blemished the legitimate sons of his race; though all of them men of singular bravery and remarkable valour.

Now you must know that the company I commanded was no other than crossbows, for at this time the use of the arquebus had not as yet been introduced amongst us. Only, three or four days before, six Gascon arquebusiers came over to us from the enemy, which I had received into my company, having by good fortune been that day upon the guard at the great gate of the city; and of those six one was a native of the territory of Monluc.[1] Would to heaven that this accursed engine had never been invented, I had not then received those wounds which I now languish under, neither had so many valiant men been slain for the most part by the most pitiful fellows and the greatest cowards; poltroons that had not dared to look those men in the face at hand, which at distance they laid dead with their confounded bullets. But it was the devil's invention to make us murder one another.

Being thus passed the river, I ordered the Bastard d'Aussan not to

[1] The name is now borne by a hamlet on the Garonne, north of Nérac.

suffer his men to shoot but only to present as if they intended to do it, to the end that he might favour mine and give them time to discharge and retire again into their order. Now when I was under the foot of the hill I could not possibly see what our men did; but being advanced a little further into the plain I saw all the enemy's three squadrons drawn up into one body and the great party on the left hand, marching upon a good round trot directly towards ours, who were rallied and stood firm, without being able either to advance forwards or to retire back by reason of some great stones that lay scattered in their rear. Here it was that Captain Carbon (who had no arms [i.e. armour] on, having been wounded in his left arm by an arquebus shot), seeing me so near him, came up to me and said: 'Oh Monluc, my dear friend, charge up boldly, I will never forsake thee.' 'Captain,' said I, 'take you only care to save yourself and your *gendarmes*,' at the same instant crying out: 'Shoot, comrades, at the head of these horse.' I was not above a dozen paces distant from the enemy when I gave them this volley, by which (as it appeared by the testimony of the prisoners who were taken a few days after) above fifty horses were killed and wounded, and two troopers slain, an execution that a little cooled their courage and caused their troops to make a halt. In the meantime Captain Carbon had leisure with his party to retire full gallop towards the brook I had passed over to relieve him; where such as had their horses lost taking hold of the others' horse tails saved themselves also, and all together passed over the river. Which haste they were necessitated to make, or otherwise the great party of horse on the left hand had charged them in the flank, had they drawn more leisurely off.

In the meantime under favour of the twenty crossbows of d'Aussan, who sustained us, we rallied again and gave another volley. So soon as Captain Carbon had passed the river with his horse, remounted Monsieur de Gramont on another horse and mounted the rest *en crouppe*, he commanded the said Sieur de Gramont to ride to the top of the hill and in all haste to draw off the ensigns both of horse and foot at a round trot directly to the other river, where the bridge was that leads towards Bayonne. Which order being given he suddenly turned back again towards me, having in his company an Italian called Signor Diomedes and the Sieur de Maignault, where he found me retreating towards a ditch upon the edge of a marsh, and of which I might be within some twelve or fourteen paces, which not only hindered him from getting up to me but moreover gave him enough to do to save himself. I notwithstanding in spite of the enemy recovered the ditch of the marsh, being still sheltered by d'Aussan, whom I commanded to climb over in great diligence and there to make head, which he accordingly performed.

The Spaniards in the meantime made a show as if they meant to charge, but they durst not attempt to break into me. Neither were my six arquebusiers idle all this while but did wonders with their shot; when having at last retreated my men within five or six paces of the ditch, I caused them all in an instant to throw themselves into it and under favour of d'Aussan almost as suddenly to mount the ditch bank on the other side, over which we all got safe and sound, saving three soldiers who were slain by lances, for not having been so nimble as the rest: and here it was that, as in a little fort, I made head against the enemy. Now you must know that that party of the enemy which came up on the left hand made a halt at the bank of the river, when they saw our horse were already got half way up the hill; and those who had fought, and to whom I had given a stop at the ditch bank, were now upon their retreat home, when seeing three squadrons of arquebusiers coming along the plain and making towards them with all the speed they could, it revived their spirits and inspired them with new courage to face about again. I in the meantime (having also discovered these fresh succours) began to shift along by the ditch till, being by the return of a corner of it slipped out of their sight, I drew my men into a very narrow meadow from whence at full speed I gained the foot of the hill I had descended before, and having repassed the river soon recovered the top of the mountain.

The danger wherein I saw myself to be, as well of the horse I had pressing upon my rear as of the battalion of infantry which I saw fast advancing towards me, did not however make me lose my judgment in a time of so great need; nor hinder me from discerning and taking this opportunity for my retreat, during which I made the little handful of men I had march very close together; and by turns encouraging and speaking to them, made them often face about and salute the cavalry, who pursued me, both with crossbow and arquebus shot. When having gained the top of the hill, I drew into an orchard, making fast the gate on the inside, that the horse might not so suddenly enter, and by favour of that and several others planted with apples, still made on towards the bridge, till I came to a little church called à Haitce [Ahetze], from whence I perceived the great road to be all covered over with the enemy's horse, there being nevertheless a great ditch betwixt them and me, from whence I bestowed upon them some arquebus and crossbow shot, which also very seldom failed of their effect and compelled (seeing they could not come up to me) some to advance forwards and others to retire. I then put some of my men into the churchyard, thinking there again to make head—the greatest folly I committed throughout the whole action—for in the meantime a good number of their horse, gliding along by the meadow straight towards the bridge, were already advanced so far that I saw myself totally enclosed without all manner of hope to escape and to save myself.

Now so soon as Captain Carbon had recovered the bridge and that the horse and foot were all passed over, he commanded Monsieur Gramont to haste away, not only a trot but a full gallop. For he already discovered the enemy's infantry in the orchards, which I could not do; neither did I ever perceive them till they began to shoot at me: and then I made a sign to my soldiers in the churchyard to come and draw up to me in the great highway. Captain Carbon in the interim, being he saw nothing of me, half concluded us all for killed or taken, and yet seeing all the enemy's troops of horse both on the right hand and on the left making directly towards the bridge, would leave Captain Compay (an admirable good soldier) at the end of the bridge with five and twenty horse and thirty crossbows of Captain Megrin's company, to try if there were any possible means to relieve me, were I yet alive, causing the bridge in the meantime to be broken down. Now because that troop of the enemy's horse which marched on the right hand made a great deal more haste towards the bridge than that of the left, I quitted the great highway and under favour of a hedge made straight towards the river, where I was again to encounter the horse, which notwithstanding I made my way through, chopped into the river, and in despite of them all passed over to the other side. Wherein, the banks of the river being high favoured me very much, they being too steep for the horse to get down: neither was our shot of both sorts idle in the meantime. At last I recovered the end of the bridge, where I found Captain Compay very busy at work to break it, and who so soon as he saw me was very importunate with me to save myself, at the same time presenting me the crupper of his horse to that end; but he had no other answer from me but this, that God had hitherto preserved me and my soldiers also, whom I was likewise resolved never to abandon till I had first brought them into a place of safety. Whilst we were in this dispute we were aware of the Spanish infantry coming directly towards the bridge, when finding ourselves too weak to stand the shock, Compay with the crossbows of Captain Megrin took the van in order to a retreat, and I remained in the rear, having gained a ditch that enclosed a little meadow, which was sufficient to defend me from the horse, it being so high that they could not come to charge.

I had now nothing left me but my six arquebusiers, my crossbows having already spent all their arrows. Nevertheless to show that their hearts were not down, I caused them to hold their swords ready drawn in the one hand and their bows in the other to serve instead of a buckler. Now Captain Compay's men had broken down the greatest part of the bridge before they went away, by reason of which impediment the cavalry could not so soon come up to us, having been constrained to ford the river two arquebus shot on the right hand, whilst the foot in the meantime with great difficulty filed it over one by one by the rails of the bridge, a posture wherein it had been a very easy matter to defeat them, had I not foreseen that then the cavalry would have come up to enclose me and our honour depended upon our retreat. Wherefore still getting ground, and from ditch to ditch, having gained about half a quarter of a league of way, I made a halt that my men might not be out of breath, when looking back I perceived the enemy had done so too and saw by his countenance that he grew weary of the pursuit, a thing at which I was very much astonished and not a little glad, for in plain truth we were able to do no more, having taken a little water and cider and some maize bread out of a few small houses we met upon the way. In the meantime Captain Compay sent out some horse to see what was become of us, believing me to be either dead or taken. And now behold us arrived in a place of safety, with the loss of only three men in the first ditch and the brave Bastard d'Aussan, who by loitering something too long in a little house by the church was unfortunately lost.

In the interim of this bustle which continued pretty long, the alarm was carried to Monsieur de Lautrec to Bayonne, together with the news that we were all totally defeated, at which he was exceedingly troubled in regard of the ill consequences that usually attend the fleshing and giving an enemy blood in the beginning of a war. However he drew out presently into the field and advanced but a very little way when he discovered our ensigns of foot conducted by the Sieur de Gramont marching upon the road towards him, who so soon as he came up presently gave him an account of what had happened, and did me the honour to tell him that I was the cause of their preservation;

but that withal I was lost in the service. Captain Carbon was not yet arrived, forasmuch as he had made a halt to stay for Captain Compay, from him to learn the issue of the business; but in the end he came up also, to whom Monsieur de Lautrec spake these words: 'Well, Carbon, was this a time wherein to commit such a piece of folly as this? Which I do assure you is not of so little moment, but that you have thereby endangered the making me lose this city of Bayonne, which you know to be a place of so great importance.' To which Carbon made answer: 'Sir, I have committed a very great fault, and the greatest folly that ever I was guilty of in my whole life: to this hour the like disgrace has never befallen me; but seeing it has pleased God to preserve us from being defeated, I shall be wiser for the time to come.' Monsieur de Lautrec then demanded of him if there was any news of me, to which he made answer that he thought I was lost; but as they were returning softly towards the city in expectation of further news, Captain Compay also arrived, who assured them that I was come safely off, relating withal the handsome retreat I had made in despite and in the very teeth of the enemy, with the loss of four men only, and that it was not possible but that the enemy must have lost a great number of men. I was no sooner come to my quarters but that a gentleman was sent from Monsieur de Lautrec to bring me to him, who entertained me with as much kindness and respect as he could have done any gentleman in the kingdom, saying to me these words in Gascon: *'Monluc, mon amie iou n'oublideray jamai lou service qu'abes fait au Rei, et m'en souviera tant que iou vivrai.'* Which is: 'Monluc, my friend, I will never forget the service you have this day performed for the King; but will be mindful of it so long as I live.' There is as much honour in an handsome retreat as there is in good fighting, and this was a lord who was not wont to caress many people; a fault that I have often observed in him; nevertheless he was pleased to express an extraordinary favour to me all the time we sat at supper, which he also continued to me ever after, insomuch that, calling me to mind four or five years after, he dispatched an express courier to me from Paris into Gascony with a commission to raise a company of foot, entreating me to bear him company in his expedition to Naples, and has ever since put a greater value upon me than I deserved. This was the first action I was ever in in the quality of a commander, and from whence I began to derive my reputation.

You captains, my comrades, who shall do me the honour to read my life, take notice that the thing in the world which you ought most to desire is to meet with a fair occasion wherein to manifest your courage in the first sally of your arms, for if in the beginning you shall prove successful, you do, amongst others, two things. First you cause yourselves to be praised and esteemed by the great ones, by whose report you shall be recommended to the knowledge of the King himself, from whom we are to expect the recompense of all our services, and labours; and in the next place, when the soldier shall see a captain who has behaved himself well and performed any notable thing at his first trial, all the valiant men will strive to be under his command, believing that so auspicious a beginning cannot fail of a prosperous issue; but that all things will succeed well with him, and that under such a man they shall never fail to be employed; for nothing can more spite a man of courage than to be left at home to burn his shins by the fire, whilst other men are employed abroad in honourable action. So that by this means you shall be sure always to be followed by brave men, with which you shall continue to get more honour and proceed to greater reputation; and on the contrary, if you chance to be baffled in the beginning, whether through your cowardice or want of conduct, all the good men will avoid you and you will have none to lead but the lees and *canaille* of the army, with whom (though you were the hero of the world) there will be no good to be done; nor other than an ill repute to be acquired. My example upon this occasion may serve for something, wherein though perhaps there were no great matters performed, yet so it is that of little exploits of war great uses are sometimes to be made. And remember, whenever you find yourselves overmatched with an enemy, that you can bridle and hold at bay with the loss of a few men, not to fear to hazard them. Fortune may be favourable to you as she was to me; for I dare confidently say that had not I presented myself to lead on these hundred foot (which all played their parts admirably well) we had certainly had all the enemy's cavalry upon our hands, which had been a power too great for so few as we were to withstand.

A new campaign is occasioned by the invasion of south-east France by the rebel Constable Bourbon, and the Imperial general Pescara, 1524. It ends at the battle of Pavia, February 1525

All these foot companies being disbanded, excepting those which were left in garrison, I who had no mind to be immured within the walls of a city again put myself into the company of Monsieur Le Marshal de

Foix, wherein I continued till such time as King Francis went his expedition against Monsieur de Bourbon,[1] who together with the Marquis of Pescara[2] laid siege to Marseilles (which Sieur de Bourbon, for an affront that had been offered to him, was revolted to the Emperor—there is nothing a great heart will not do in order to revenge), where seeing the king would permit the Marshal de Foix to carry no more than twenty men at arms of his own company along with him, and finding myself at my arrival to be excluded that election and none of the number, I took such snuff at it that I went with five or six gentlemen who did me the honour to bear me company, to be present at the battle, with a resolution to fight volunteer amongst the foot. But Monsieur de Bourbon, after having lain six weeks only before the city, raised the siege. The Signor Rance de Cère [Renzo da Ceri], a gentleman of Rome, a brave and experienced captain, together with the Sieur de Brion,[3] were within with a sufficient garrison his Majesty had thither sent for the defence of the town. So that Monsieur de Bourbon found himself to be deceived in his intelligence, and that he had reckoned without his host. The French did not as yet know what it was to rebel against their prince; for so soon as he had notice of the King's approach, he retired himself over the mountains and descended into Piedmont, by the Marquisate of Saluzzo and Pignerol, and not without very great loss fled away to Milan, which also both he and the Viceroy of Naples[4] were constrained to abandon and to fly out at one gate whilst we entered in at another.

Signor Don Antonio de Leva [Leiva][5] (who was one of the greatest captains the Emperor had, and who I do believe, had he not been hindered by the gout, with which he was infinitely tormented, would have surpassed all others of his time) was chosen in this posture of affairs to be put into Pavia with a strong garrison of German soldiers, supposing that the King would infallibly fall upon that place, as in

[1] Charles de Bourbon, Constable of France (1490–1527), had renounced his allegiance to Francis I in 1521, and allied with the Emperor and Henry VIII of England.

[2] Fernando-Francesco d'Avalos, Marquis of Pescara (1490–1525), celebrated *condottiere* of Spanish origin, who was in command of the Imperial forces.

[3] Philippe Chabot, Sieur de Brion (1492–1543), Admiral of France, 1526, was the favourite of Francis I until disgraced in 1538.

[4] Charles de Lannoy (d.1527), Imperial general, created Viceroy of Naples in 1522; the victor of Pavia.

[5] Antonio de Leiva (1480–1536), Imperial general. He died, Monluc remarks later, of grief at the failure of the expedition to Marseilles; see below, p. 71.

effect he did. The siege continued for the space of eight months,[1] in which time Monsieur de Bourbon went into Germany, where he so bestirred himself with the money he had borrowed from the Duke of Savoy that he thence brought along with him ten thousand German foot, together with four or five hundred men at arms from the kingdom of Naples, with which forces encamping himself at Lodi he came to offer the King battle upon St Matthias day,[2] our army being very much weakened as well by the length of the siege as by sickness, with which it had been miserably infected. To which disadvantages the King had moreover unluckily disbanded three thousand Grisons commanded by a colonel of their own called *le grand Diau* [*Diable*], I suppose to contract the charges of the war. Oh that these little pieces of good husbandry do very often occasion notable losses! Also a few days before Monsieur d'Albanie[3] was, by the King's command, departed with great forces towards Rome, from thence to fall into the kingdom of Naples. But in the end all vanished away in smoke; for to our great misfortune we lost the battle and all these enterprises came to nothing.

The description of this battle is already published in so many places that it would be labour lost therein to waste my paper. I shall therefore only say that the business was not well carried in several places on our side, which occasioned their ruin who behaved themselves best upon that occasion. The King was taken prisoner, Monsieur the Marshal de Foix both taken and wounded with an arquebus shot in his thigh, which moreover entered into his belly, Monsieur de St Pol[4] taken and wounded with thirteen wounds, with which he had been left for dead upon the place and was stripped to his shirt; but a Spaniard coming to cut off his finger for a ring he could not otherwise pull off, he cried out, and being known, was carried with the said Marshal into Pavia to the lodging of the Marquise d'Escaldasol. Several other great lords lost their lives, as the brother to the Duke of Lorraine, the Admiral de Chabannes, and many others taken, amongst whom were the King of Navarre, Messieurs de Nevers, de Montmorency, de Brion and others. But I shall not tax the memory of anyone for the loss of this battle, nor

[1] In fact the siege lasted only four months, October 1524–February 1525.

[2] The battle of Pavia was fought on 24 February 1525.

[3] John Stuart, Duke of Albany (*c.* 1482–1536), Scots soldier in the service of France, Governor of Bourbonnais.

[4] Bourbon, François de, Comte de St Pol (1491–1545).

set a mark upon those who behaved themselves ill enough, even in the presence of their King.

During all the time of my abode in the army I was continually with a captain called Castille de Navarre, without any pay, which captain having the fortune to command the forlorn hope in the day of battle, entreated me to bear him company, which accordingly I did, as also the five gentlemen who came in company with me. I was taken prisoner by two gentlemen of the company of Don Antonio de Leiva, who upon the Saturday morning let me go, together with two of my comrades; for they saw they were likely to get no great treasure of me. The other three were killed in the battle. Being now at liberty I retired myself into the house of the Marquise, where Monsieur le Marshal lay wounded. I found him with Monsieur de St Pol, both together in one bed, and Monsieur de Montejan [Montjehan] lodged in the same chamber, who was also wounded in his leg. There I heard the discourse and dispute betwixt Sieur Federic Bogé [de Baugé], who was prisoner, and Captain Sucre [de Succre], who belonged to the Emperor, upon the loss of this battle, who accused our French of many great oversights, particularly nominating several persons whose names I am willing to forbear. But I judged their opinions to be very good, being both of them very great soldiers, and what I then heard has since been serviceable to me upon several occasions: an use that everyone ought to make of such controversy who intends to arrive at any degree of perfection in the practice of arms. A man must seek not only all occasions of presenting himself at all rencounters and battles, but must moreover be curious to hear and carefull to retain the opinions and arguments of experienced men concerning the faults and oversights committed by commanders, and the loss or advantages to the one side and the other ensuing thereupon; for it is good to learn to be wise and to become a good master at another man's expense.

The kingdom of France has long bewailed this unfortunate day, with the losses we have sustained, besides the captivity of this brave prince who thought to have found fortune as favourable to him here as she was at his battle with the Swiss.[1] But she played the baggage and turned her tail, making him to know how inconvenient and of how dangerous consequence it is to have the person of a King exposed to the uncertain event of battle; considering that his loss brings along with it the ruin of his kingdom. Almighty God nevertheless was pleased to look upon this with an eye of pity, and to preserve it; for

[1] Ten years before, at the battle of Marignano, September 1515.

the conquerors, dazzled with the rays of victory, lost their understanding and knew not how to follow their blow; otherwise, had Monsieur de Bourbon turned his forces towards France, he would have put us all to our trumps.

The Monday following Monsieur de Bourbon gave order that such as were taken prisoners, and had not wherewithal to pay their ransom, should avoid the camp and return home to their own houses. Of which number I was one; for I had no great treasure. He gave us indeed a troop of horses and a company of foot for our safe conduct; but the devil a penny of money or a bit of bread, insomuch that not one of us had anything but turnips and cabbage-stalks, which we broiled upon the coals, to eat till we came to Ambrun [Embrun].[1] Before our departure Monsieur le Marshal commanded me to commend him to Captain Carbon and the rest of his friends, whom he entreated not to be dejected at this misfortune, but to rouse up their spirits and endeavour to do better than ever, and that they should go and join themselves to Monsieur de Lautrec his brother. After which he made me a very notable remonstrance, which was not ended without many tears, and yet delivered with a strong accent and an assured countenance, though he was very sore wounded; and so much that the Friday following he died.[2] I travelled on foot as far as La Redorte in Languedoc, where his company then lay.

The expedition to Naples set on foot, 1527

In the meantime Madame the Queen Regent, mother to the King, and with her all the confederate princes of the crown, had set several treaties on foot and laboured on all hands the King's deliverance with great integrity and vigour, and to so good effect that in the end this mighty Emperor, who in his imagination had swallowed up the whole kingdom of France, gained not so much as one inch of earth by his victory, and the King had the good fortune in his affliction to derive assistance even from those who at other times were his enemies, yet to whom the Emperor's greatness stood highly suspected. His Majesty being at last returned home, and mindful of the injuries and indignities had been offered to him during his captivity, having in vain tried all other ways to recover his two sons out of the Emperor's

---

[1] Hautes-Alpes, east of Gap.

[2] Lescun died on 3 March 1525.

hands, was in the end constrained to have recourse to arms and to re-commence the war.

And then it was that the expedition to Naples was set on foot under the command of Monsieur de Lautrec, who (as I have already said) dispatched a courier to me into Gascony to raise a company of foot, which I also in a few days performed, and brought him betwixt seven and eight hundred men of which four or five hundred were arquebusiers, though at that time there was but very few of them in France. Of these Monsieur d'Aussun entreated of me the one half for the completing of his company, which I granted to him, and we made our division near to Alexandrie [Alessandria], which at this time was surrendered to the said Monsieur de Lautrec,[1] who from thence sent Messieurs de Gramont and de Monpezat [Montpezat][2] to besiege the castle de Vigeve [Vigevano]; before which place, as we were making our approaches and casting up trenches to plant the artillery, I was hurt with an arquebus shot in my right leg, of which shot I remained lame a long time after; insomuch that I could not be at the storming of Pavia, which was carried by assault and half burnt down to the ground. Nevertheless I caused myself to be carried in a litter after the camp, and before Monsieur de Lautrec departed from Parme [Parma] to march away to Bouloigne [Bologna] I again began to walk.

The attack on Forcha di Penne, where Monluc is wounded, February 1528

Now near unto Ascolly [Ascoli][3] there is a little town called Forcha di Penne seated upon the top of a mountain, of so difficult access that the ascent is very steep on all sides, saving on those of the two gates, into which a great number of the soldiers of the country had withdrawn and fortified themselves. The Count Pedro de Navarre,[4] who was our colonel, commanded our Gascon companies to attack this post, which we accordingly did and assaulted the place. We caused some mantelets to be made wherewith to approach the wall, in which we made two holes of capacity sufficient for a man easily to enter in, about fifty or

[1] Alessandria, Piedmont, on the Tanaro, fell on 12 September 1527. See map, p. 59.

[2] Antoine de Lettes, Sieur de Montpezat (died c. 1544), achieved fame in Piedmont and was made Marshal of France in 1543.

[3] Ascoli Piceno, Marches, on the Tronto, which marks the north-eastern boundary of the Kingdom of Naples.

[4] Pedro Navarro (c. 1460–1528), celebrated military engineer, born the son of a Pyrenean shepherd, at this time in the service of France.

threescore paces distant the one from the other; whereof I having made the one, I would myself needs be the first to enter at that place. The enemy on the other side had in the meantime pulled up the planks and removed the boards and tables from the roof of a parlour into which this hole was made, and where they had placed a great tub full of stones. One of the companies of Monsieur de Luppé, our lieutenant-colonel, and mine prepared to enter at this place, and now God had granted me the thing that I had ever desired, which was to be present at an assault, there to enter the first man or lose my life. I therefore threw myself headlong into the parlour, having on a coat of mail such as the Germans used in those days, a sword in my hand, a target upon my arm and a morion upon my head. But as those who were at my heels were pressing to get in after me, the enemy poured the great tub of stones upon their heads and trapped them in the hole, by reason whereof they could not possibly follow.

I therefore remained all alone within, fighting at a door that went out into the street. But from the roof of the parlour, which was un-planked and laid open for that purpose, they peppered me in the meantime with an infinite number of arquebus shot, one of which pierced my target and shot my arm quite through, within four fingers of my hand, and another so battered the bone at the knitting of my arm and shoulder, that I lost all manner of feeling, so that letting my target fall I was constrained to retire towards my hole, against which I was borne over by those who fought at the door of the parlour; but so fortunately nevertheless for me that my soldiers had, by that means, opportunity to draw me out by the legs, but so leisurely withal, that they very courteously made me tumble heels over head from the very top to the bottom of the graffe, wherein rolling over the ruins of the stones I again broke my already wounded arm in two places. So soon as my men had gathered me up, I told them that I thought I had left my arm behind me in the town, when one of my soldiers, lifting it up from whence it hung, as in a scarf, dangling upon my buttocks, and laying it over the other, put me into a little heart. After which, seeing the soldiers of my own company gathered round about me: 'Oh, my comrades,' said I, 'have I always used you so kindly and ever loved you so well, to forsake me in such a time as this?' Which I said, not knowing how they had been hindered from following me in.

Upon this my lieutenant, who had almost been stifled to death in the hole, called La Bastide (father to the Savaillans now living, and one of the bravest gentlemen in our army) proposed to two Basque captains called Martin and Ramonet, who always quartered near unto my company; that if they would with ladders storm by a canton of the wall hard by, he would undertake at the same time to enter by the hole itself, and either force his entry that way or lose his life in the attempt. To which I also encouraged them, as much as my weakness would permit. The ladders being therefore presently brought and tied together, because they proved too short, La Bastide made towards the hole, having sent to the other captains to do as much to the other; but they did no great feats. In the interim that La Bastide was fighting within, having already gained the hole, Martin and Ramonet gave a brave scalado to the canton, and with so good success that they beat the enemy from the wall and entered the town. Of this being presently advertised, I sent to La Bastide to conjure him to save me as many women and maids as he possibly could, that they might not be violated (having that in devotion for a vow I had made to our Lady of Loretto, hoping that God, for this good act, would please to be assisting to me): which he did, bringing fifteen or twenty, which were also all that were saved; the soldiers being so animated to revenge the wounds I had received and to express their affection to me that they killed all before them, so much as to the very children, and moreover set the town on fire. And although the Bishop of Ascoli (this being a member of his diocese) was very importunate with Monsieur de Lautrec in behalf of the town, the soldiers could notwithstanding never be made to leave it till they saw it reduced to ashes.

The next day I was carried to Ascoli where Monsieur de Lautrec sent Messieurs de Gramont and de Montpezat to see how I did, with whom he moreover sent two surgeons the King had given him at his departure, the one called Master Alesme and the other Master George; who, after they had seen how miserably my arm was mangled and shattered, positively pronounced that there was no other way to save my life but to cut it off, the execution whereof was deferred till the next morning. Monsieur de Lautrec thereupon commanded the said Sieurs de Montpezat and de Gramont to be present at the work, which they promised they would, but not without some difficulty, out of the friendship they both had for me, especially the Sieur de Gramont.

Now you must understand that my soldiers had a few days before taken prisoner a young man, a surgeon, who had formerly belonged to Monsieur de Bourbon. This young fellow, having understood the determination to cut off my arm (for I had entertained him into my service), never ceased to importune me by no means to endure it; representing to me that I was not as yet arrived to the one half of my age, and that I would wish myself dead an hundred times a day when I should come to be sensible of the want of an arm. The morning being come, the forementioned lords and the two surgeons and physicians came into my chamber with all their instruments and plasters, without more ceremony or giving me so much as leisure to repent, to cut off my arm, having in command from Monsieur de Lautrec to tell me that I should not consider the loss of an arm to save my life, nor despair of my fortune. For although his Majesty should not regard my service nor take it into consideration to settle a subsistence for me, yet that nevertheless his wife and himself had forty thousand *livres* a year revenue wherewith to recompense my valour and to provide that I should never want; only he wished me to have patience and to manifest my courage upon this occasion.

Everything being now ready and my arm going to be opened to be cut off, the young surgeon standing behind my bed's head never desisted preaching to me by no means to suffer it, insomuch that (as God would have it) though I was prepared and resolved to let them do what they would with me, he made me to alter my determination. Whereupon without doing any thing any more, both the lords and the surgeons returned back to Monsieur de Lautrec to give him an account of the business, who (as they have all of them several times since assured me) said these words: 'I am glad to hear he is so resolved, and should also myself have repented the causing of it to be done. For had he died, I should ever have suspected myself to have been the occasion of his death; and had he lived without an arm, I should never have looked upon him but with exceeding great trouble to see him in such a condition. Let God therefore work his will.'

Immediately after the two forenamed surgeons came to examine mine, whether or no he was sufficient to undertake the cure for otherwise it was ordered that one of them should remain with me. But they found him capable enough; to which they also added some instructions what was to be done upon such accidents as might happen. The next day, which was the fourth after my hurt, Monsieur de Lautrec caused me to be carried after him to Termes de Brousse [Termine, dei Abruzzi], where he left me in his own quarters to the care of the man of the house, who was a gentleman, and for the further assurance of my person carried hostages with him, two of the most considerable men of the town, whereof one was brother to the gentleman of the house, assuring them that if any the least foul play was offered to me those two men should infallibly be hanged. In this place I remained two months and a half, lying continually upon my back, insomuch that my very backbone pierced through my skin, which is doubtless the greatest torment that any one in the world can possibly endure.

And although I have written in this narrative of my life that I have been one of the most fortunate men that have borne arms these many years, in that I have ever been victorious wherever I commanded, yet have I not been exempt from great wounds and dangerous sicknesses, of which I have had as many and as great as any man ever had who outlived them. God being still pleased to curb my pride that I might know myself and acknowledge all good and evil to depend upon his pleasure: but all this notwithstanding a scurvy, sour, morose and choleric nature of my own (which savours a little, and too much of my native soil) has evermore made me play one trick or another of a Gascon, which also I have no great reason to repent.

So soon as my arm was come to a perfect suppuration, they began to raise me out of bed, having a little cushion under my arm, and both that and my arm swathed up close to my body. In this posture I continued a few days longer, until mounting a little mule that I had, I caused myself to be carried before Naples, where our camp was already sat down, having first sent away a gentleman of mine on foot to our Lady of Loretto to accomplish my vow, I myself being in no condition to perform it. The pain I had suffered was neither so insupportable nor so great as the affliction I had not to have been present at the taking of Melphe [Melfi] and other places; nor at the defeating of the Prince of Orange, who after the death of Monsieur de Bourbon (slain at the sack of Rome) commanded the Imperial Army.[1] Had not this valiant prince (of deplorable memory, for the foulness of his revolt from his lord and master) died in the very height of his victories, I do believe he had sent us back the Popes into Avignon once again.

The expedition jeopardized by the treason of Andrea Doria

At my arrival at the camp, Monsieur de Lautrec and all the other great persons of the army received me with great demonstrations of kindness and esteem, and particularly Count Pedro Navarro, who caused a confiscation to be settled upon me of the value of twelve hundred ducats' yearly revenue called la Tour de la Nunciade [Torre

---

[1] Melfi fell on 23 March: Orange defeated at Troja on 15 March 1528.

dell' Annunziata], one of the fairest castles in all the territory of
Labour [Lavoro], and the first barony of Naples, belonging to a rich
Spaniard called Manferdino. I then thought myself the greatest lord
in all the army, but I found myself the poorest rogue in the end, as you
shall see by the continuation of this discourse. I could here dilate at full
how the kingdom of Naples was lost, after it was almost wholly conquered, a story that has been writ by many; but it is great pity they
would not or durst not relate the truth, being that kings and princes
might have been taught to be so wary by this example as not to
suffer themselves to be imposed upon and abused, as they very often
are. But nobody would have the great ones learn to be too wise, for
then they could not play their own games with them so well as they
commonly do. I shall therefore let it alone, both for that I do not
pretend to record the faults of other men, as also because I had no
hand in these transactions, and shall only write my own fortunes to
serve for instruction to such as shall follow after, that the little Monlucs
my sons have left me may look with some kind of glory into the life
of their grandfather and aim at honourable things by his example.

There were no great matters performed after my coming to the
camp, neither did they busy themselves about anything but the city
of Naples, which also they intended to overcome by famine, and it
must suddenly have fallen into our hands, had it not been for the
revolt of Andrea Doria,[1] who sent to Count Philippin [Filippino
Doria] his nephew to bring back his galleys to Genoa, with which he
kept the city of Naples so close blocked up by sea that a cat could not
have got in; which he immediately did, and thereupon an infinite of
provision was put into the town by sea, whilst our galleys delayed to
come. God forgive him who was the cause thereof, without which
accident the town had been our own, and consequently the whole
kingdom. This Filippino, lieutenant or vice-admiral to Andrea Doria,
near unto Capo-d'Orso obtained a famous naval victory over Ugo de
Moncada and the Marquis de Guast [del Vasto][2], who came to the
relief of Naples. But from this victory proceeded our ruin; for
Filippino, having sent his prisoners to his uncle to Genoa, and the
King being importunate to have them delivered over to him, Andrea
Doria would by no means part with them, complaining that he had
already delivered up the Prince of Orange to the King, without any

---

[1] Andrea Doria (1466-1560), celebrated Genoese Admiral.

[2] For del Vasto see Appendix I, 'Avalos, Alfonso d'.' The naval victory of Doria, then in
the service of France, was that of Salerno, April 1528.

recompense. Upon which occasion the Marquis del Vasto (a man of as great dexterity and cunning as any of his time, and a great warrior) knew so well how to manage Andrea Doria's discontent that in the end he turned his coat and with twelve galleys went over to the Emperor's side. The King our master was well enough informed of all his practices and might easily enough have prevented the mischief, but his heart was so great and he was so highly offended with Doria that he would never seek to him, whereof he repented at leisure; for he has since been the cause of many losses that have befallen the King, and particularly of the kingdom of Naples, Genoa, and other misfortunes. It seemed as if the sea stood in awe of this man; wherefore without a very great and more than ordinary occasion, he was not fit to have been provoked or disgusted. But perhaps the King might have some other reason.

Monluc, his arm in a scarf, distinguished himself in a skirmish at the Maddalena, outside Naples. Despite such actions, the French expedition to Naples was doomed: Lautrec died, and the siege was raised, August 1528

This was the last engagement where I had anything to do, wherein though I did not command in chief, yet had I notwithstanding the command of a very good company of foot and had my full share of the fight that was very handsome, but not for all; which I have set down to acquit myself of my promise, to wit, that I would give a particular account of all those passages wherein I had the honour to command: passing the rest lightly over, as I do the remainder of this unfortunate siege, which we were at last constrained to raise, Monsieur de Lautrec being dead, to the great misfortune of all France which never had a captain endowed with better qualities than he was; but he was unhappy and ill assisted by the King after his Majesty had engaged him, as he did first at Milan and now lastly before Naples. For my part with that little that was saved, which was almost nothing, I returned the greatest part of my journey on foot, with my arm in a scarf (having above thirty ells of taffeta about me, forasmuch as they had bound my arm and my body together with a cushion between), wishing a thousand times rather to die than to live; for I had lost all my masters and friends who knew and loved me, being all dead excepting Monsieur de Montpezat (the father of this now living),[1] and poor Don Pedro [Navarro] our colonel taken and carried prisoner

[1] Jacques des Prez, bishop of Montauban, was the only son of Montpezat living in 1571.

into the Rock of Naples, where they put him to death, the Emperor
having commanded that for the reward of his revolt they should cut
off his head. He was a man of great understanding, in whom Monsieur
de Lautrec (who confided in few persons) had a very great confidence.
I do also believe (and am not single in that opinion) that he counselled
him ill in this war, but what! we only judge by events.

In this handsome equipage I came home to my father's house
where, poor gentleman, I found him engaged in too many necessities
of his own to be in any capacity of much assisting me; forasmuch as
his father had sold three parts of four of the estate of the family and
had left the remainder charged with five children by a second venture,
besides us of my father's who were no less than ten. By which anyone
may judge in what necessities we who are come out of the family of
Monluc have been constrained to follow the fortunes of the world.
And yet our house was not so contemptible but that it had near upon
five thousand *livres'* yearly revenue belonging to it, before it was sold.
To fit myself in all points I was constrained to stay three years at home,

without being able to get any cure for my arm; and after I was cured I was to begin the world again as I did the first day I came out from a page, and as a person unknown seek my fortune in all sorts of necessities and with extreme peril of my life. I praise God for all, who in all the traverses of my life has ever been assisting to me.

Upon the first motions of war King Francis instituted his *Légionnaires*,[1] which was a very fine invention had it been well pursued (for a start all our laws and ordinances are observed and kept, but after a while neglected and let down), for it is the true and only way to have always a good army on foot (as the Romans did) and to train up the people to war, though I know not whether that be good or evil. It has been much controverted, though I for my part had rather trust to my own people, than to strangers.

The years of peace, and Monluc's inactivity, were ended when Charles V invaded Provence in the summer of 1536 and laid siege to Marseilles. An attack on the flour mills near Aix, supplying the Imperial army, is debated at Marseilles

Whilst the Emperor lay very long at Aix, in expectation of his great cannon wherewith to come and batter the walls of Marseilles, his provisions did every day more and more waste and diminish. In which point of time the King arrived at Avignon,[2] where his Majesty was advertised that if means could be made to destroy some mills the Emperor had seized into his hands towards Arles, and especially one within four leagues of Aix called the mill of Auriole [Auriol], the enemy's camp would soon suffer for want of bread. Upon which advice the King committed the execution of the burning of those mills about Arles to the Baron de la Garde, who had a company of foot, to Captain Thorines, standard-bearer to the Count de Tandes [de Tende], and some others, who accordingly executed the design. Which notwithstanding the spies still brought word to the King that he must also burn those of Auriol, forasmuch as they alone ordinarily nourished not the Emperor's whole household only but moreover the six thousand old Spanish foot which he always kept about his own person. His Majesty sent therefore several times to Messieurs de Barbezieux[3]

[1] Francis I introduced the Legions, to provide native French infantry for the army, on a regional basis, in 1534.

[2] On 12 September, 1536.

[3] Antoine de La Rochefoucauld, Sieur de Barbezieux, French general.

and de Montpezat[1] to hazard a regiment of men to go and burn the said mills of Auriol.

The first to whom they recommended the execution thereof was to the foresaid Christofle Goast [Christophe Guasco], who positively refused to undertake it, alleging that it was five leagues to the aforesaid mills, where they were to fight threescore guards that were within it and an entire company that were quartered in the town, so that he should have five leagues to go and as many to return, by means whereof he should going or coming be infallibly defeated upon the way, for the Emperor could not fail of intelligence, it being no more than four leagues only from the said Auriol to Aix; and on the other side the soldiers would never be able to travel ten long leagues without baiting by the way. This answer was sent back to the King, who notwithstanding would not take it for current pay but on the contrary sent another more positive order than the former, that it should be proposed to some others and that though a thousand men should be lost in the enterprise, yet let them not concern themselves, for the benefit that would accrue by burning the mills would countervail the loss (such easy markets princes make of the lives of men).

Whereupon it was offered to Monsieur de Fonteraille, who was once in mind to undertake it, but some of his friends representing to him his certain ruin in the attempt, he pissed backwards and would by no means touch. All which being sent word of to his Majesty (who continually had the manifest advantage the destroying of the other mills had brought to his Majesty's affairs, reminded to him), he still persisted to press the aforesaid lords to send someone or another to demolish these. Now one day, after I had heard how discontented the King was, and the excuses that had been alleged by those to whom it had hitherto been recommended (which in truth were very rational and just), I began to meditate with myself which way I might execute this design, and to consider that if God would give me the grace to bring it about, it would be a means to bring me to the knowledge of the King and to restore me to the fame, reputation and acquaintance I had formerly acquired, and that now by three years' idleness and the length of my cure was as good as vanished and lost; for it is nothing to get a good repute if a man do not uphold and improve it. Having therefore taken with myself a resolution to execute this design or to die in the attempt, I informed myself at full of my landlord of the situation and condition of the place where these mills were; who told

[1] See above, p. 52 n. 2.

me that Auriol was a little town enclosed with high walls, where there was a castle well fortified and a *bourg* composed of many houses with a fair street through the middle of it, and at the end of the said *bourg*, which led from the town towards the mill, was a little on the left hand the mill itself. That at the gate of the said town there was a tower which looked directly down the great street towards the mill, before which no man could stand without running great hazard of being either slain or wounded; and that beyond the mill was a little church at the distance of about thirty or forty paces. He told me moreover that I was to go to Aubaigne [Aubagne], two leagues from Marseilles, and that from thence to Auriol it was three more if we went by the mountains which the horse could not possibly do; but must be constrained to go near upon a league about, where they were moreover to pass a river that was deep to the saddle skirts, by reason that the bridges had been broken down.

My landlord having told me all this, I considered that if I should undertake this affair with a great party, I should be defeated; for the place being only four leagues distant from the Emperor's camp, he would have present intelligence and would send out his horse to intercept me in my return, as it also fell out; for immediately upon our coming to the mill, the captain of the castle dispatched away in all haste to the Emperor. So that I conceived it much better for me to undertake it with a small number of men, and those light and active fellows; to the end that if I did the work I went for, I might either have means to retire by one way or another, or at the worst if I should throw myself away and those who were with me, yet they being but a few, the city of Marseilles would by that miscarriage be in no manner of danger to be lost, which was the thing most disputed in the Council; whereas by losing a thousand or twelve hundred men, which were thought a necessary proportion for such an enterprise, the said city might be exposed to some danger, especially in a time when they expected a siege.

I then desired my landlord to provide me three fellows who were expert in the ways, to guide me by night to the said Auriol, and so that, as near as could be guessed, they should bring me to the mills two hours before day; which he accordingly did, when after having some time consulted with them, I found the men were fearful and loth to go; but at last mine host so encouraged them that they were all resolved. Whereupon I gave to each of them a brace of crowns and caused them to be kept up in my lodging, which was about noon; and having computed with my landlord how many hours the nights were then long, we found that provided I should set out about the twilight, I should have time enough to do my business.

All this being done, that my design might not be known, I went myself first to Monsieur de Montpezat to acquaint him with what I intended to do, and moreover that I was resolved to take with me no more than six score men only, which I would choose out of the Seneschal's Regiment to which I was lieutenant.[1] In all places wherever I have been, I have still made it my study to discern betwixt the good men and the bad, and to judge what they were able to do; for all men are not proper for all uses.

The said Sieur de Montpezat thought my resolution very strange, and out of friendship advised me not to do so ridiculous a thing as to hazard myself with so few men; telling me that I might as well have five hundred if I would. To which I made answer that I would never demand five hundred men for the execution of an enterprise that I could better perform with six score, and tormented him so that in the end he was constrained to go along with me to Monsieur de Barbezieux, who yet thought it more strange than the other and would needs know of me my reasons and by what means I would execute this design with so few people. To whom I made answer that I would not declare to anyone living which way I intended to proceed, but that nevertheless (if they so pleased) I would undertake it. Whereupon Monsieur de Montpezat said to him: 'Let him go; for though he should be lost and all those with him, the city will not for that be in the more danger to be lost, and it will give his Majesty content.' Monsieur de Villebon,[2] who was present at the deliberation, laughed and jeered at me, saying to Monsieur de Barbezieux: 'Let him go, he will infallibly take the Emperor and we shall all be ashamed when we see him bring him into the city tomorrow morning.' Now this man did not love me, for some words that had passed betwixt us at the Port Royal;[3] neither could I forbear to tell him that he was like a dog in a manger that would neither eat himself nor suffer others. All was passed over in jest, though in plain truth I was half angry, for a little spurring would serve to make me start. The Seneschal de Toulouse, my colonel, adhered to my opinion, whereupon I had immediate

[1] Monluc was at this time lieutenant in the Languedoc legion, commanded by the *Sénéchal* of Toulouse.

[2] Jean d' Estouteville, Sieur de Villebon, Provost of Paris.

[3] One of the gates at Marseilles.

leave granted me to go choose out my six score men and no more, which I did, taking only one *centenier* and the *caps d'escouade*,[1] the rest were all gentlemen, and so brave a company that they were better than five hundred others. It is not all to have a great number of men, they sometimes do more hurt than good, which made me entreat Monsieur de Barbezieux to cause the gate of the city to be shut, being well assured that otherwise I should have had more company than I desired; which he also did, and it happened well for another reason, for in less than an hour my design was spread all over the whole city.

The raid on the mills at Auriol, 19 August 1536

Just at sunset I with my six score men repaired to the gate, the wicket whereof was only open, but the street was so full of soldiers, ready to go out with me, that I had much ado to distinguish my own, and was therefore constrained to make them all take hands, for I very well knew them every one. As I was going out of the gate, Monsieur de Tavannes[2] (who was since Marshal of France and at this time standard-bearer to the *Grand Ecuyer* Galiot)[3] came to me with fifteen or twenty gentlemen of their own company, telling me that he with those friends of his were come to offer themselves, resolved to run all hazards with me in the execution of my design. I used all the arguments I could to divert him from that resolution, but it was time and labour lost, for both he and those with him were all positively resolved. Messieurs de Barbezieux, de Montpezat, de Botières [de Boutières], de Villebon and the Seneschal de Toulouse were all without the gate and before the wicket, drawing us out one by one, when Monsieur de Tavannes offering to pass, Monsieur de Barbezieux would not permit him, telling him that he should be none of the party, and there some words and a little anger passed both on one side and the other; but Monsieur de Tavannes overcame at last and passed the wicket, for which cause they detained from me fifteen or twenty men of those I had chosen; but I lost nothing by the exchange, only these disputes deferred the time so long that the night was shut up before we began to march. Monsieur de Castelpers, lieutenant to Monsieur de Mont-

---

[1] *Centenier* (= centurion) and *cap d'escouade* were the more junior officers in the Legions, the equivalent of captain and lieutenant.

[2] Gaspard de Saulx–Tavannes (1509–73), French commander and Marshal of France.

[3] Ricard, Jacques, Sieur de Genouilhac, called Galiot (d. 1546), was the celebrated Grand Master of the Artillery to Francis I, as well as *Grand Ecuyer* (Master of the Horse).

pezat (who was my very particular friend), having heard how I had been railled and jeered amongst them, determined to get to horse with some fifteen or twenty men at arms of the said company, being all very well mounted, and to that end had spoken to Monsieur de Montpezat at his going out of the gate, to entreat him that he would not be displeased if he made one in the enterprise, telling him that I was a Gascon and that if I failed in the attempt, it would beget matter of sport for the French and they would laugh us to scorn. Monsieur de Montpezat was at first unwilling to it but, seeing him begin to grow into a little heat, at last consented, whereupon he presently ran to mount to horse and there might be nineteen or twenty of the party.

Now to give a full account of this enterprise (which although it was not the conquest of Milan, may nevertheless be of some use to such as will make their advantage of it), so soon as we came to the Plan Sainct Michel [Place St Michel],[1] I gave to Captain Belsoleil (*centenier* to our company) threescore men; and threescore I kept for myself (Monsieur de Tavannes and his followers being comprised in that number), to whom I also delivered a good guide, telling him withal that he was not to come near me by a hundred paces and that we would continually march at a good round rate. Which order being given and Monsieur de Tavannes and I beginning to set forward, up comes Monsieur de Castelpers, of whose deliberation we till then knew nothing, forasmuch as it had been resolved upon at the very moment of our going out at the wicket, which hindered us another long half hour. But in the end we agreed that he should go the horse way and gave him another of my guides which he mounted behind one of his men; so that we had three parties, and to every party a guide. At our parting I gave him instructions that so soon as he should arrive at the end of the *bourg*, he should draw up behind the church, for should they enter into the street, the company quartered in the town would either kill them or their horses, and that therefore he was not to appear till first he heard us engaged.

We now began to set forward and marched all night, where as far as Aubagne we found the way to be exceeding good; but from thence to Auriol we were fain to crawl over the sides of mountains where, I believe, never anything but goats had gone before; by which abominable way, having got within half a quarter of a league of Auriol, I made a halt, bidding Monsieur de Tavannes to stay there for me, for I must go speak with Belsoleil. I therefore went back and met him

[1] Nowadays part of the city of Marseilles.

within a hundred paces of us or less; where speaking to him and his guide, I told him that when he should arrive at the *bourg* he was by no means to follow me, but to march directly to the gate of the town, betwixt the *bourg* and the said town, and there make a stand at the gate, it being necessary that he should gain two houses next adjoining to the said gate, which he must suddenly break into to keep the enemy from sallying out to disturb us; and that there he was to stay and fight, without taking any care to relieve us at all. After which order given to him, I moreover passed the word from hand to hand to all the soldiers that no-one was to abandon the fight at the gate to come to us to the mill; but that they were punctually to observe whatever Captain Belsoleil should command them.

Returning then back to Monsieur de Tavannes, we again began to march, when being come near to the castle, under which and close by the walls of the town, we were of necessity to pass, their sentinels twice called out to us: 'Who goes there?' To which we made no answer at all but still went on our way, till coming close to the *bourg* we left the way that Captain Belsoleil was to take and slipped behind the houses of the said *bourg*, when being come to the further end where the mill stood we were to descend two or three stone steps to enter into the street, where we found a sentinel that never discovered us till we were within a pike's length of him, and then he cried: '*Qui vive?*' To which I made answer in Spanish: '*Espaigne*' (wherein I was mistaken, for the word was not then '*Espaigne*', but '*Impery*'); whereupon without more ceremony he gave fire, but hit nothing.

The alarm being by this means given, Monsieur de Tavannes and I threw ourselves desperately into the street and were bravely followed; where we found three or four of the enemy without the door of the mill, but they immediately ran in. The door of this mill was made with two folding leaves, both which were to be bolted fast with a great iron bar on the inside; one of these had a great chest behind it and the other the foresaid bar held more than half shut, and had these fellows behind it. The mill was full of men, both above stairs and below (for there was threescore men in it, with the captain, who had no dependence upon the governor of the town, each of them having his command apart), and we were one by one to enter this place.

Monsieur de Tavannes would very fain first have entered and pressed forward with that intent, but I, pulling him back by the arm, withheld him and pushed in a soldier that was behind me; the enemy made but two arquebus shot, having leisure to do no more, being all

fast asleep excepting these three or four who had been placed as
sentinels before the mill door in the street. So soon as the soldier was
got in, I said to Monsieur de Tavannes: 'Now enter if you will';
which he presently did, and I after him, where we began to lay about
us to some purpose, there being no more but one light only to fight
by within. In this bustle the enemy by a pair of stone stairs of indifferent wideness recovered the upper room, where they stoutly defended the said stairs from the floor above, whilst I in the meantime
sent a soldier to tell the rest that were without that they should get up
upon the outside of the mill and, uncovering the roof, shoot down
upon their heads, which was immediately performed; so that the
enemy perceiving our men to be got upon the roof and that they
already let fly amongst them, they began to throw themselves into
the water out of a window on the backside of the mill. But we
nevertheless mounted the stairs and killed all those that remained, the
captain excepted, who with two wounds and seven others all wounded
were taken prisoners. Hereupon I presently sent one away to Captain
Belsoleil to bid him take courage and stoutly to dispute the gate of the
town, for the mill was our own.

The alarm in the meantime in the town was very great, and those
within three times attempted to sally; but our men held them so short
that they durst never open their gates. I sent Captain Belsoleil moreover most of my men to assist him and in the meantime, with the rest,
fell to burning the mill, taking away all the ironwork, especially the
spindles and rinds, that it might not be repaired again, never leaving it
till it was entirely burnt down to the ground and the millstones rolled
into the river. Now you must know that Captain Tavannes took it a
little to heart that I had pulled him back by the arm, and asked me
afterwards upon our return why I would not permit him to enter
the first, suspecting I had more mind to give the honour of it to the
soldiers; to whom I made answer that I knew he was not yet so crafty
to save himself as those old soldiers were, and that, moreover, that was
not a place considerable enough for a man of his worth and condition
to die in, but that he was to reserve himself for a noble breach and not
to lose his life in a paltry mill.

Whilst these things were in doing, Monsieur de Castelpers arrived
and, leaving his party behind the church, came up to us on foot, and
upon this the day began to appear. Wherefore I entreated Monsieur
de Tavannes and de Castelpers to retire behind the church (for the
shot flew very thick in the street, where they could see anyone pass),

telling them that I would go draw off Belsoleil. Whereupon they both accordingly retired, and as I was drawing off our men one after another running down on both sides the street, Monsieur de Castelpers presented himself with his twenty horse at the end of the street by the church, wherein he did us very great service for the enemy might otherwise have sallied out upon us. I had only seven or eight men hurt, who nevertheless were all able to march, one gentleman only excepted, called Vignaux, whom we set upon an ass of those we had found in the mill, and presently began to retire towards the top of a mountain, which was almost the same way by which Monsieur de Castelpers had come, when the enemy, discovering us to be so few, they all sallied out in our rear. But we had already gained the top of the hill when they arrived but at the foot of it, and before they recovered the height we were got into the valley on the other side, ready to climb another (there being many little hills in that place), and yet we never marched faster than a foot pace, and so went straight on to Aubagne.

I had given order to the soldiers that went along with us that everyone should take with him a loaf of bread, which they ate by the way, and I also had caused some few to be brought, which I divided amongst the *gendarmes* of Monsieur de Tavannes, and we ourselves ate as we went; which I here set down to the end that when any captain shall go upon an enterprise where he is to have a long march, he may take example to cause something to be brought along to eat wherewith to refresh the soldiers, that they may be the better able to hold out; for men are not made of iron.

So soon as we were come to Aubagne, two leagues from Marseilles,[1] where we had thought to have halted and to have taken some refreshment, we heard the artillery of the galleys and of the town, which at that distance seemed to be volleys of arquebus shot, an alarm that constrained us without further delay, or taking any other refreshment than what we had brought along with us, to march forwards and to enter into consultation amongst ourselves what course we were best to take. We already took it for granted that the Emperor was arrived before the town and that he would certainly sit down before it, and then concluded it impossible for us to get in again, which made us often repent and curse the enterprise that had shut us out, the misfortune whereof was wholly laid to my charge as the author of all. In this uncertainty what course to steer, Monsieur de Castelpers was once resolved to go charge desperately through the

[1] In fact, 17 kilometres.

enemy's camp to get into the city; but when he came to acquaint us with his determination we remonstrated to him that that would be to throw himself away out of an humour, and that since we had together performed so brave a service, and with which the King would be so highly pleased, we ought likewise together either to perish or to save ourselves. Captain Trebons, *guidon* to the company of Monsieur de Montpezat, told him the same, so that we concluded in the end to leave the great highway, and crossing the mountains on the left hand to fall down behind Nostre Dame de la Garde,[1] making account, that in case we could not enter into the city, the captain of the said citadel would receive us in there. So we turned out of the way, and it was well for us that we did so, for Vignaux and the wounded, keeping on the great road straight to Marseilles, had not gone on five hundred paces but they met with four or five hundred horse which the Emperor (having had intelligence from those of Auriol of what had been done) had sent out to meet and fight us upon the way. And had not the Emperor parted from Aix by night to go before Marseilles, so that the messengers of a long time could meet with nobody to whom to deliver their errand, I do believe we had certainly been defeated: but the Emperor knew nothing of it till break of day, whereupon he presently sent out those four or five hundred horse upon the road to Aubagne, who did no other harm to Vignaux and those who were with him but only took away their arms.

In this manner we travailed all day from mountain to mountain in the excessive heat, without finding one drop of water, insomuch that we were all ready to die for thirst; always within sight of the Emperor's camp and ever within hearing of the skirmishes that were made before the town, Monsieur de Castelpers and his *gendarmes* marching all the way on foot, as we did, and leading their horses in their hands, till coming near to Notre Dame de la Garde, the captain of the castle taking us for the enemy let fly three or four pieces of cannon at us, which forced us to shift behind the rocks. From thence we made signs with our hats, but for all that he ceased not to shoot till in the end, having sent out a soldier to make a sign, so soon as he understood who we were he gave over shooting, and as we came before Notre Dame de la Garde we saw the Emperor, who was retiring by the way he came, and Christophe Guasco, who had all day maintained the skirmish, beginning also to retreat towards the city.[2] We then began

[1] Notre Dame de la Garde, close to Marseilles.
[2] i.e. Marseilles.

to descend the mountain; when so soon as Monsieur de Barbezieux and Monsieur de Montpezat (who, with some other captains, were standing without the gates of the city) had discovered us, they would have gone in again, taking us for the enemy. But somebody saying that then those of the castle would have shot at us, the said Sieur de Montpezat presently knew Monsieur de Castelpers, and we thereupon arrived at the gate of the city where we were mightily caressed, especially when they heard of the good success of our enterprise, and they talked with the captain of the mill who was wounded in the arm and in the head, and after everyone retired to his own quarters.

I made no manner of question but that Monsieur de Barbezieux, so soon as the King should come to Marseilles, would have presented me to his Majesty and have told him that I was the man who had performed this exploit, that his Majesty might have taken notice of me. But he was so far from doing me that friendship that on the contrary he attributed all the honour to himself, saying that it was he who had laid the design of this enterprise and had only delivered it to us to execute, and Monsieur de Montpezat was by ill fortune at that time very sick and could say nothing in my behalf, so that I remained as much a stranger to the King as ever. I came to know all this by the means of Henry King of Navarre, who told me that he himself had seen the letters which the said Sieur de Barbezieux had writ to the King to that effect, wherein he attributed to himself the whole honour of that action. Monsieur de Lautrec would not have served me so, neither is it handsome to rob another man of his honour, and there is nothing that does more discourage a brave heart: but Monsieur de Tavannes, who is now living, can testify the truth. So it is that the destroying of these mills, both the one and the other, especially those of Auriol, reduced the Emperor's camp to so great necessity that they were fain to eat the corn pounded in a mortar after the manner of the Turks, and the grapes they ate put their camp into so great a disorder and brought so great a mortality amongst them, especially the Germans, that I verily believe there never returned a thousand of them into their own country. And this was the issue of this mighty preparation.

The captains who shall read this relation may perhaps observe that in this enterprise there was more of fortune than of reason, and that I went upon it as it were in the dark, though it was happily brought about: but I do not suspect however that anyone will conclude it to be wholly an effect of my good fortune, but will also take notice that I forgot nothing of what was necessary to make the design succeed;

and on the other side they may observe that my principal security was that the enemy within the town by the rule of war ought not to sally out of their garrison till they should first discover what our forces were, a thing in the obscurity of the night which they could very hardly do; all which notwithstanding, I did not yet so much rely upon their discretion but that I moreover put a bridle in their mouths, which was Belsoleil and his company. A man must often hazard something, for no-one can be certain of the event. I concluded the conquest of the mill for certain, but I ever thought it would be a matter of great difficulty and danger to retreat.

Thus did the Emperor Charles, both with shame and loss, retire, where that great leader Anne de Montmorency (at that time *Grand Maistre*, and since Constable of France) obtained renown. It was one of the greatest baffles the Emperor ever received, and for grief whereof his great captain Antonio de Leiva (as was reported) afterwards died. I have sometimes heard the Marquis del Vasto say that this expedition was the sole contrivance of the said Antonio de Leiva, and yet both he and his master very well knew what it was to attack a King of France in his own kingdom.

Little of moment occurs in the years immediately following, which were, after the Truce of Nice (1538), mainly peaceful. Hostilities were resumed, however, in 1542, and one of the main theatres of war was Piedmont, where Monluc arrived in the summer of 1543. The French held several strongholds, the Imperialists an equal number, and the war consisted of raids, sorties and skirmishes between forces from opposing garrisons. Monluc took part in those around Savigliano,[1] where de Thermes was Governor. In December 1543 he plotted, with de Thermes, the downfall of an Imperialist Governor, Pietro Porto: this was the enterprise of the merchant of Barge

Some time after Monsieur de Thermes[2] carried on an enterprise that was never discovered to any but to Monsieur Boutières and myself, not so much as to Monsieur de Tès [Taix],[3] though he was our colonel, and it was thus. There was a merchant of Barges [Barge], a great friend and servant to Monsieur de Thermes and a good Frenchman, called Granuchin, who, coming from Barge to Savillan [Savigliano], was taken by some light horse belonging to Count Pietro Porto,

---

[1] For this, and other places in Piedmont, see map, p. 59.

[2] For de Thermes, see Appendix I, 'La Barthe, Paul de'.

[3] For de Taix, see Appendix I, 'Taix, Jean de'.

Governor of Fossan [Fossano], and being a prisoner was sometimes threatened to be hanged and sometimes promised to be put to ransom, with so great uncertainty that the poor man for seven or eight days together was in despair of his life. But in the end he bethought himself to send word to the Count that if he would be pleased to give him leave to talk with him, he would propound things that should be both for his advantage and honour.

The Count thereupon sent for him where, being come, Granuchin told him that it should only stick at himself if he were not lord of Barge, for that it was in his power to deliver up the castle into his hands, the city not being strong at all. The Count, greedy to listen to this enterprise, presently closed with him about it, agreeing and concluding that Granuchin should deliver up his wife and his son in hostage. And the said Granuchin proposed the manner of it to be thus: saying that he was very intimate with the captain of the castle, and that the provisions that were put into it ever passed through his hands, and that moreover he had a share in some little traffic they had betwixt them: to wit, betwixt the said captain of the castle, called la Mothe, and himself; and that the Scotchman who kept the keys of the castle was his very intimate friend, whom he also evermore had caused to get something amongst them and whom he was certain he could make firm to his purpose. Not the captain de la Mothe nevertheless, but that he was sick of a quartan ague that held him fifteen or twenty hours together so that he almost continually kept his bed; and that so soon as he [Granuchin] should be at liberty he would go and complain to Monsieur de Thermes of two men that were reputed Imperialists, who had told him and given the enemy intelligence of his journey, and that after having left his wife and his son in hostage he would go and demand justice of Monsieur de Boutières by the mediation of Monsieur de Thermes and then would go to Barge to the castle, and that upon a Sunday morning he would cause fifteen or twenty soldiers that la Mothe had there to go out (leaving only the Scotchman, the butler and the cook within) to take those who had told him as they should be at the first mass in the morning; and in the meantime the Count should cause forty soldiers to march, who before day should place themselves in ambush in a little copse about an arquebus shot distant from the postern gate, and that so soon as it should be time for them to come he would set a white flag over the said postern.

Now there was a priest of Barge, who being banished thence lived at Fossano, that was a great friend to Granuchin and had laboured very much for his deliverance, and he also was called into the council, where amongst them it was concluded that the said priest on a night appointed should come to a little wood the half way betwixt Barge and Fossano, where he was to whistle to give notice that he was there, and that if he had corrupted the Scot he should bring him along with him to resolve amongst themselves how the business should be further carried on. Things being thus concluded, Granuchin wrote a letter to Monsieur de Thermes, wherein he entreated him to procure for him a safe conduct from Monsieur de Boutières, that his wife and his son might come to Fossano, there to remain pledges for him, for he had prevailed so far by the intercession of certain of his friends that the Count was at last content to dismiss him upon a ransom of six hundred crowns. But that if he was not abroad and at liberty no man would buy his goods, out of which he was to raise that sum; which safe conduct if he should obtain in his behalf he desired he would please to deliver it to a friend of his he named in Savigliano, to whom he also had writ to desire him to make what haste he could to send his wife and son to the said Fossano.

All this being accordingly procured and done, and the said Granuchin set at liberty, he forthwith came to Savigliano to find out Monsieur de Thermes, to whom he gave an account of the whole business. Whereupon Monsieur de Thermes (who already began to feel himself falling sick of a disease that commonly held him fourteen or fifteen days at a time) sent for me, to whom he communicated the enterprise, where it was by us all three concluded that Granuchin should go talk with Monsieur de Boutières and inform him at large of the whole design. To which purpose Monsieur de Thermes gave him a letter to Monsieur de Boutières who, having received and read it, made no great matter of the business, only writing back to Monsieur de Thermes that if he knew Granuchin to be a man fit to be trusted he might do as he thought fit. By which slight answer Monsieur de Thermes entered into an opinion that Monsieur de Boutières would be glad he should receive some baffle or affront (and indeed he did not much love him), which made him once in mind to break off the design and to meddle no more in it. But seeing the said Granuchin almost in despair to think that the business should not go forward, and I being more concerned than he that such an opportunity of trapping the enemy should be lost, earnestly entreated Monsieur de Thermes to leave the whole business to my care; which he made great difficulty to grant, ever fearing that should anything happen amiss, Monsieur de

Boutières would do him a courtesy to the King, as the custom is: for when anyone bears a man a grudge he is glad when he commits any oversight, that the master may have occasion to be offended and to remove him from his command, condemning him for that he would not be governed by the wise; but in the end with much importunity he was content to refer the management of the business wholly to my discretion.

The said Granuchin departed then to go to Barge, where he made discovery of all to Captain la Mothe and the Scotchman, to whom Monsieur de Thermes writ also; and the night appointed being come they both went out, and alone (for Granuchin was very well acquainted with the way), and came to the wood where they found the priest; with whom they agreed, first, that the said Count should acquit Granuchin of his ransom, giving him as much as the soldiers that took him had taken from him, and moreover appoint him an apartment in the castle with the captain he should put into it, with a certain pension for his support; and secondly, that he should marry the Scotchman to an inheritrix there was in Barge, and also find out some handsome employment for him, forasmuch as he was never after to return either into Scotland or into France. All which was agreed and concluded betwixt them, and moreover that the priest should bring all these articles signed and sealed with the arms of the said Count to a summer house in the fields belonging to the brother of the said priest to which he sometimes repaired at nights; and that the Sunday following the business should be put in execution.

Having accordingly received all these obligations, Granuchin returned again to Savigliano, where he gave us an account of all and showed us the bond. Now there was only three days to Sunday, wherefore we made him presently to return, having first agreed that he should bring along with him two guides of the very best he could find out; not that he should however discover anything to them of the business but only show them some counterfeit letters, wherein mention should be made of some wine he had bought for me.

The guides came accordingly by Saturday noon to Savigliano, when seeing them come I took Captain Fabas my lieutenant apart and privately in my chamber communicated to him the whole design, telling him withal that I had made choice of him for the execution of it; which he made no scruple to undertake (for he had mettle enough) and it was agreed that he should tie the guides together and that they were by no means to enter into any highway or road but to march across the fields. We had much ado to persuade the guides to this, forasmuch as they were to pass three or four rivers and there was snow and ice all along, so that we were above three hours disputing this way. But in the end the two guides were content, to each of which I gave ten crowns and moreover a very good supper.

We were of advice that we should not take many men, that less notice might be taken; and at that time we were making a rampire at that gate towards Fossano where, in order to that work, we had broken down a little part of the wall and made a bridge over the graffe, over which to bring in earth from without. By this breach I put out Captain Fabas, and with him four and thirty more only, and so soon as we were without we tied the guides for being lost and so he set forwards. The enemy's assignation and ours was at the same hour, so that Granuchin had directed them the way on the right hand to come to this copse, and ours he had ordered to march on the left hand near to the walls of the city; who so soon as they were come to the postern there found Granuchin and the Scot ready to receive them, it being the hour that the Scotchman used to stand sentinel over the said postern, so that they were never discovered, and he disposed them into a cellar of the castle where he had prepared a charcoal fire with some bread and wine. In the meantime the day began to break, and as the bell rung to mass down in the town the Scot and Granuchin commanded all the soldiers in the castle to go take these two men (that Granuchin had accused to have betrayed him) at mass, so that there remained no more in the castle but only la Mothe himself, his *valet de chambre* who also trailed a pike, the butler, the cook, the Scotchman and Granuchin.

The Scot then pulled up the bridge and called out Captain Fabas, making him to skulk behind certain bavins in the base court, kneeling upon one knee, which being done they went to set up the white flag upon the postern. Soon after the priest arrived and with him about forty soldiers, who were no sooner entered in but the Scotchman shut the gate and at the same instant Captain Fabas and his company flew upon them, who made some little resistance, insomuch that seven or eight of them were slain, but Granuchin saved the priest and would not endure he should have the least injury offered to him. In the meantime a country fellow, as he was coming from a little house below the castle, saw the Spanish soldiers with their red crosses enter in at the postern gate and thereupon ran down into the town to give the alarm and to tell them that the castle was betrayed, at which news the soldiers who had been sent out to take the two men at mass would have returned into the castle. But ours shot at them, though so high as not to hit them, taking upon them to be enemies and crying out: '*Imperi, Imperi, Savoy, Savoy*', which was the reason that the soldiers fled away to Pignerol carrying news to Monsieur de Boutières that Granuchin had betrayed the castle and that the enemy was within it. Monsieur de Boutières thereupon in a very great fury dispatched away a courier to Monsieur de Thermes who lay sick in his bed and almost distracted at the disaster, often crying out: 'Ah, Monsieur Monluc, you have ruined me. Would to God I had never hearkened to you'; and in this error we continued till the Wednesday following. In the meantime the soldiers who had entered were clapped up in the cellar, my soldiers taking the red crosses and moreover setting up a white flag with a red cross upon a tower of the castle and crying out nothing but '*Imperi, Imperi*'.

Things being in this posture, Granuchin immediately made the priest to subscribe a letter, wherein he had writ to the Count that he should come and take possession of the town and castle, for that Granuchin had kept his word with him, and then sent for a labourer who was tenant to the brother of the said priest, to whom he caused the letter to be given by the priest himself, saying and swearing to him that if he made any kind of sign, either in giving the letter or otherwise, that he would presently kill him; making him moreover deliver several things to the messenger by word of mouth. The fellow went away and upon a mare of his own made all the haste he could to Fossano, it being but twelve miles only, immediately upon whose coming the Count resolved that night to send away a corporal of his called Janin, with five and twenty of the bravest men of all his company, who about break of day arrived at Barge. So soon as he came to the castle, Granuchin, the Priest and the Scot were ready to let him in at the foresaid postern whilst Captain Fabas went to plant himself behind the bavins as before, although Granuchin was something long in opening the gate, both because he would clearly see and observe whether the priest made any sign, and also for that he had a mind those of the city should see them enter. When so soon as it was broad day he opened the postern, telling them that the soldiers who came in with the priest were laid to sleep being tired out with the long labour they had sustained the day before, and so soon as they were all in the Scot suddenly clapped to the gate, and as suddenly Captain Fabas started up and fell upon them without giving them time, saving a very

few, to give fire to their arquebuses, as ours did who had them all
ready. Nevertheless they defended themselves with their swords, so
that six of mine were hurt and fifteen or sixteen of this company were
slain upon the place, of which Corporal Janin was one (which was a
very great misfortune to us) together with a brother of his; the rest
were led into the cellar tied two and two together, for there were
already more prisoners in the castle than soldiers of our own.

Now this fight continued longer than the former, the enemy in
fighting still cried out '*Imperi*' and ours '*France*'; insomuch that their
cries reached down into the city, and especially the rattle of the
arquebus shot, so that to avoid being so soon discovered, their design
being to train the Count thither (for to that end tended all the farce)
they all got upon the walls of the castle and from thence cried out
'*Imperi*' and '*Savoy*', having on their red crosses, as I said before. Now
the country fellow that had been sent with the letter to the Count did
not return with those men up to the castle but stayed at his master's
country house by the way; wherefore he was again suddenly sent for
and another letter delivered to him by the hands of the priest to carry
to the said Count to Fossano, wherein he gave him to understand that
Corporal Janin was so weary he could not write but that he had given
him in charge to render him an account of all and that he was laid
down to sleep. So soon as the Count had read this letter, he put on a
resolution to go, not the next day which was Tuesday, but the
Wednesday following (when God intends to punish us, he deprives us
of our understandings, as it happened here in the case of this gentleman). The Count in the first place was reputed one of the most
circumspect (and as wise as valiant) leaders they had in their whole
army, which notwithstanding he suffered himself to be gulled by two
letters from this priest, especially the last, which he ought by no
means to have relied upon; nor to have given credit to anything without having first seen something under his corporal's own hand, and
should have considered whether or no it were a plausible excuse to say
that the said corporal was laid down to sleep. But we are all blind
when we have once set our hearts upon anything of moment.

Believe me, gentlemen, you that are great undertakers of enterprises, you ought maturely to consider all things and weigh every the
least circumstance, for if you be subtle, your enemy may be as crafty
as you. '*A trompeur trompeur et demy*', says the proverb: 'Harm watch
harm catch'; and 'The cunningest snap may meet with his match.'
But that which most of all deceived the Count was that on the

Tuesday those of the town who thought themselves to be become Imperialists, and yet were in some doubt by reason of the various cries they had heard during the fight, had sent five or six women to the castle under colour of selling cakes, apples and chestnuts, to see if they could discover anything of treason (for all those that remained in the town had already taken the red cross). So soon as our people saw them coming up the hill they presently suspected their business, and resolving to set a good face on the matter, went to let down the little drawbridge to let them in. My soldiers then fell to walking up and down the base court with their red crosses, all saving three of four that spake very good Spanish, who fell to talk with the women, and bought some of their wares, taking upon them to be Spaniards; insomuch that they afterwards returning to the town assured the inhabitants that there was no deceit in the business: and moreover brought a letter which la Mothe writ to a friend in the town, wherein he entreated him to go to Monsieur de Boutières and to tell him that he had never consented to Granuchin's treachery, which letter he delivered to one of the women, knowing very well that the party to whom it was directed was not there to be found but would be one of the first to run away, as being a very good Frenchman. But their design was that the letter should fall into the hands of those of the Imperial party, as accordingly it did.

As the Count was coming on Wednesday morning, our people in the castle discovered him marching along the plain, and the people of the town went to meet him without the gate, where being come he asked if it were certainly true that the castle was in his hands, to which they made answer that they believed it so to be; but that at the entrance of his men the first time there were a great many arquebuses shot off within and a very great noise was made; and that on the Monday morning, when the others entered, they likewise heard a very great noise that continued longer than the former, and that they once thought they heard them cry one while 'France' and another 'Imperi' and 'Duco'. But that notwithstanding they had yesterday sent their wives into the castle with fruit, buns and chestnuts, whom they had permitted to enter, where they saw all the soldiers with red crosses. The Count hearing this commanded his lieutenant to alight and to refresh his horses and men, bidding those of the town speedily get something ready for him to eat; for so soon as he had taken order in the castle he would come down to dinner, after which he would take their oath of fidelity and so return back again to Fossano.

Now you must know it is a very steep and uneasy ascent from the town to the castle, by reason whereof the Count alighted and walked it up on foot, accompanied with a nephew of his, another gentleman and his trumpet. So soon as he came to the end of the bridge, which was let down and the gate shut but the wicket left open, so that a man might easily pass and lead his horse after him, Granuchin and the priest being above in the window, saluting him, desired him to enter, to which nevertheless he made answer that he would advance no further till he had first spoken with Corporal Janin. Seeing then that he refused to enter, Granuchin in his hearing said to the priest (to get him from thence): 'Pray father go down and tell Corporal Janin that my lord is at the gate, where he stays to speak with him'; and at the same time himself also departed from the window, pretending to go down; whereupon Captain Fabas and his soldiers ran to open the gate, which was only bolted, and all on a sudden leaped upon the bridge. Seeing this, the Count, who was one of the most active men of all Italy and who held his horse by the bridle (the best one of them that ever that country bred, and which I afterwards gave to Monsieur de Taix) vaulted over a little wall which was near to the bridge, drawing his horse after him with intent to have leaped into the saddle (for there was no horse so tall—provided he could lay his hand upon the pommel—but he could, armed at all pieces,[1] vault into the seat), but he was prevented by the bastard of Bazordan, called Janot (yet living, and then of my company), who by misfortune being he either could not or would not get over the wall to lay hands upon him, let fly at him an arquebus, which taking the default of his arms went into his belly, piercing through his bowels almost to the other side, of which shot he sunk down to the ground.

Captain Fabas took his nephew and another the trumpet, but the other gentleman escaped down the hill crying out that the Count was either killed or taken; whereupon the lieutenant and all his company scuttled to horse in so great a fright that they never looked behind them till they came to Fossano. Had it so fallen out that Janin at the second entry had not been slain, they had not only snapped the Count and by degrees all his whole troop (for they might have compelled him to have spoken to them with a dagger at his back ready to stab him should he make a sign), but moreover might perhaps from hence have spun out some contrivance against Fossano itself, for one enterprise draws on another.

[1] i.e. in full armour.

The Imperial forces under Caesar of Naples withdrew to the east bank of the Po, to Carmagnola. The French now prepared to cross the river (January 1544), despite the winter season

I thought fit to discourse this affair[1] and commit this passage to writing to rouse up our captains' spirits, that they may look about them and whenever they shall find themselves engaged upon the same account, may carefully compute what time the enemy may have wherein to be advertised of their motion, and also what time is required wherein to make their retreat. Whereupon if you shall find that your enemy has time enough to take you upon your march and that you are not strong enough to fight them, never scruple to turn out of your way for the trouble of going three or four leagues about; for it is better to be weary than to be killed or taken. You must not only have your eye at watch but your understanding also. It is under your vigilance and care that your soldiers repose. Consider therefore everything that may happen, always measuring the time and taking things at the worst, and despise not your enemy. If you have the art with cheerful and frolic expressions to cajole and rouse up the soldier, by times representing to him the danger of a little delay, you may make them do what you list and without giving them leisure to sleep, convey them and yourselves into a place of safety without engaging your honour, as several whom I have known taken a bed *à la Françoise* (as the saying is) have done. Our nation cannot suffer long, as the Spaniard and German can, yet is not the fault in the air of France nor in the nature of the people, but in the leader. I am a Frenchman, impatient (they say) and moreover a Gascon, who exceed the other French in choler and impatience as I think they do in valour. Yet have I ever been patient of all sorts of toil and suffering, as much as any other could be, and have known several of my time and others whom I have bred that have inured and hardened themselves to all pain and travail, and believe me (you that command in arms) if you yourselves be such, you will make your soldiers the same in time. I am sure, had not I done so, I had been killed or taken. But let us return to our subject.

The next day we went to pass the river of Pau [Po], over which we made a bridge of waggons for the foot only, the horse fording it over at great ease, it being no more than belly deep. We were all night in passing and at break of day when they were almost all got over, I

[1] An action related by Monluc, here omitted.

with a company of arquebusiers went up close to the town, where I fell to skirmishing, having some horse also with me. Caesar of Naples then immediately put his men in order to quit Carmagnolle [Carmagnola] and began to march, retiring towards a river there to retreat to Quier [Chieri]. Where had it not been that our cavalry fetched a great compass to get clear of the ditches, we had certainly fought and perhaps defeated them, as (to say the truth) we might have done however, had some been so disposed. I'm sure it stuck not at our companies nor at Monsieur de Taix. But Monsieur le President Birague,[1] if he will speak the truth, knows very well where the fault lay, for he was then in the army with Monsieur de Boutières and both heard and saw all they said and did and knows very well that I with two hundred arquebusiers pursued them upon their retreat, firing all the way for above a mile and a half together, and ready to tear my flesh to see how faintly they advanced, which showed they had no great stomach to fight.

Tis an ill thing when a general is in fear of being beaten and whoever goes timorously to work will never do anything to purpose. Had there been no greater men in the company than myself, without trifling after that manner, I had done as I did by the Spaniards which I defeated but fifteen days before. There were a great many excuses however on all sides why we did not fight, and not only there but also throughout all Piedmont, where they spoke of us God knows with what characters of honour. After the report of this cowardice (for it can be called by no other name) was spread abroad, Monsieur de Boutières was not very well satisfied with himself; but I shall leave this discourse and fall upon some other subject, only this I must say, that the world had after no great opinion of him. He was ill obeyed and worse respected. If there was any fault on his part or not I leave others to judge, and there are enough yet living that can tell better than I; yet was he a prudent and a good cavalier; but God makes nobody perfect at all points.

The destruction of the bridge across the Po at Carignano, January 1544

Three or four days after came Ludovic de Birague[2] who proposed an enterprise to Monsieur de Boutières, which was, that in case he would

---

[1] René de Birague (1507–83), Italian statesman, President of the Turin Parlement, and later Chancellor of France and Cardinal.

[2] Cousin of President Birague.

leave Monsieur de Taix about Bourlengue [Verolengo] (where he was
Governor) with seven or eight companies of foot, that then he would
engage to take Crassentin [Crescentino], Sainct Germain [San
Bermano] and Saincthia [Santhià];[1] a thing that because Monsieur de
Goutières was upon the design of breaking the bridge at Carignano,[2]
he made very great difficulty to consent unto until the said bridge
should first be broken down. But Monsieur de Thermes being come
with his own company and the two companies of the Baron de
Nicolas, it was concluded amongst them that Monsieur de Taix
might be spared to go with Signor Ludovic with seven ensigns, being
that still there would remain five or six; the three companies of
Monsieur de Dros which he had again recruited, and seven or eight
others of Italians. I do not well remember whether Monsieur des Cros
was himself yet arrived or no for the last named were his men; but it
may suffice that we made up, French and Italians, eighteen ensigns
besides the Swiss. It was therefore concluded in the council that before
they should take in hand the breaking of the bridge they should first
see how the enterprise of the said Signor Ludovic should succeed,
which should it miscarry and that they were defeated, all Piedmont
would be in very great danger. But in a few days after news was
brought to Monsieur Boutières, that they had taken San Germano and
Santhià, with four or five other little enclosed towns. Neither must I
forget that Monsieur de Taix stiffly insisted to have had me along
with him, insomuch that there arose some dispute about it; but
Monsieur de Boutières protested he would not undertake to break the
bridge unless I was there; Monsieur de Thermes, Monsieur d'Aussun,
the President Birague and Signor Francisco Bernardino stood very high
on Monsieur Boutières his side, so that I was constrained to stay, very
much against my will, I having a very great desire to have gone along
with Monsieur de Taix, both because he loved me and had as great
confidence in me as in any captain of the regiment, as also that he was
a man of exceeding great mettle and would seek all occasions of
fighting. However, the forementioned news being brought, the breaking of the bridge was concluded, and after this manner.

It was ordered that I with five or six companies of Gascons should
go fight the hundred Germans and hundred Spaniards that had every
night kept guard at the end of the bridge, ever since our army had

[1] All Imperial-held fortresses, to the north-east of Turin: see map, p. 59.

[2] Bridge over the Po, south of Turin.

been at Piobes [Piobesi Torinese].[1] To which I made answer that I would not have so many; for being to pass through narrow ways so great a number of men would make so very long a file that the sixth part of them could never come up to fight, and in short that I would only have an hundred arquebusiers and an hundred corslets, to be equal to the enemy, not doubting but before the game was done to make it appear that our nation were as good as either German or Spaniard, but withal that Boguedemar, La Pallu, and another captain (whose name I have forgot) should bring all the rest of the men after, at the distance of three hundred paces, to assist me in case the enemy should sally out of Carignano to relieve their own people. Which accordingly was left to my discretion.

There was a house on the left hand the bridge which it was ordered the Italians (who might be between twelve and fourteen ensigns) should possess themselves of, to favour me should the enemy make a sally; that Monsieur de Boutières should advance with all the cavalry and the Swiss within half a mile; that Captain Labardac with his company should advance on the other side of the river with two pieces of cannon to make some shot at a little house which was on the bridge end on our side, where the enemy kept their guard, and that Monsieur de Salcède [de Salcedo][2] (who but a little before was come over to us) with three or fourscore country fellows (everyone bringing a hatchet along with him) should attempt to break the bridge. For whom also seven or eight boats were prepared wherein to convey themselves under the said bridge where they were to cut the posts not quite through but to the thickness of a man's leg, and that being done, to cut the long beams that supported the bridge above, which dividing from one another the pillars would totter and break of themselves; they had moreover certain fireworks delivered to them which they were made to believe, being applied to the pillars, would in a short time burn them down to the water. Everyone then going to execute the orders they had received, I with my two hundred men chosen out of all the companies went full drive directly towards the bridge, where I could not however so soon arrive but that the cannon had already made one shot at the little house, had broken into it and killed a German, whom at my coming I found there not quite dead. And

---

[1] Boutières had occupied Piobesi, south of Turin, in December 1543.

[2] Pierre de Salcedo (d. 1572), Spanish soldier who changed sides and took a prominent part in several actions for France thereafter.

although it was night yet the moon shone out so clear that we might easily see from the one end to the other, saving that by intervals there fell a mist which continued sometimes half an hour and sometimes less, during which we could not see a yard's distance from us.

Now either frighted at the report of the cannon or at the noise I made at the house (it being not above an hundred paces distant from the bridge), the enemy took to their heels and fled away towards Carignano, after whom I sent some arquebus shot but followed no further than the end of the bridge. At the same time also Monsieur de Salcedo, with his boors and his boats, arrived underneath, who at his first coming presently fastened his artificial fires to the pillars; but it was only so much time thrown away and he must of force make the fellows fall to it with their axes, who having tied their boats fast to the said pillars began to lay on at that end where the Swiss were, cutting on straight towards me, who kept the other end of the bridge towards the enemy.

This fury of the clowns lasted for four long hours, continually laying on upon the pillars, insomuch that though they were ranked four and four together and of a very great thickness, yet before we had any disturbance they were all cut to the very place where I was. Monsieur de Salcedo ever caused one company to rest themselves upon the bank of the river, where he had caused a little fire to be made, and from hour to hour made them to relieve one another. During which employment the enemy sent out thirty or forty arquebusiers to discover what we were doing just at a time when the fog fell, whom I could neither see nor hear for the noise of the axes, till they were got within four pikes' length of me and let fly amongst us, which having done they immediately retired yet could they not see us by reason of the mist. Messieurs de Thermes then and de Moneins [de Monein][1] with three or four horse came up to us to know the meaning of those arquebus shots and sent back to Monsieur de Boutières to tell him that it was nothing and that for them we nothing desisted from the work, themselves alone still remaining with me. They had not stayed an hour but that the mist again began to fall and the enemy as soon returned upon us. That is to say, six hundred Spaniards chosen men and six hundred German pikes, Pierre Colonne [Pedro Colonna][2] (as I have

---

[1] Tristan de Monein (d. 1548), Béarnais gentleman who rose in the service of the King of Navarre to become Lieutenant Governor of Guienne.

[2] Italian *condotiere* in the pay of the Empire, at this time commander of the forces at Carignano.

since understood) having ordered the business thus: that two hundred arquebusiers again chosen out of the six hundred should charge full drive directly upon us, the other four hundred to march at an hundred paces distance in the rear of them, and the six hundred Germans two hundred paces after all.

Now I had placed the captains who led the ensigns after me against a great ditch bank some two hundred paces behind me, and sometimes Captain Fabas my lieutenant and sometimes Boguedemar came to me to see what we did, and again returned back to their place. On that side of the bridge towards the Swiss we peradventure had broken down some twenty paces, having begun to cut the beams above, and found that as the bridge divided it fell down for fifteen or twenty paces together, which gave us hope that we should make an end of the work. In the meantime Monsieur de Salcedo still made the pillars to be cut over again, yet not quite through, but only a little more than before, which was the reason that he had divided his workmen into three parts, whereof one was in the boats, the other upon the bridge cutting the traverse beams, and ten or twelve by the fireside. As God is pleased sometimes to be assisting to men he this night wrought a real miracle, for in the first place the two hundred arquebusiers came up to me, finding me in such a posture that scarce one soldier had his match cocked, for they went by turns ten or a dozen at a time to the countrymen's fire to warm their hands, having two sentinels out a hundred paces from me, upon the way towards the city and not doubting but the Italians on their side would also have the same, for they were a little nearer than I but it was a little on one side. How they ordered their business I cannot tell, for I had no more than my two sentinels who came running in to me, and as they came in with the alarm the Spaniards also arrived crying out *'Espagne, Espagne'*, all the two hundred arquebusiers firing upon us together.

Whereupon Messieurs de Thermes and de Monein, being on horseback and alone, ran unto Monsieur de Boutières, who had already seen the beginning of the disorder, and note that almost all the two hundred men I had at the end of the bridge ran away straight to the ensigns and on a sudden the ensigns also fled, and in like manner at the same time the Italians who were on our left hand did the same, neither once looking behind them till they came to the head of the cavalry, where Monsieur de Boutières himself stood. Our word was *'St Pierre'*, but that did me no good, seeing which I began to cry out 'Monluc, Monluc you cursed cowardly whelps will you forsake me thus?' By good fortune I had with me thirty or forty young gentle-men, who had never a hair on their faces, the handsomest and the bravest youth that ever was seen in one little company, who thought I had run away with the rest; but hearing my voice, returned im-mediately towards me; with whom, without staying for any more, I charged straight to the place from whence the shot came whizzing by our ears. But to see one another was impossible for the mist that fell together with the thick smoke that was mixed with it, and in running up to them my men discharged all together, crying out '*France*' as they cried out '*Espagne*', and I dare affirm that we fired at less than three pikes' distance; by which charge their two hundred arquebusiers were overturned upon the four hundred, and all of them upon the six hundred Germans. So that all in a rout and confusion they fled full speed towards the city, for they could not discover what we were.

I pursued them about two hundred paces; but my pursuit was interrupted by the great noise in our camp (I never heard the like). You would have sworn they had been all stark staring mad, calling and bawling upon one another, yet these great bawlers are none of the greatest fighters. There are a sort of men who bustle up and down, call, command, and keep a great clutter, and in the meantime for one step they advance retire two paces backward. But this hideous noise was the reason that I could never discover the enemy's disorder; neither could they discover ours by reason of the great outcry they made at their entrance into the city, which was no other than a postern near to the castle, into which three or four men only could march abreast.

Thus then I returned to the end of the bridge, where I found Monsieur de Salcedo all alone with ten or a dozen of the country fellows whose turn it was to rest, for the others that were in the boats cut the ropes and fled away with the current of the river straight to Montcallier [Moncalieri],[1] those on the top that were cutting the traverse beams on that side towards the Swiss, leaving their axes and hatchets upon the bridge, cast themselves into the water, which was there no more than waist deep, they being not yet come to the depth of the river. The Swiss, likewise, who heard this dismal noise, fell to running towards Carmagnola, having an opinion that both we and all our camp were in a rout, and taking the two cannons along with them made all the haste they possibly could to recover Carmagnola. I sent one of my soldiers after the runaways to enquire news of my

[1] On the right bank of the Po, downriver from Carignano: see map, p. 59.

lieutenant Captain Fabas, whom he met (having rallied thirty or forty of his men) returning towards the bridge to see what was become of me, believing me to be slain; who presently dispatched away to Boguedemar, La Pallu and some other captains, who had made a halt, rallying some part of their men; whom he caused in all haste to march directly towards the bridge, telling them that I had beaten back the enemy, who thereupon came at a good rate to seek me. Captain Fabas was the first that came, all torn and tattered like a scarecrow, forasmuch as the soldiers in a crowd all run over his belly as he thought to have rallied, who found Monsieur de Salcedo and me at the end of the bridge consulting what we were best to do. So soon as he came he gave us an account of his fortune and that of the rest of his companions, when seeing him so accoutred we turned all into laughter; but the hubbub in our camp continued above a long hour after.

The other captains being come up to us, we concluded to make an end of breaking down the bridge or there to lose our lives, whereupon I presently took fifty or threescore soldiers, and Monsieur de Salcedo the ten or twelve country fellows he had left, giving order to Captain Fabas, Boguedemar and La Pallu to remain at the end of the bridge and to set our sentinels almost as far as the gates of the city. I believed that the Italians notwithstanding the hurly-burly in our camp were yet at their post, and therefore commanded Captain Fabas himself to go and see if they were there or no; who at his return found that I had caused fifteen or twenty soldiers to take up the axes the peasants had left upon the bridge, who together with the ten or twelve country fellows were cutting the cross beams above; where he told us that he had been at the house but that he had found nobody there.

This news put us a little to a stand, what we were best to do; but nevertheless we stopped not to execute our former resolution, and so soon as the tumult was a little over came Messieurs de Thermes and de Monein, who brought me a command from Mr de Boutières immediately to retire. The said Sieur de Monein alighted from his horse, for Monsieur de Thermes could not for his gout, and came to me on foot where he found that since the disorder we had at two cuttings made above thirty paces of the bridge to fall and were falling upon the third, each of them being fifteen or twenty paces long, who thereupon returned to Monsieur de Boutières to acquaint him how all things had passed, Monsieur de Salcedo having lost almost all his peasants, but that our soldiers had taken their axes with which they did wonders in cutting, and that all the captains and soldiers, Monsieur de Salcedo and I were resolved to die rather than depart from thence till first the bridge was totally broken down. Monsieur de Boutières thereupon sent him back to protest against me for any loss that might happen contrary to his command, which the said Sieur de Monein did, telling us moreover that the said Sieur de Boutières was already upon his march to return though he halted within a mile of us, which I conceive he did to the end that by that means he might draw me off; for he wanted no courage but he was always in fear to lose. Whoever is of that humour may perhaps make a shift to save himself but shall never achieve any great conquests.

Monsieur de Thermes had made a stop at the end of the bridge so soon as he had heard Monsieur de Boutières to be upon his march, and returned no more back with Monsieur de Monein to carry my answer but presently sent orders to his company not to stir from the place where he had left them, and so we cut on all the remainder of the night till within an hour of day, that we marched towards the little house upon the hill. Monsieur de Monein returned again to us just at the instant when the last blow was given, and Monsieur de Thermes ran to his company to cause them to advance a little towards us that they might favour our retreat, and Monsieur de Monein ran towards Monsieur de Boutières whom he found expecting his return. So that having deprived the enemy of a great convenience, we retired without any manner of impediment at all. I was willing to commit this to writing, not to magnify myself for any great valour in this action, but to manifest to all the world how God has ever been pleased to conduct my fortune. I was neither so great a fop nor so foolhardy, but that could I have seen the enemy, I should have retired and perhaps have run away as fast as the rest, and it had been madness and not valour to have stayed. Neither is there any shame attends a rational fear when there is great occasion, and I should never have been so senseless as with thirty or forty foot only to have stood the fight.

Captains by this may take example never to run away or (to put it into a better phrase) to make a hasty retreat, without first discovering who there is to pursue them, and moreover having seen them, to attempt all ways of opposition till they shall see there is no good to be done. For after all the means that God has given to men have been employed and to no purpose, then flight is neither shameful nor unworthy. But believe me (gentlemen) if you do not employ all, everyone will be ready to say (nay, even those who have run away with you) if he had done this, or if he had done that, the mischief had been prevented and things had fallen out better than they did; and such a one vapours most and speaks highest who perhaps was himself the first that ran away. Thus shall the reputation of a man of honour (let him be as brave as he will) be brought into dispute with all the world. When there is no more to be done, a man ought not to be obstinate but to give way to fortune, which does not always smile. A man is no less worthy of blame for wilfully losing himself when he may retire and sees himself at the last extremity, than he who shamefully runs away at the first encounter; yet the one is more dirty than the other, and this difference there is betwixt them, that the one will make you reputed rash and harebrained, and the other a poltroon and a coward.

Part II   From Book II
The Habsburg-Valois Wars,
1544–1553

The youthful d'Enghien arrived in Piedmont to take charge of the French army, which was now to embark on the campaign which ended in the great victory of Cérisoles: but not before Monluc is sent to the King (March 1544) to persuade him to allow the army to hazard a battle

At the arrival of this brave and generous prince,[1] which promised great successes under his conduct, he being endued with an infinite number of shining qualities, as being gentle, affable, valiant, wise and liberal, all the French and all those who bore arms in our favour did very much rejoice, and particularly I because he had a kindness for me and was pleased to set a higher esteem upon me than I could any way deserve. After he had taken a view of all the forces, magazines and places that we held, and that he had taken order for all things after the best manner he could, about the beginning of March he dispatched me away to the King to give his Majesty an account how affairs stood, and withal to acquaint him that the Marquis del Vasto was raising a very great army, to whom new succours of Germans were also sent, and moreover that the Prince of Salerne [Salerno][2] was also coming from Naples with six or seven thousand Italians under his command. It was at the time when the Emperor and the King of England were agreed and combined together jointly to invade the kingdom of France, which they had also divided betwixt them.

I had waited at court near upon three weeks for my dispatch, having already acquitted myself of my commission, which was in sum only to demand some succours of the King and to obtain leave to fight a battle. And about the end of the said month came letters also to the King from Monsieur d'Anguyen [d'Enghien], wherein he gave him notice that seven thousand Germans were already arrived at Milan, of the best of those the Emperor had had before Landrecy

---

[1] For d'Enghien, see Appendix I, 'Bourbon-Vendôme, François de'.

[2] Fernando, Prince of Salerno (1507–70), at times in the service of the Empire.

[Landrecies][1], where there were seven regiments of them; but being he could not at that time fight with the King, he commanded the seven colonels to choose each a thousand out of their respective regiments, ordering them to leave their lieutenants to get their regiments ready, and so sent them into Italy to join with the Marquis del Vasto. Wherefore the said Monsieur d'Enghien humbly besought his Majesty to send me speedily away to him, and also requested him that he would please to do something for me as a reward for my former services and an encouragement to more for the time to come. Upon which letter his Majesty was pleased to confer upon me the office of a gentleman waiter (which in those times was no ordinary favour, nor so cheap as nowadays) and made me to wait upon him at dinner, commanding me in the afternoon to make myself ready to return into Piedmont, which I accordingly did.

About midday Monsieur the Admiral d'Annebaut[2] sent for me to come to the King, who was already entered into the council, where there was assisting Monsieur de St Pol, the Admiral, *Monsieur le Grand Ecuyer* Galiot, Monsieur de Boissy [Boisy][3] (since *Grand Ecuyer*) and two or three others whom I have forgot, together with the Dauphin[4] who stood behind the King's chair; and none of them were sat but the King himself, Monsieur de St Pol, who sat hard by him, and the Admiral on the other side of the table over against the said Sieur de St Pol.

So soon as I came into the chamber the King said to me: 'Monluc, I would have you return into Piedmont to carry my determination, and that of my council, to Monsieur d'Enghien and will that you hear the difficulties we make of giving him leave to fight a battle according to his desire'; and thereupon commanded Monsieur de St Pol to speak. The said Monsieur de St Pol then began to lay open the enterprise of the Emperor and the King of England, who within six or seven weeks were determined to enter into the kingdom, the one on the one side and the other on the other, so that should Monsieur d'Enghien lose the battle, the whole kingdom would be in danger to be lost; forasmuch as all the King's hopes (for what concerned his foot) resided in the regiments he had in Piedmont, for that in France there were no other but

[1] In north-eastern France, where Charles V was also campaigning in 1544.

[2] For whom see Appendix I, 'Annebaut, Claude d."

[3] Claude Gouffier, Sieur de Boisy (d. 1570), became *Grand Ecuyer* on the death of Jacques Galiot in 1546.

[4] The later Henry II.

what were now legionary soldiers, and that therefore it was much better and more safe to preserve the kingdom than Piedmont. Concerning which they were to be on the defensive part and by no means to hazard a battle; the loss whereof would not only lose Piedmont but moreover give the enemy footing on that side of the kingdom. The Admiral said the same, and all the rest, everyone arguing according to his own fancy.

I twittered to speak, and offering to interrupt Monsieur de Galiot as he was delivering his opinion, Monsieur de St Pol made a sign to me with his hand, saying 'Not too fast, not too fast', which made me hold my peace and I saw the King laugh. Monsieur le Dauphin said nothing. I believe it is not the custom, though the King would have him present that he might learn, for before princes there are evermore very eloquent debates but not always the soundest determinations; for they never speak but by halves and always sooth their master's humour, for which reason I should make a very scurvy courtier, for I must ever speak as I think.

The King then said these words to me: 'Monluc, have you heard the reasons for which I cannot give Monsieur d'Enghien leave to fight?' To which I made answer, that I had both heard and weighed them very well, but that if his Majesty would please to give me leave to deliver my opinion I would very gladly do it, not that nevertheless for that his Majesty should any ways alter what had already been determined in his council. His Majesty then told me that he would permit me so to do and that I might freely say whatsoever I would. Whereupon I began after this manner. I remember it as well as it had been but three days ago. God has given me a very great memory in these kind of things, for which I render him hearty thanks, for it is a great contentment to me now that I have nothing else to do, to recollect my former fortunes and to call to mind the former passages of my life, to set them truly down without any manner of addition; for be they good or bad you shall have them as they are.

'Sir, I think myself exceedingly happy, as well that you are pleased I shall deliver my poor opinion upon a subject that has already been debated in your Majesty's council, as also that I am to speak to a warlike King. For both before your Majesty was called to this great charge which God has conferred upon you, and also since, you have as much tempted the fortune of war as any King that ever ruled in France, and that without sparing your own royal person any more than the meanest gentleman of your kingdom; wherefore I need not fear freely to deliver my opinion, being to speak both to a King and a soldier.' Here the Dauphin, who stood behind the King's chair and just over against me, gave me a nod with his head by which I guessed he would have me to speak boldly, and that gave me the greater assurance, though in plain truth I had ever confidence enough and fear never stopped my mouth.

'Sir,' said I, 'we are betwixt five and six thousand Gascons upon the list, for your Majesty knows that the companies are never fully complete, neither can all ever be at the battle, but I make account we shall be five thousand, and five or six hundred Gascons complete, that I dare make good to your Majesty upon my honour. Of these every captain and soldier will present you with a list of all their names and the places from whence we are come and will engage our heads to you, all of us to fight in the day of battle, if your Majesty will please to grant it and give us leave to fight. 'Tis the only thing we have so long expected and desired, without sneaking thus up and down from place to place and hiding our heads in corners. Believe me, sir, the world has not more resolute soldiers than these are, they desire nothing more than once to come to the decision of arms. To these there are thirteen ensigns of Swiss, of which the six of St Julien I know much better than those of le Baron [de Sisnech], which Fourly [Frölich] commands, yet I have seen them all mustered and there may be as many of them as of ours. These will make you the same promise we do who are your natural subjects, and deliver in the names of all to be sent to their cantons, to the end that if any man fail in his duty he may be cashiered and degraded from all practice of arms for ever: a condition to which they are all ready to submit, as they assured me at my departure. And being of the same nation, I make no doubt but those of le Baron will do the same. Your Majesty may have taken notice of them all before Landrecies. Here then, sir, are nine thousand men or more, on which you may depend, and assure yourself that they will fight to the last gasp of their lives.

'As for the Italians and Provençals which are under Monsieur des Cros, and also the Gruiens [Gruyériens] that came to us before Yvrée [Ivrée], I shall not take upon me to become security for them, but I hope they will all do as well as we, especially when they shall see how we lay about us.' At which I lifted up my arm—in the earnestness of speaking—as if I were going to strike, whereat the King smiled. 'You should also, sir, have four hundred men at arms in Piedmont, of which there may well be three hundred, and as many archers, as well disposed

93

as we. You have four captains of light horse, which are Messieurs de Thermes, d'Aussan, Francisco Bernardino and Mauré, each of which ought to have two hundred light horse, and amongst them all they will furnish you with five or six hundred horse, all of which are ambitious to manifest the zeal they have to your service. I know what they are and what they will do very well.'

The King then began to be a little angry to hear that the companies of the *gendarmes* were not all complete, but I told him that it was impossible, forasmuch as some of them had obtained leave of their captains to go home to their own houses to refresh themselves, and others were sick; but that if his Majesty would please to give leave to those gentlemen who would beg it of him to be present at the battle, they would very well supply that default. 'Since then, sir,' said I, continuing my discourse, 'that I am so happy as to speak before a soldier King, who would you have to kill ten thousand foot and a thousand or twelve hundred horse, all resolute to overcome or die? Such men as these, and so resolved, are not so easily defeated, neither are they novices in war. We have several times attacked the enemy upon equal terms and for the most part beaten them. And I dare boldly say that had we all of us one arm tied behind us, it would not be in the power of the enemy to kill us all in a whole day's time without losing the greatest part of their army and the choicest of their men. Imagine then when we have both our arms at liberty and our weapons in our hands, how easy it will be to beat us. Truly, sir, I have heard great captains discourse and say that an army of twelve or fifteen thousand men is sufficient to confront an army of thirty thousand, for 'tis not the crowd but the courage that overcomes, and in a battle the one half of them never comes to fight. We desire no more than we have, let us deal it out.'

The Dauphin all this while stood laughing behind the King's chair and still made signs to me, for by my behaviour I seemed already to be in battle. 'No, no, sir, these are not men to be beaten, and if these lords who have spoken had once seen them at their work, they would alter their opinion, and so would your Majesty too. These are not men to lie dozing in a garrison, they require an enemy and have a mind to show their valour. They beg leave of you to fight, and if you deny them you take away their spirits and give it to your enemies, who will be puffed with vanity to see themselves feared, whilst your own army shall moulder away to nothing. By what I have heard, sir, all that these lords stumble at, who have delivered their opinions before you, is the apprehension of losing the battle, and that makes them always cry: If we lose, If we lose. But I have not heard one of them tell you, if we win it, what great advantages will thereby accrue. For God's sake, sir, fear not to grant our request, and let me not return with such a shame upon me that men shall say you durst not trust the hazard of a battle in our hands, who so voluntarily and cheerfully make a tender of our lives to do you service.'

The King, who had very attentively hearkened to me, and that was delighted at my gestures and impatience, turned his eyes towards Monsieur de St Pol, who thereupon said to him: 'Sir, will you alter your determination at the importunity of this coxcomb, that cares for nothing but fighting and has no sense of the misfortune nor the inconveniences that the loss of a battle would bring upon you? Believe me, sir, 'tis a thing of too great importance to be referred to the discretion of a young harebrained Gascon.' To whom I made answer in these very words: 'My lord, assure yourself I am neither a braggadoccio nor so arrant a coxcomb as you take me for. Neither do I say this out of bravado, and if you will please to call to mind all the intelligences his Majesty has received since we returned from Perpignan into Piedmont, you will find that wherever we encountered the enemy, whether on horseback or on foot, we have always beaten them, excepting when Monsieur d'Aussun was defeated, who also miscarried through no other default than for attempting to retreat at the head of an army, which a prudent captain never ought to do. It is not yet three months (I am sure you have heard it, for it is known to all the world) since the two brave combats we fought both on foot and on horseback in the plain over against St Fré, [Sanfré] first against the Italians and since against the Spaniards, and both in ten days' time; and Monsieur d'Aussun, fifteen days before he was taken, fought and defeated an entire regiment of Germans.

'Consider then we that are in heart and they in fear. We that are conquerors and they beaten. We who despise them whilst they tremble at us: what difference there is betwixt us. When should it be that the King should give us leave to fight, if not now that we are in this condition in Piedmont? It must not be when we have been beaten that his Majesty ought to do it, but now that we are in breath and fleshed with conquest. Neither is there any thought to be taken, save only to take good heed that we assault them not in a fortress as we did at the Bicocca; but Monsieur d'Enghien has too many good and experienced captains about him to commit such an error, and there will be no other question if not how to tempt them into the open field, where there shall be neither hedge nor ditch to hinder us from coming to grapple with them, and then, sir, you shall hear news of one of the most furious battles that ever was fought, and I most humbly beseech your Majesty to expect no other news but that of a great and glorious victory, which if God give us the grace to obtain (as I hold myself assured we shall) you will so stop the Emperor and the King of England in the midst of their career that they shall not know which way to turn them.'

The Dauphin still continued laughing more than before and still making signs, which gave me still the greater assurance to speak. All the rest then spoke everyone in his turn, and said that his Majesty ought by no means to rely upon my words. Only the Admiral said nothing but smiled, and I believe he perceived the signs the Dauphin made me, they being almost opposite to one another. But Monsieur de St Pol replied again, saying to the King: 'What, sir, it seems you have a mind to alter your determination and to be led away at the persuasion of this frantic fool.' To which the King made answer: 'By my faith, cousin, he has given me so great reasons and so well re-presented to me the courage of my soldiers that I know not what to say.' To which Monsieur de St Pol replied: 'Nay, sir, I see you are already changed.' Now he could not see the signs the Dauphin made me, as the Admiral could, for he had his back towards him. Where-upon the King, directing his speech to the Admiral, asked him what he thought of the business, who again smiling returned his Majesty this answer: 'Sir, will you confess the truth? You have a great mind to give them leave to fight, which if they do I dare not assure you either of victory or disgrace, for God alone only knows what the issue will be. But I dare pawn my life and reputation that all those he has named you will fight like men of honour, for I know their bravery very well as having had the honour to command them. Do only one thing, sir (for we see you are already half overcome and that you rather incline to a battle than otherwise), address yourself to Almighty God and humbly beg of him, in this perplexity, to assist you with his counsel what you were best to do.' Which having said, the King, throwing his bonnet upon the table, lifted up his eyes towards heaven and, joining his hands, said: 'My God, I beseech thee that thou wilt be pleased to direct me this day what I ought to do for the preserva-tion of my kingdom, and let all be to thy honour and glory.' Which having said, the Admiral asked him, 'I beseech you, sir, what opinion are you now of?' When the King, after a little pause, turning towards me with great vehemency cried out, 'Let them fight, let them fight.' 'Why then,' says the Admiral, 'there is no more to be said. If you lose the battle, you alone are the cause. And if you overcome the same, alone shall enjoy the satisfaction, having alone consented to it.'

This being said, the King and all the rest arose and I was ready to leap out of my skin for joy. The King then fell to talking with the Admiral about my dispatch and to take order for our pay which was a great deal in arrear. Monsieur de St Pol in the meantime drew near unto me and smiling said, 'Thou mad devil, thou wilt be the cause either of the greatest good or the greatest mischief that can possibly befall the King.' Now you must know that the said Sieur de St Pol had not spoken anything for any ill will that he bore me, for he loved me as well as any captain in France, and of old, having known me at the time when I served under Marshal de Foix; and moreover told me that it was very necessary I should speak to all the captains and soldiers and tell them that the confidence his Majesty reposed in our worth and valour had made him condescend to permit us to fight, and not reason, considering the condition he was then in. To whom I replied, 'My lord, I most humbly beseech you not to fear, or so much as doubt but that we shall win the battle, and assure yourself that the first news you will hear will be that we have made them all into a *fricassée* and may eat them if we will.'

The King then came to me and laid his hand upon my shoulder, saying, 'Monluc, recommend me to my cousin d'Enghien and to all the captains in those parts, of what nation soever, and tell them that the great confidence I have in their fidelity and valour has made me condescend that they shall fight, entreating them to serve me very well upon this occasion, for I never think to be in so much need again as at this present; that now therefore is the time wherein they are to manifest the kindness they have for me, and that I will suddenly send them the money they desire.' To which I made answer, 'Sir, I shall obey your commands and this will be a cordial to cheer them and a spur to the good disposition they already have to fight, and I most humbly beseech your Majesty not to remain in doubt concerning the issue of our fight, for that will only discompose your spirit; but cheer up yourself in expectation of the good news you will shortly hear of us; for my mind presages well, and it never yet deceived me.' And thereupon, kissing his hand, I took my leave of his Majesty.

The Admiral then bid me go and stay for him in the wardrobe, and whether it was Monsieur de Marchemon [Marchaumont][1] or Monsieur de Bayart [Bayard][2] that went down with me I cannot tell, but going out I found at the door Messieurs de Dampierre,[3] de St André[4] and d'Assier,[5] with three or four others, who demanded of me if I carried leave to Monsieur d'Enghien to fight, to whom I made answer in Gascon, '*Hares y harem aux pics et patacs.*[6] Go in presently, if you have any stomach to the entertainment, before the Admiral depart from the King.' Which they accordingly did, and there was some dispute about their leave, but in the end his Majesty consented they should go, which nothing impaired their feast; for after them came above a hundred gentlemen post to be present at the battle. Amongst others the Sieurs de Jarnac,[7] and de Chastillon [de Châtillon],[8] since Admiral, the son of the Admiral d'Annebaut,[9] the Vidame of Chartres[10] and several others, of which not one was slain in the battle, save only Monsieur d'Assier, whom I loved more than my own heart, and Chamans who was wounded when I fought the Spaniards in the plain of Perpignan; some others there were that were hurt but none that died. There is not a prince in the world who has so frank a gentry as ours has, the least smile of their King will inflame the coldest constitution, without any thought of fear, to convert mills and vineyards into horses and arms, and they go volunteers to die in that bed which we soldiers call the bed of honour.

Being arrived soon after at the camp, I acquitted myself of my charge towards Monsieur d'Enghien and presented him my letters from the King, who was infinitely overjoyed and embracing me in his arms, said these very words: 'I knew very well that thou wouldst not bring us peace,' and turning to the gentlemen about him, 'Well my masters,' said he, 'the King is pleased to gratify our desire, we

[1] Cosme Clausse, Seigneur de Marchaumont (d. 1558), secretary to the Dauphin.

[2] Gilbert Bayard, secretary of finance.

[3] Claude de Clermont, Seigneur de Dampierre (d. 1545), general and courtier.

[4] For whom see Appendix I, 'Albon, Jacques d', Sieur de St André.'

[5] François Ricard de Genouilhac, Sieur d'Assier (c. 1516–44), son of Jacques Galiot.

[6] 'Now we're off there to play at cut and thrust.'

[7] Guy Chabot, Sieur de Jarnac (d. after 1572), defeated La Châtaigneraie in the famous duel (1547): see below, p. 126.

[8] For whom see Appendix I, 'Coligny Gaspard de.'

[9] Jean d'Annebaut (d. 1562).

[10] François de Vendôme, Vidame de Chartres (d. 1562).

must go to it.' I then gave him an account of the difficulty I had met with in obtaining that leave and that the King himself was the only cause of it, which ought the more to encourage us to behave ourselves bravely in the battle. He was moreover very glad when I told him that the forementioned lords were coming after me, being certain that several others would also follow after them, as they did. Bidding me by all means go discharge myself of his Majesty's commands to all the colonels, captains of the *gendarmes*, light horse and foot, which I did, not observing one that did not mightily rejoice when I gave them to understand what assurance I had given the King of the victory. Neither did I satisfy myself with speaking to the officers only but moreover went amongst the soldiers, assuring them that we should all be highly recompensed by the King, making the matter something better than it was, for a man must now and then lie a little for his master.

Preliminaries to the battle

During the time of my absence Monsieur d'Enghien had blocked up Carignano, being he could not carry it by fine force without infinite loss, quartering in the meantime at Vimeus [Vinovo] and Carmagnola, and soon after the arrival of these gentlemen, the Marquis del Vasto departed with his camp upon Good Friday from Ast [Asti], and came to lodge at [Montà] near Carmagnola and upon Easter Day removed his camp to Serizolles [Cérisoles].[1] The company of the Count de Tande [Tende][2] was this day upon the guard, to which Captain Taurines[3] was lieutenant, who sent word to Monsieur d'Enghien that the camp was upon their march and that their drums were plainly heard. Monsieur d'Enghien thereupon commanded me presently to mount to horse and to go in all haste to discover them and to bring him certain intelligence of their motion, which I also did, Captain Taurines giving me twenty lancers for my guard. I went so far that I discovered the cavalry, who marched through the woods belonging to the Abbey of ....[4] and heard the drums, some marching before and some following after, which put me to a stand to guess what

[1] See map, p. 59.

[2] Claude de Savoie, Comte de Tende (d. 1566), Governor of Provence.

[3] Pierre Guitart, Sieur de Taurines.

[4] Left blank by the author.

the meaning of this order might be. At my return I found Monsieur d'Enghien, Messieurs de Châtillon, de Dampierre, de St André, d'Escars (the father of these now living),[1] d'Assier and de Jarnac in the chamber of the said Seigneur d'Enghien talking with him, having caused their arms to be brought and laid upon the beds in the said chamber; where I made a report to him of what I had seen. Whereupon all the gentlemen cried out to him, 'Let us go, sir, let us go to fight today, for it is a good day and God will assist us.' Upon which the said seigneur commanded me to go bid Messieurs de Taix and de St Julien to draw out their regiments into the field, at the same time sending another gentleman to the *gendarmes* and the light horse to do the same, which was performed in an instant, and we drew out of Carmagnola into a plain leading toward Cérisoles, where we were all drawn up into battalia.

Monsieur de Mailly,[2] master of the ordnance, was there ready with his artillery as soon as any of us all, and we heard the enemy's drums almost as plainly as we heard our own. In my life did I never see so cheerful an army nor soldiers so well disposed to fight as this of ours was, excepting some of the great ones of the army, who were evermore persecuting Monsieur d'Enghien not to put it to the hazard of a day, representing to him what a blow it would be to the King should he lose the battle, which might perhaps occasion the loss of the kingdom of France. And others were still persuading him that he ought to fight, the King having granted leave and expecting he should now so do. So that amongst them they put this poor prince, being yet very young, into so great a perplexity that he scarce knew which way to turn him nor what to do. You may imagine whether I was not mightily pleased with these doings and whether I would not have spoken loudly, had I had to do with my match, neither as it was could I altogether forbear. The lords who were lately come from court were all for fighting, and I could very well name both the one and the other if I so pleased; but I shall forbear to do it, for I have not taken my pen in hand to blemish anyone, but the Admiral Châtillon and Monsieur de Jarnac, who are both living, know it as well as I. Both the one and the other had reason for what they said and were not prompted by any fear of their own persons; but only the apprehension of losing all

[1] Jacques de Peyrusse, Sieur d'Escars, *Sénéchal* of Marsan, had three sons by his first marriage.

[2] René, Baron de Mailly (d. 1583), later Governor of Montreuil.

withheld them, and some perhaps (as I have often seen) argue against their own inclinations and the plurality of voices, to the end that if anything falls amiss, they may afterwards say, 'I was of a contrary opinion, I told him as much, but I was not to be believed.' Oh there is great cunning in the world, and in our trade especially of all others.

Just as we should have marched to go to fight, four or five drew Monsieur d'Enghien aside, alighting from their horses, where they entertained him walking up and down for above half an hour, whilst everyone gnashed their teeth for rage that they did not march. In the end the result of all was that all the regiments of foot should return to their quarters and also the artillery and the *gendarmes*, and that Monsieur d'Enghien with four or five hundred horse and some of the captains of his council should go to the plain of Cérisoles to discover the enemy's camp; that I should bring after him four hundred arquebusiers, and all the rest to retire to their quarters. I then saw a world of people ready to run mad for vexation, and do verily believe that if God had so pleased that Monsieur d'Enghien had marched according to his determination he had won the battle with very little difficulty, for the drums that I had heard return into the enemy's rear were all the Spanish foot, who went back to draw off two pieces of cannon which were set fast in such manner that they could not be stirred either backward or forward; so that we had had nothing to fight with but the Germans, the Italians and the horse, none of which, nor even the Marquis himself, could have escaped us. But after we had stood above three hours facing the enemy, which were in a plain betwixt Somarive [Sommariva] and Cérisoles, who expected no other but to fight (and the Marquis told Monsieur de Thermes since—being a prisoner—as he has assured me, that he was never in his life in so great fear of being lost as that day, for his chiefest hopes was in the Spanish arquebusiers); Monsieur d'Enghien returned back to Carmagnola as discontented as ever prince was, and at the descent of a wood as we were upon our return to the said Carmagnola, I said to him as we rid along, Messieurs de Dampierre and de St André being by, these words: 'Sir, sir, this morning when you arose what could you have desired of God Almighty more than what he has this day given you; which is to find the enemy you have so much desired in the open field, where there was neither hedge nor ditch to obstruct you? But I perceive you are more inclined to believe those who counsel you not to fight than those who advise you to it.' At which he fell to swear and curse, saying that hereafter he would believe no-one but himself, by which I well perceived him to be nettled, so that still going on to appease him I said, 'No sir, no, in God's name believe nobody but yourself, for we all know very well that you desire nothing more than to fight, and God will prosper you,' and so went on straight to Carmagnola, vexed to the blood, remembering what I had so largely promised to the King in his council.

So soon as the said Seigneur came to Carmagnola, he presently called a council of war, and I at my arrival found our whole regiment both officers and soldiers up to the ears in mutiny, demanding their pay; but they held them in hand with the coming of Monsieur Langey,[1] who brought some money along with him. I was then entreated by Monsieur de La Molle the elder, who commanded two ensigns, and the next day was slain, to speak to Monsieur d'Enghien in the behalf of all, and that he would bear the blame. And as we were all waiting in the hall, by fortune Messieurs de Dampierre and de St André came in, and finding all in mutiny said to us these words: 'Have a little patience I beseech you, till Monsieur d'Enghien rise from the council' (and I do believe they had been talking to him by the way, for I found him riding betwixt them) and so they entered into the chamber, where they stayed not long but came out again. Monsieur de Dampierre came out first, who because Monsieur d'Enghien immediately followed him, looking at me, he laid his finger upon his mouth for a sign that I should say nothing, and Monsieur d'Enghien all in rage went straight to his chamber and the other colonels and captains every one to his own quarters, but we stirred not from thence. Presently after Messieurs de Dampierre and de St André came out into the hall and said to us these words: 'Get you home to your quarters and prepare yourselves, for tomorrow we must fight.' As they came out we took notice of those who were for fighting, all of them smiling upon us, by which also we guessed beforehand how the matter went.

In the evening when I accompanied Monsieur de Dampierre to his lodging, he told me the whole story and what Monsieur d'Enghien had propounded to the council, insisting upon the error he saw he had committed in not fighting, by which he had lost an advantage that he could not again recover, entreating them all to consider of it and to resolve upon a battle. Whereupon some fell again to discourse the same thing they had said before, of what a loss it would be to the King, with many other reasons to divert him from that resolution; and others

[1] Martin du Bellay, Sieur de Langey (d. 1560), brother of Guillaume whose *Memoirs* Monluc drew upon for the composition of his *Commentaries*.

maintained the opinion they had ever done, that he ought to put it to a battle. But Monsieur d'Enghien, who saw himself fallen into the same dispute as before, broke out in a violent passion, saying that he was resolved to fight at what price soever, and that if anyone should any more dispute the contrary he should never think so well of that man again, so long as he lived. Whereupon one in the company, who before had so highly argued against it, made answer: 'Oh sir, is it then a resolution you have taken that you will fight?' 'Yes', replied Monsieur d'Enghien. 'Then,' says the other, 'there is no more to be said'; and thereupon it was concluded that everyone should repair to his command, and that an hour before day we should be all in the same plain where we had been the day before, to march directly towards the enemy, wherever he was to be found; which was accordingly performed, some remonstrating in the meantime to the captains and soldiers that it would be out of season to stand upon telling them out their pay in the face of the enemy and that they were to stay till the battle was over, which was only a device to amuse those who were so importunate for their pay.

Now being we had the day before left the enemy in the plain betwixt Sommariva and Cérisoles, Monsieur d'Enghien did not very well know whether they might be at Sommariva or at Cérisoles, notwithstanding that the Governor of Sommariva had sent him word that the camp intended to quarter there. Signor Francisco Bernardino therefore sent out three or four of his light horse towards the said Cérisoles, who went so near that they discovered their camp, which was already in arms and the drums beginning to beat. That which had made them return to Cérisoles was to stay for the Spanish foot, who were gone for the two pieces of cannon, as has been said before. Monsieur de Thermes likewise sent out again three or four of his people also, and in the meantime we marched underneath toward Sommariva, but so soon as the light horse returned with the same intelligence we turned on the left hand and came up into the plain, where the whole army was, and there made a halt. And there Monsieur d'Enghien and Monsieur de Taix gave me all the arquebusiers to lead, for which honour I returned him my most humble thanks, telling him that I hoped, by God's assistance, to acquit myself so well of my charge that he should remain satisfied with my service, and said as much to Monsieur de Taix, who was my colonel and who came and commanded all the captains and lieutenants that I would take to obey me equally with himself.

The battle of Cérisoles, 14 April 1544

I then took four lieutenants, namely le Breil (whom I have mentioned before), le Gasquet, Captain Lyenard and Captain Fabas, who was my own lieutenant. To Fabas and Lyenard I gave the right wing and myself with the two others took the left, leading towards the little house that was afterwards so much disputed; and it was ordered that the Swiss which were commanded by Monsieur de Boutières (who a little before the rumour of the battle had been recalled from his own house) and we should fight together in the vanguard.[1] The battle was to be conducted by Monsieur d'Enghien, having under his cornet all the young lords that came from court, and the rearguard was com- manded by Monsieur Dampierre wherein were four thousand Gruyériens and three thousand Italians led by the Sieur de Dros[2] and des Cros, together with all the guidons and archers of companies.[3]

Now there was a little eminence that dipped towards Cérisoles and Sommariva which was all on a little copse but not very thick. The first of the enemy that we saw enter into the plain to come towards us were the seven thousand Italians conducted by the Prince of Salerno and in the flank of them three hundred lancers commanded by Rodolphe Baglion [Rodolfo Baglione], who belonged to the great Duke of Florence. The skirmish began by this little hill on the descent whereof the enemy had made a halt just over against us, and so soon as the skirmish was begun I gave one squadron to Captain Breil, being that which was nearest to me, and the hindmost to Captain Gasquet, about two hundred paces distant the one from the other, and of my own I gave forty or fifty arquebusiers to a sergeant of mine called Arnaut, of St Clar, a valiant man and one that very well understood his business, and I myself stood for a reserve. Being at the foresaid little house, I discovered three or four companies of Spanish arque- busiers who came full drive to possess themselves of the house, and in the meantime Fabas and Lyenard fought the Italians in the valley on the right hand. The skirmish grew hot on both sides, the enemy one while beating me up to the house and I again other whiles driving

---

[1] The army was drawn up for battle in the customary way, in three bodies—vanguard, 'battle' and rearguard. At Cérisoles the vanguard was on the right flank, the rearguard on the left. Monluc's arquebusiers were placed in front of the van.

[2] Carlo Vagnone, Sieur de Dros, a Piedmontese soldier in French service.

[3] The archers, the light horsemen attached to the lances of the *gendarmerie*, fought independently of the others in battle.

them back to their own party, for they had another that was come up to second the first, and it seemed as if we had been playing at base; but in the end I was constrained to call Captain Breil up to me, for I saw all their foot embody together, with a troop of horse to flank them. Now had I not so much as one horse with me, notwithstanding that I had advertised Monsieur d'Enghien that their cavalry was also with the arquebusiers that came up to me. Let it suffice that of a long time nobody came, insomuch that I was constrained to quit the house, but not without a great dispute which continued for a very great space. I then sent back Captain Breil to his place, the skirmish continued for almost four hours without intermission, and never did men acquit themselves better.

Monsieur d'Enghien then sent Monsieur d'Aussun unto me, commanding me to repossess myself of the house, which was neither of advantage nor disadvantage to me; to whom I made answer, 'Go and tell Monsieur d'Enghien that he must then send me some horse to fight these horse that flank their arquebusiers', (which he also saw as well as I) 'for I am not to fight horse and foot together in the open field.' He then said to me, 'It is enough for me that I have told you,' and so returned to carry back my answer to Monsieur d'Enghien, who thereupon sent Monsieur de Monein to tell me that one way or another he would that I should regain it, with whom also came the Seigneur Cabry, brother to Seigneur Maure, bringing with him threescore horse, all lancers, and Monsieur de Monein might have about some five and twenty, he being then but beginning to raise his troop. To whom I returned the same answer I had given before to Monsieur d'Aussun, and that I would not be cause of the loss of the battle, but that if they would go charge those horse that flanked the arquebusiers I would quickly regain the house. They then answered that I had reason and that they were ready to do it. Whereupon I presently sent to Captain Breil to come up to me, and to Captain Gasquet to advance to his place, and immediately Captain Breil coming up on the right hand and the horse in the middle, we marched at a good round trot directly up to them, for we were not above three hundred paces distant from one another. All this while the skirmish never ceased and as we drew within a hundred or sixscore paces off them we began to fire, upon which the cavalry faced about and their foot also, and I saw their lancers turn their backs, retreating to their troops. Monsieur de Monein and Seigneur Cabry went immediately hereupon to Monsieur d'Enghien to tell him what they had seen their cavalry do, and that if he did not send me up horse to second me I could not choose but be routed. I sent back Captain Breil and Gasquet into their places.

Now there was a little marsh near unto Cérisoles and a great hollow way, which hindered the enemy that they could not come up to us drawn up in battalia, and the Marquis del Vasto had caused six pieces of artillery to pass over this marsh and they were already advanced a good way on this side when seeing their people driven back, they were afraid that the whole army followed the pursuit and that they should lose their cannon. Wherefore they presently made the Germans to pass over this marsh and through the said hollow way, who, so soon as they came into the plain, drew up again into battalia, for it was not possible for them to pass but in great disorder, and in the meantime the cavalry and Spanish arquebusiers came up to me as before; insomuch that having no horse with me I was necessitated to quit them the place and to retire to the place from whence I came.

Now I had discovered their German foot and their artillery, and as I was retiring Monsieur de Thermes and Signor Francisco Bernardino came and placed themselves on the right hand of our battalion and upon the skirt of the hill (which was very straight), and over against the battalion of the Italians; for their lancers were exactly opposite to our pikes. Monsieur de Boutières with his company and that of the Count de Tende advanced on the left hand of our battle, and the Swiss were three or fourscore paces behind us and a little on the one side. In the meantime our arquebusiers that were conducted by Lyenard and Captain Fabas sometimes beat back the enemy as far as their main battle, and sometimes the enemy repelled them up to ours. I saw then that I must of necessity disarm our battalion of arquebusiers that made our flank on that side where Monsieur de Boutières stood and give them to them, wherewith to make a charge; which they did, and with great fury beat them up to their battle, and it was high time, for their arquebusiers had almost gained the flank of our horse. I therefore ran up to them and we began a furious skirmish, which was great and obstinately fought, for all our squadrons were closed up together, and it continued a long hour or more.

Now the enemy had placed their cannon by the side of the little house, which played directly into our battle. Monsieur de Mailly then advanced with ours and placing himself close by us, began to shoot at those of the enemy by the little house, for there where we maintained the skirmish he could not do it without killing our own men; when, looking towards our own battle, I saw Monsieur de Taix, who began to march with his pikes, charge directly towards the Italians, whereupon I ran up to him saying, 'Whither do you go, sir, whither do you go, you will lose the battle; for here are all the Germans coming to fight you and will charge into your flank.' The captains were the occasion of this, who ceased not to cry out to him, 'Sir, lead us on to fight, for it is better for us to die hand to hand than stand still here to be killed with the cannon.' 'Tis that which terrifies the most of anything and oftentimes begets more fear than it does harm. But however so it was that he was pleased to be ruled by me, and I entreated him to make his men kneel on one knee with their pikes down, for I saw the Swiss behind laid at their full length squat to the ground, so as hardly to be seen; and from him I ran to the arquebusiers. The enemy's arquebusiers by this time were beginning to retire behind the house when, as I was going up to charge straight up to them, I discovered the front of the Germans' battle and suddenly commanded the captains Breil and Gasquet to retire by degrees towards the artillery, for we were to make room for the pikes to come up to the fight, and I went to our battle, where being come I said to my men these words.

'Oh my fellow soldiers let us now fight bravely, and if we win the battle we get a greater renown than any of our nation ever did. It was never yet read in history that ever the Gauls fought the Germans pike to pike but that the Germans defeated them, and to set this honourable mark upon ourselves that we were better men than our ancestors, this glory ought to inspire us with a double courage to fight so as to overcome or die and make our enemies know what kind of men we are. Remember, comrades, the message the King sent to us and what a glory it will be to present ourselves before him after the victory. Now, sir,' said I to Monsieur de Taix, 'it is time to rise,' which he suddenly did, and I began to cry out aloud: 'Gentlemen, it may be there are not many here who have ever been in a battle before, and therefore let me tell you that if we take our pikes by the hinder end and fight at the length of the pike, we shall be defeated; for the Germans are more dexterous at this kind of fight than we are. But you must take your pikes by the middle as the Swiss do and run headlong to force and penetrate into the midst of them, and you shall see how confounded they will be.' Monsieur de Taix then cried out to me to go along the battle and make them all handle their pikes after this manner, which I accordingly did, and now we were all ready for the encounter.

The Germans marched at a great rate directly towards us and I ran to put myself before the battle, where I alighted from my horse, for I ever had a lackey at the head of the battalion ready with my pike. And as Monsieur de Taix and the rest of the captains saw me on foot they all cried out at once, 'Get up, Captain Monluc, get up again and you shall lead us on to the fight.' To whom I made answer that if it was my fate to die that day, I could not die in a more honourable place than in their company, with my pike in my hand. I then called to Captain la Burte [de la Burthe], who was sergeant major, that he should always be stirring about the battalion when we came to grapple, and that he and the sergeants behind and on the sides should never cease crying 'Put home, soldiers, put home', to the end that they might push on one another.

The Germans came up to us at a very round rate, insomuch that their battle being very great, they could not possibly follow, so that we saw great windows in their body and several ensigns a good way behind, and all on a sudden rushed in among them, a good many of us at least, for as well on their side as ours all the first ranks, either with push of pikes or the shock at the encounter, were overturned, neither is it possible amongst foot to see a greater fury. The second rank and the third were the cause of our victory, for the last so pushed them on that they fell in upon the heels of one another, and as ours pressed in the enemy was still driven back. I was never in my life so active and light as that day and it stood me well so to be, for above three times I was beaten down to my knees. The Swiss were very sly and cunning, for till they saw us within ten or a dozen pikes' length of one another they never rose, but then like savage boars they rushed into their flank and Monsieur de Boutières broke in at a canton. Monsieur de Thermes and Signor Francisco in the meantime charged Rodolfo Baglione, whom they overthrew, and put his cavalry to rout. The Italians, who saw their cavalry broken and the landsknechts and Germans overthrown and routed, began to take the descent of the valley and as fast as they could to make directly towards the wood. Monsieur de Thermes had his horse killed under him at the first encounter, and by ill fortune his leg was so far engaged under him in the fall that it was not possible for him to rise, so that he was there by the Italians taken and carried away prisoner and, to say the truth, his legs were none of the best.

Now you are to take notice that the Marquis del Vasto had composed a battalion of five thousand pikes, namely two thousand Spaniards and three thousand Germans, out of the number of six thousand, being the same that Count Laudron [Lodrone] had brought into Spain where he had remained ten years or more, and who all spoke as good Spanish as natural Spaniards. He had formed this battalion only to claw away the Gascons, for he said that he feared our battalion more than any of the others and had an opinion that his Germans (being all chosen men) would beat our Swiss. He had placed three hundred arquebusiers only in the nature of a forlorn hope, at the head of this battle, which he reserved to the forenamed effect, and all the rest maintained the skirmish. Now as he was by the little house on the same side with the Germans, he saw the Gruyériens, who were all armed in white, and took them for the Gascons, and thereupon said to his men: '*Hermanos, hermanos, aqui estan lous Gascones; sarrais à ellos.*'[1] They were not gone two hundred paces from him but that he perceived our battle, which started up, and saw his error when it was too late to help it, for we all wore black arms.

This battle of five thousand pikes marched then at a good round rate directly upon the Gruyériens and they were of necessity to pass hard by Monsieur d'Enghien, who by somebody or other was very ill advised, for as they passed by he charged with his *gendarmes* quite through their battalion in the flank, and there were slain and wounded a great many brave and worthy men and some of very considerable quality, as Monsieur d'Assier, le Sieur de La Rochechouard with several others, and yet more at the second charge. There were some who passed and repassed quite through and through, but still they closed up again and in that manner came up to the Gruyériens, who were soon overthrown without so much as standing one push of pike, and there died all their captains and lieutenants who were in the first rank and the rest fled straight to Messieur des Cros. But this battalion of Spaniards and Germans still at a very great rate pursued their victory and overthrew the said Sieur des Cros, who there died and all his captains with him. Neither could Monsieur d'Enghien any way relieve him, forasmuch as all the horses almost of his cavalry in these two furious and inconsiderate charges were wounded and walked fair and softly over the field towards the enemy.

He was then in the height of despair and cursed the hour that ever he was born, seeing the overthrow of his foot and that he himself had scarce an hundred horse left to sustain the shock; insomuch that Monsieur de Pignan of Montpellier (a gentleman of his) assured me that he twice turned the point of his sword into his gorget, to have offered violence to himself, and himself told me at his return that he

[1] 'Brothers, brothers, there are the Gascons; up and at them.'

was then in such a condition he should have been glad anyone would have run him through. The Romans might have done so, but I do not think it becomes a Christian. Everyone at that time passed his censure upon it according to his own fancy. For our parts we were as well as heart could wish and as much pleased as the enemy was afflicted; but let us return to the blows, for there were yet both to give and to take. The cowardice of the Gruyériens occasioned a great loss on that side of the field. In my life I never saw such great lubbers as those were, unworthy ever to bear arms, if they have not learnt more courage since. They are indeed neighbours to the Swiss, but there is no more comparison betwixt them than betwixt a Spanish horse and an ass. It is not all to have a great number of men upon the list but to have those that are true bred, for a hundred of them are worth a thousand of the other. And a brave and valiant captain with a thousand men that he knows he may trust to will pass over the bellies of four thousand.

After the same manner that Monsieur d'Enghien had seen his people massacred before his eyes, without any power to relieve them, did the Marquis del Vasto behold his people also trampled under foot by an equal fortune, so wantonly she played on both hands with these two generals. For as he saw Rodolfo Baglione and his Germans, both of them routed and overthrown, he took his horse and retreated towards Asti. Monsieur de St Julien, who that day discharged the office of camp-master and colonel of the Swiss, was on horseback (and, to say the truth, he was but weak of person and wanted strength to support any great burden of arms on foot), saw their battle overthrown on the one side and ours on the other, and before he went to Monsieur d'Enghien saw us Swiss and Gascons amongst the five thousand Spaniards and Germans, killing on all hands. And then it was that he turned back and overtook Monsieur d'Enghien near to the wood that leads towards Carmagnola, but very poorly accompanied, and cried out to him, 'Sir, sir, face about, for the battle is won, the Marquis del Vasto is routed and all his Italians and Germans cut to pieces.' Now this battalion of the Spaniards and Germans had already made a halt, giving themselves for lost when they saw neither horse nor foot of their own come up to them, by which they very well knew that they had lost the battle, and began to take on the right hand straight towards [La Monta] from whence they had departed the day before.

I thought I had been the cunningest snap in all the whole army having contrived to place a row of arquebusiers betwixt the first and second rank to kill all the captains first, and had said to Monsieur de

Taix three or four days before that before any of ours should fall I
would kill all their captains in the first rank; but I would not tell him
the secret till he had given me the command of the arquebusiers, and
then he called to him de la Burthe the sergeant major, bidding him
presently make choice of the arquebusiers and to place them after that
manner. Upon my faith I have never seen nor heard of the like before
and thought myself to be the first inventor of it; but we found that
they were as crafty as we, for they had also done the same thing, who
never shot no more than ours till they came within a pike's length, and
there was a very great slaughter, not a shot being fired but it wrought
its effect.

So soon as Monsieur d'Enghien understood the battle to be won,
which before (by the defeat of those on his side of the field and those
cowardly Gruyériens, to encourage whom he had done all that in him
lay) he had given over for lost, he presently put himself in the rear of
those Germans and Spaniards, which as he was doing, several of those
who had taken fright and were shifting for themselves rallied up to
him, some of which now appeared wonderful eager of the pursuit,
who had run away but a little before, and others had broke their
bridles on purpose to lay the fault of their own fear upon the poor
horses, who by this means were to bear more than the weight of their
masters. He had a little before the battle, by good fortune, sent to
Savigliano for three companies of very good Italian foot to be present
at the business, who being as far as Reconis [Racconigi] upon their way
from thence heard the thunder of the artillery, by which being assured
that the battle was begun they mounted all the arquebusiers they could
on horseback, and coming all the way a gallop arrived in so opportune
a season that they found Monsieur d'Enghien in pursuit of the enemy,
not having one arquebusier in company with him; where alighting
from their horses they put themselves in the rear of them whilst the
said Seigneur d'Enghien with his cavalry, one while in their flank and
another in their front, still pushed on the victory. He then sent a
trooper to us in all haste to bid us turn that way for there was more
work to do, which messenger found us at the chapel hard by the gate
of Cérisoles, having just made an end of killing with so great fury and
slaughter that not so much as one man remained alive save only a
colonel called Aliprand de Mandruce [Alisprando Madruzzo], brother
to the Cardinal of Trent,[1] who being laid amongst the dead with seven
or eight wounds upon him, Caubios, a light horse belonging to

[1] Christophe Madruzzo, created Cardinal in 1542.

Monsieur de Thermes, as he came through the dead bodies saw him, being yet alive but stripped stark naked, spoke to him and caused him to be carried to Carmagnola to redeem Monsieur de Thermes in case he should recover and live, as he afterwards did. The Swiss, in killing and laying on with their two-handed swords, still cried out 'Mondovi, Mondovi', where those of their nation had received no quarter,[1] and in short all that made head against us on our side of the field were slain.

We had no sooner received the command from Monsieur d'Enghien, but that immediately the battle of the Swiss and ours turned towards him. I never saw two battalions so soon reunited as these were, for of ourselves we rallied and drew up into battalia as we went, marching all the way side by side. In this posture the enemy, who went off at a great rate firing all the way, and by that means keeping the horse at distance, discovered us coming up to them, who so soon as they saw us advanced within five or six hundred paces and the cavalry in front ready to charge in amongst them, they threw down their pikes, surrendering themselves to the horse. But here the game began, some killing and others endeavouring to save, there being some who had fifteen or twenty men about him, still getting as far as they could from the crowd for fear of us foot, who had a mind to have cut all their throats; neither could the cavalry so well defend them but that above half of them were slain, for as many as we could lay our hands on were dispatched. Now you shall know what became of me.

Monsieur de Valence, my brother, had sent me a Turkish horse from Venice,[2] one of the fleetest coursers that ever I yet saw, and I had an opinion which all the world could not dispossess me of, that we should win the battle. Wherefore I gave my said horse to a servant I had, an old soldier in whom I reposed a very great confidence, bidding him be sure always to keep behind our battalion of pikes and telling him that if it pleased God I did escape from the skirmish I would then alight and engage with the pikes, and that when we came to close, if he should see our battle overthrown that then he might conclude me to be slain and should save himself upon the horse; and on the contrary, if he should see us prevail over the enemy's battle, that then he should still follow (without offering to break in) in the rear of our battalion, when so soon as I should be certain of the victory I would

[1] When it was taken by del Vasto in November of the previous year.

[2] Jean de Monluc, later Bishop of Valence, was at this time French envoy to Venice: see Appendix I, 'Monluc, Jean de.'

leave the execution and come to take my horse to pursue the cavalry and try to take some prisoner of condition.

I had a whimsy came into my head that I should take the Marquis del Vasto or die in the attempt, trusting to the swiftness of my horse, for which I had already in my imagination swallowed a mighty ransom or at least some remarkable recompense from the King. Having then a while followed the victory, I stayed behind, thinking to find my man; and indeed I was so weary with fighting, running, and moreover so spent with straining my voice to encourage the soldiers that I was able to do no more, when I was assaulted by two great mastiff Germans, who had thought presently to have done my business. But having rid myself of one of them the other betook him to his heels but he went not very far; in truth I there saw very brave blows given. I then went to seek out that son of a whore my man, but the devil a man that I could find, for as the enemy's artillery played upon our battle and very often shot over, the shot falling behind it, had removed my gentleman from the place where I thought to find him; who very discreetly went and put himself behind the Swiss; when seeing the disorder of the Gruyériens and Provençals he very learnedly concluded us to be in the same condition and thereupon fled back as far as Carmagnola.

Thus are men oftentimes deceived in their choice; for I should never have suspected that this fellow would so soon have had his heart in his breeches and have run away with so little ado. I then found Captain Mons, having no more than one servant only with him, who had done a great deal better than mine, for he had kept a little pad nag ready for him upon which he took me up behind him, for I was extremely weary, and so we passed on, still seeing the Germans knocked down all the way as we went; till being sent for by Monsieur d'Enghien we both alighted and went on foot, till the entire defeat of the Germans and Spaniards. When presently I saw my man come back, calling him a hundred rogues and cowards for so basely running away; who replied that he had not done it alone but in company with better men and better clad than himself, and that he had only run away to bear them company. By which pleasant answer my anger was appeased, and upon my word he hit upon it in a lucky hour for I was very near showing him a trick of a Gascon.

We then rallied together some twenty or five and twenty horse, what of those of Monsieur de Thermes, of Signor Francisco Bernardino and the Sieur de Maure, and rid a round gallop after the Marquis del

Vasto, and with us moreover a gentleman whose name I have forgot but he was one of those who came post from court to be at the battle, and as we went we met by the way two light horse leading prisoner Signor Carles de Gonzague [Carlo Gonzaga], whom they had taken in the rear of the enemy's party, which still more encouraged us to spur forward. So soon as we came so near to the enemy as to discover what posture they were in, we perceived that they were rallied and closed up to the crupper, still marching on in very good order at a good round trot and their lances ready in the rest. Which made me say to those of our company: 'These people are ready for us and therefore I do not think it convenient to charge in amongst them, lest instead of taking some of the chief of them it fare with us as with the Scotchman who took a Tartar.' So that we returned without attempting anything more upon them. But I am yet of opinion that had not that rascally man of mine played me that dog-trick I had taken some man or other of command amongst them. As we were upon our return, the gentleman I spoke of before accosting me said these words, 'Jesu! Captain Monluc, what danger was this battle in once today of being lost?' To which I (who had neither seen nor heard of any disorder and thought that the last we had defeated had been those of Carignano, who were drawn out of their garrison to be present at the battle) made answer, 'Why, which way were we in any danger, seeing that all day we have had the victory in our hands?' 'I perceive then,' said he, 'that you know nothing of the disorder has happened.' And thereupon told me all that had befallen in the battle. As God shall help me, I do believe that had he given me two stabs with a dagger I should not have bled, for my heart was shrunk up and I was sick at the news, in which fright I continued for three nights after, starting up in my sleep and dreaming continually of a defeat.

Thus then we arrived at the camp where Monsieur d'Enghien was, to whom I went, and making my horse curvet, said to him sportingly these words: 'What think you, sir, am I not as pretty a fellow on horseback as I am on foot?' To which he made answer (though yet very melancholy), 'You will always behave yourself very well, both in the one posture and in the other,' and bowing his body was pleased to embrace me in his arms and knighted me upon the place; an honour I shall be proud of so long as I live, both for being performed upon the field of battle and by the hand of so generous and so great a prince. Accursed be he that so basely deprived us of him.[1] But no more of

[1] The Italian *condottiere* Bentivoglio—later Monluc's ally at Siena—killed d'Enghien in 1546.

that. I then said to him, 'Sir, have I served you today to your satisfaction?'; for Monsieur de Taix had already told him that I had fought with them on foot. To which he replied, 'Yes, Captain Monluc, and so well that I will never forget how bravely you have behaved yourself, neither, do I assure you, will I conceal it from the King.' 'Why then, sir,' said I, 'it lies in your power to do me the greatest kindness that ever you can do a poor gentleman so long as you live.' At which words, drawing me apart, that nobody might hear, he asked me what it was that I would have him do for me; to which I made answer that it was to dispatch me suddenly away with news of the success of the battle to the King; telling him withal that it was an office more properly belonging to me than any other, considering what I had said to his Majesty and his council to obtain leave to fight, and that the last words I had said to the King were that he was only to expect news of the victory. To which, turning towards me, he made answer that it was all the reason in the world and that I should be sent before any other. And so all the army returned victorious to Carmagnola.

But as I expected to have been sent away post in the night I was told that Monsieur d'Escars had gained everyone to speak for him that he might go. Monsieur de Taix had also passed his word to me; but in the end he suffered himself to be overcome, as also did Monsieur d'Enghien, which was the greatest misfortune that possibly could have befallen me; for having overcome the King's council and their deliberation and that his Majesty had done me the honour to condescend to my opinion, here to have carried him the certain news of what I had promised and assured him so few days before, I leave everyone to judge whether I should have been welcome or no; and what wrong I had done me, especially having been that day in a great and honourable command and acquitted myself of it to my general's content. It had been a great good fortune for me and also a great honour, to have carried to the King what I had before promised and assured him of. There was however no remedy and I was forced to submit, though they had much ado to appease me, but it was to no purpose to be angry or to complain of the injury was done me. I have since repented me a thousand times that I did not steal away the same night, which if I had done I would have broke my neck or have been the first that should have brought the news to the King, and I am confident he would not only himself have taken it in good part but moreover have made my peace with others. But I, from that time forward, gave over all thoughts of advancement and never after expected to come to anything, which made me beg leave of Monsieur d'Enghien to be dismissed that I might return into my own country. Which said Seigneur promised me great matters (knowing me to be discontented) and Monsieur de Taix did the same, using all the persuasions he could to make me stay. But I pressed my departure so much that at last I obtained leave, upon my promise to return; and for further assurance of me the said Sieur d'Enghien made me accept a commission from him for the speedy raising of one thousand or twelve hundred foot to bring into Piedmont, to recruit the companies, for in plain truth we had lost a great many men.

Now I shall tell you what advantages accrued to the King from this victory, which I only had from Monsieur de Thermes to whom the Marquis del Vasto had told it, lying wounded in bed of an arquebus shot in his thigh. He told him that the Emperor and the King of England were agreed at one and the same time to enter the kingdom of France, each on his own side, and that the Emperor had sent him the seven thousand Germans purposely to make him so strong that Monsieur d'Enghien might not dare to fight him; and afterwards to march directly to Lombriasse [Lombriasco][1] there to throw a bridge over the river and to put into Carignano the provisions that he brought along with him and as much more as he could provide besides; and thence to draw out the four thousand Spanish and German foot, who were to return towards Ivrée, leaving four thousand Italians in their stead. Which being done he was to send back the seven German colonels with their regiments to the Emperor. That then there would still remain with him in his camp five thousand Germans and as many Spaniards, with which at the same time that the King of England should enter the kingdom he was to descend by the Val d'Oste [Valle d'Aosta], through which he should march straight to Lyons, where he should meet nobody to oppose him but the inhabitants of the city nor any fortress at all; where lying between the two rivers he might command all the territories of the Duke of Savoy, together with Dauphiné and Provence. All this was told me by Monsieur de Thermes after his return; an enterprise that had not been hard to execute had we not won the battle, in which betwixt twelve and fifteen thousand men of the enemy were slain.[2] The victory was very important, both in respect of the prisoners, which were many of them very consider-

---

[1] On the Po, south of Carignano.

[2] In fact, probably not half as many: F. Lot, *Recherches sur les Effectifs des Armées Francaises ... 1494–1562*, 85.

able, as also for the baggage, which was exceedingly rich. And besides many places surrendered out of fear and in the end Carignano itself, of which I shall not meddle with the particulars because I was not present at the surrender. Had they known how to make their advantage of this battle, Milan had been in a tottering condition, but we never knew how to improve our victories to the best. It is also very true that the King had at this time enough to do to defend his kingdom from two such powerful enemies.

The victory of Cérisoles was negatived, as Monluc saw, by events elsewhere. The Imperialists defeated France's allies in Italy, and Charles V encouraged Henry VIII to invade Picardy, while he himself concluded the Peace of Crépy with Francis. Monluc was among the 'old soldiers of Piedmont' who were transferred to the northern front to resist the English (summer 1544)

The thirst of revenge had prompted the Emperor (contrary to the faith he had engaged to the Pope) to league and confederate himself with the King of England, who was fallen off from his obedience to the holy chair out of despite; which two princes (as it was said) had divided the kingdom (for so both the Marquis del Vasto told Monsieur de Thermes, and I have since heard the same from an English gentleman at Boulogne). But however it was but disputing the bear's skin. France well united within itself can never be conquered till after the loss of a dozen battles, considering the brave gentry whereof it is fruitful and the strong places wherewith it abounds. And I conceive they are deceived who say that Paris being taken, France is lost. It is indeed the treasury of the kingdom and an unexhausted magazine, where all the richest of the whole nation unlade their treasure, and I do believe in the whole world there is not such a city, for 'tis an old saying that there is not a crown in Paris but yields ten sols revenue once a year. But there are so many other cities and strong places in the kingdom as are sufficient to destroy thirty armies. So that it would be easy to rally together and to recover that from them again before they could conquer the rest, unless the conqueror would depopulate his own kingdom to repeople his new conquest. I say this because the design of the King of England was to run directly up to Paris whilst the Emperor should enter into Champagne. The forces of these two princes being joined together consisted of fourscore thousand foot and twenty thousand horse with a prodigious train of artillery, by which any man may judge whether our King had not enough to do and whether it was not high time to look about him. Without all doubt these poor princes have greater care and trouble upon them than the inferior sorts of men, and I am of opinion the King did very well to call back his forces out of Piedmont, though some are pleased to say that the state of Milan might otherwise have been won and that the Emperor would have been necessitated to have called back his forces out of France to defend that duchy; but all this depended upon event.

So it was that God would not suffer these princes to agree betwixt themselves, each of them being bent upon his own particular advantage; and I have often heard, and sometimes seen, that when two princes jointly undertake the conquest of a kingdom they never agree, for each of them is always suspicious of being overreached by his companion and evermore jealous of one another. I have not, I confess, much conversed with books; but I have heard say that after this manner we first lost the kingdom of Naples and were cheated by the King of Spain. This suspicion and jealousy at this time preserved us, as it has at other times done several others as the historians report. For my part I should more apprehend one great single enemy than two who would divide the cake between them; there will always be some exceptions taken and two nations do not easily agree, as you see here. The English King came and sat down before Boulogne, which was basely surrendered to him by the Sieur de Vervins, who lost his life for his labour; an example that ought to be set before all such as undertake the defence of strongholds.[1] This by no means pleased the Spaniard, who reaped no advantage by it and saw very well that his confederate would only intend his own business.

Our colonel, Monsieur de Taix, brought three and twenty ensigns to the King, being all the same which had been at the battle, saving one new company. But I fell sick at Troyes and came not up to the army till they were advanced near to Boulogne, where the said Sieur de Taix delivered me the patent his Majesty had sent me for the office of camp-master; but there was nothing done worthy remembrance till the camisado of Boulogne. As we arrived near to La Marquise,[2] the Dauphin who commanded the army had intelligence that it was three or four days since the town had been taken (though he knew it before) and that the King of England was embarked and gone for England. It is to be presumed that this prince had made such haste away only

[1] Boulogne fell to Henry VIII, 14 September 1544: Vervin was executed at Paris, July 1549.

[2] Marquise lies between Boulogne and Calais: see map, p. 133.

to avoid fighting, forasmuch as he had left all things in so great disorder; for in the first place we found all his artillery before the town in a meadow that lies upon the descent towards the Tour d'Ordre;[1] secondly there was found above thirty casks full of corslets, which he had caused to be brought[5] out of Germany therewith to arm his soldiers, which he had left for the defence of the town; thirdly he had left all the ammunition of victual, as corn, wine and other things to eat in the lower town, insomuch that if Monsieur de Téligny be yet living (as I am told he is), the father of this who is a Huguenot and who treated the peace during these troubles,[2] and was taken upon the camisado in the lower town (where not one man but himself escaped alive), he will bear witness that there was not in the higher town provision to serve four days, for himself told it me.[3]

The camisado at Boulogne, the night of the 6–7 October 1544

The occasion of the camisado was this. A son-in-law of the Marshal du Biès [du Biez][4] (not this fine Monsieur de Vervins but another whose name I have forgot[5]) came to Monsieur de Taix and told him that a spy of his, who came from Boulogne, had assured him that as yet nothing had been removed to the higher town, but that all still remained below, and that if they would speedily attempt to take the lower town (which might easily be done) they would in eight days' time have the upper come out to them with ropes about their necks; and that if Monsieur de Taix so pleased he would in the morning lead him where he might himself discover all; the spy moreover affirming that as yet not one breach in the wall was repaired but that all lay open as if it were a village.

Upon this information Monsieur de Taix was impatient to go to take a view of all and took me along with him, together with this son-

---

[1] The Tour d'Ordre was a fortified lighthouse, a strongpoint commanding Boulogne town and harbour.

[2] Louis de Téligny, Sieur de Lierville, whose son Charles, a follower—and son-in-law—of Coligny, helped draw up the Peace of St Germain (August 1570) and was killed in the massacre of St Bartholomew.

[3] The old fortified town lies on a hill; to the west and close to the harbour lay Basse Boulogne. A large contemporary English plan of Boulogne, its defences, and the French positions, is in the British Museum, Cotton Aug. I, suppt. 5.

[4] Oudard du Biez, *Sénéchal* of the Boulonnais and Marshal of France.

[5] Jacques de Fouquesolles, husband of du Biez's daughter: Vervin, the commander who surrendered Boulogne, was also son-in-law to du Biez.

in-law of the marshal. We might be about a hundred horse drawn out of the several troops, and just at the break of day we arrived before the town, leaving the tower of Ordre some two or three hundred paces on the right hand, and saw five or six pavilions upon the descent in the great highway leading to the gate of the city. We were no more than five or six horse only, Monsieur de Taix having left the rest behind a little hill. This son-in-law of the marshal and I therefore went down to the first pavilion and passed close by it into the camp on the left hand, till we came to the second, from whence we discovered all their artillery at no further distance than fourscore paces only, neither did we see any more than three or four English soldiers that were walking up and down by the cannon, and in the foresaid second pavilion we heard them jabber English. The marshal's son-in-law then made me return back to Monsieur de Taix, who immediately upon my telling him what we had seen, went down with me to the place from whence I came and there with the foresaid gentleman stood still. In the meantime it grew to be fair broad day, so that the sentinels very well perceived us to be none of their own people and thereupon presently gave the alarm. But for all that we saw not a man offer to sally out of the tower (I have indeed since been told that Doudellet,[1] whom Monsieur de St Pol had bred up of a page, had the guard at the tower) and so we returned.

Monsieur de Taix then with the said gentleman presently went to find out the Dauphin and Monsieur d'Orléans,[2] where it was concluded that the next morning at break of day a camisado should be given, and that Monsieur de Taix with our companies should give the first onset by three breaches that were in the wall on that side where we had been to discover; which were breaches that had only been made for pleasure. The Rheingrave[3] then entreated the Dauphin that he and his Germans might go on with us to the assault; but Monsieur de Taix had already promised Count Pedemarie de Sainct Segond[4] that he would speak to the Dauphin to give him leave to go on with us, which was a very great misfortune; for had the Germans gone on with us to the breach the enemy had never fired one shot, which would have invited a great many more to come in to our relief much sooner than they did.

[1] Probably Dudley, an English officer.

[2] Dauphin Henry's younger brother Charles, Duke of Orléans (1522–45).

[3] Jean Philippe, Count of Rheingau, commanded the German reiters in French service.

[4] Pier Maria Rossi, Count of San Secondo, commanded the Italian troops in French service.

We set out in the night with shirts over our arms[1] and met the Rheingrave with his Germans ready and resolved to pass over a bridge of brick there was near unto Marquise, which resolution he was not to be persuaded from, but would pass over after us, what promise soever he had made to the Count. Of which Monsieur de Taix sent present word to the Dauphin, and whilst they were in dispute about it came the Admiral d'Annebaut, who so far prevailed with the Rheingrave that at last he was persuaded to retire behind, giving us leave to pass and the Italians after us, but for his own part he would not stir from the battle of the *gendarmes* that was drawn up near to Marquise and Monsieur Dampierre also, who was colonel of the Grisons,[2] came up as far as the Tour d'Ordre where he drew up his men into battalia. Now Monsieur de Taix had given me one part of his men with them to fall on by the highway on his right hand, being the same he had discovered the day before. I then charged up straight to the artillery, and those who remained with Monsieur de Taix and the Italians fell on by the three breaches, which they bravely carried; and being there was neither gate nor breach on that side where the artillery was, I was fain to go all along by the wall on that side towards the river, where I at last found a breach of some ten or twelve paces wide, which I entered without any manner of opposition and went on straight to the church; where I saw no captain of ours save one only who was running along by the river directly to the forementioned breaches, and him I called to but he heard me not.

Now you must know that Monsieur de Taix was wounded and enforced to retire. What became of Count Pier Maria I know not, but I was afterwards told that all the captains, both Gascons and Germans, were gone out of the town and had made no stay there, by reason of an alarm that the English had recovered the breaches by the outside of the town, as it was true; but there were of them not above two hundred men that were sallied out on the outside from the higher town, and I was moreover told that it was Doudellet who fled from the Tour d'Ordre straight to the town. All our ensigns were left in the town but I never perceived anything of all this, for had I seen the disorder I do believe I should have done as the rest did; I will not pretend to be braver than I am. Before the church I found two Italian captains only with their companies and colours, where so soon as I arrived I

[1] Dark shirts were worn over armour for concealment: hence the term 'camisado', from camisade, for a surprise attack of this kind.

[2] Dampierre (see above p. 104) now was in command of Swiss mercenaries.

fell to assaulting three or four houses and forced them, wherein were
a great number of English and most of them without arms; some of
which were clad in white and red, others in black and yellow, and a
great many soldiers also without those colours. But I soon understood
that all those in liveries were pioneers, because they had no arms as
the other had who defended themselves, and so that above two
hundred of them were slain in the houses. I then marched straight to
the church, where I found the said Italian captains (the one called
Cezar Port and the other Hieronym Megrin, and with these Italians
Messieurs d'Andelot[1] and de Navailles who was lieutenant to Monsieur
de Nemours),[2] asking them where all our captains were, who returned
me answer that they knew not what was become of them. I then
began to perceive there was some disorder in the case, not seeing one
man of all our companies excepting those who were entered with me
and about fifty or threescore others who had stayed behind to plunder
and were rallied to me at the assault of the houses.

Whilst I was considering with myself what the matter should be,
all on a sudden there came a great number of English full drive
directly upon us as we stood before the church, and in the street
adjoining, crying out, 'Who goes there?' To which I made answer in
English, 'A friend, a friend' (for of all the languages that are scattered
amongst us I have learned some words, and the Italian and Spanish
passably well, which has sometimes been very useful to me). But the
English proceeding to further interrogatories, they soon put me to the
end of my Latin; by which perceiving what we were they presently
fell on, crying out, 'Kill, kill, kill'.[3] I then called out to the Italian
captains, saying, '*Aiutate mi et state appreso me, perche io me ne vo
assaglir li; non bisogno lassiar mi investire.*'[4] Which having said, I ran full
drive upon them, who immediately faced about, and pursued them,
laying on in their rear, to the end of the street where they turned off
on the right hand along by the wall of the upper town, from whence

[1] François de Coligny, Sieur d'Andelot (1521–69): later Colonel-General of Infantry,
and a leader of the Huguenots after 1562. See below, p. 175.

[2] François de Navailles, cavalry officer under the command of Jacques de Savoie, Duke
of Nemours.

[3] The original reads: ' "Who goeth there?" c'est-a-dire: "Qui va la?" Je leur respondis
en anglois: "A frind, a frind", qui veut dire: "Amis, amis." ... Comme ces Anglois
eurent faict d'autres demandes et que je fuz au bout de mon latin, ils poursuivirent en
criant: "Quil, quil, quil", c'est-a-dire: "Tue, tue, tue".' *Commentaires*, ed. P. Courteault,
174.

[4] 'Aid me and stand by me. While I attack them don't let me be surrounded.'

they discharged at us some small pieces and a whole cloud of arrows. I then retired back to the Italians, where I was no sooner come and settled in my former order but that they returned to charge me again, but I had taken a little heart, having found them so easily to run away, and therefore gave them leave to come up close to us, where I then charged them and we thought they ran away with greater facility than before.

I therefore retired once more before the church, but then there fell such a furious storm of rain that it seemed as if God Almighty had been disposed to drown us all, during which shower there came up ten or twelve ensigns of ours from one of the breaches at which they had entered, not having above six soldiers with them, and I might have about as many ensigns with me. One of the ensigns then told me that the breaches were all taken and that the captains were fled away; which having heard I desired the two Italian captains that they should a while make good that canton where the church stood (for there was a wall before the door of it) and I would go dispute the breach by which I had entered, which so soon as I should recover I would send them word that they might draw off and come to me, and if peradventure the enemy in the meantime should come up to them, that then they should remember what they had seen me do and boldly charge them.

I then went to the breach, where I saw already ten or twelve English got thither, two of which stood upon their defence, but of the rest some leaped over the breach and others slipped on the right hand along the inside of the wall, and so soon as we were got out we saw moreover fifteen or twenty that came running towards us along on the outside the wall, and seeing us turned on the right hand towards the other breaches by which our people before had entered. I then entreated a gentleman of Burgundy (whose name I have forgot), who was mounted upon a horse he had taken, that he would go to Cezar Port and Hieronym Megrin to call them away, which he was very willing to do, provided I would promise to stay for him, which I assured him upon my life I would do and that dead or alive he should find me at this breach. The rain still continued more and more violent, when the said gentleman returning told me that he could not possibly get to them and that they were either retreated into the church or all dead. When behold on a sudden three or four hundred English came at a good round trot directly upon us all along by the wall, just as we were upon the point to enter again to go relieve the Italians, but seeing them come full drive upon us, we were constrained to alter that resolution.

Messieurs d'Andelot, de Navailles, this Burgundian gentleman and three or four others had never stirred from my side from the time they had first met me before the church (and it was well for them, for if they had they had gone to pot with the rest), and as the English came on in this fury, there arose a hubbub amongst us, some crying out to me to fly towards the river and others towards the mountain:[1] but upon the instant I resolved to remonstrate to them. 'What have you to do to go to the mountain? In our way thither we must of necessity pass close by the higher town, for to go directly to the river do you not see that it is rising and got so high already that we shall all be drowned? Let no-one therefore think any more of that, but let us make ourselves ready, for we must fight these people.' Whereupon Monsieur d'Andelot cried out aloud, 'I, I, Captain Monluc, I pray you let us fight them, for that is the best.' He was a man of very great courage, and 'tis great pity he afterwards turned Huguenot, for I do believe he was one of the bravest gentlemen in the kingdom. We therefore marched directly up to them, when so soon as we came within four or five pikes' length of them they let fly a great shower of arrows upon us, and we ran up to them to push a pike, for there were but two arquebus shot fired, and immediately they faced about and fled the same way they came. We followed after and very close, and when they came to the canton of the town towards their own people, who kept almost all our ensigns enclosed, they seeing them come, and we pursuing in the rear of them, quitted the breaches to relieve their own men and rallying all together came running directly upon us, who were all at the foot of the mountain of the tower of Ordre.

I then cried to Monsieur d'Andelot and to all the ensigns and soldiers, 'Get away as fast as you can and climb the mountain,' for I, for my own part, with four or five pikes, would stay to see the event of all, retiring towards a rivulet which was by the artillery. So soon as the English had quitted the breach to come to us, our ensigns leaped out of the town towards the valley by which they had come, and being got to the foot of the mountain, where Monsieur d'Andelot and the ensigns were marching up, the enemy saw that our ensigns were again passed over the breaches and that the said d'Andelot with the other ensigns were got half way up the hill. They then thought to turn after the others, as they did, but could never overtake above eight or ten soldiers at the most, whom they cut all to pieces. Five or six

[1] The river is the Liane, the mountain the hill close to the Tour d'Ordre.

English then came up to me and I passed the rivulet, where the water was knee deep. From its banks they bestowed some arrows upon me and shot three into the target, and another through a sleeve of mail I wore upon my right arm, which for my part of the booty I carried home to my quarters, and having received them went to mount the hill on the backside of the Tour d'Ordre. Monsieur le Dauphin, having with him Monsieur d'Orléans and the Admiral [d'Annebaut], made his landsknechts to march to relieve us within the town, but before they could come near the disorder was already happened and they found Messieurs d'Andelot and de Navailles with the ensigns, who were got up to the top of the mountain.

In the interim of this confusion the Vidame of Chartres and my brother Monsieur de Lious [Lioux][1] advanced as far as the bottom of the hill to see if they could learn any news of me, but they were sent back with a vengeance and told the Dauphin that they did certainly believe I was slain within the town, forasmuch as they had seen all the captains, me only excepted; and whilst they were in this discourse Monsieur d'Andelot arrived, of whom the Dauphin demanded if he knew what was become of me, to whom he made answer that I had been the preservation of him and all those that were with him, but that (it seemed) I had not known how to save myself, which I might have done if I had so pleased, as well as the rest. The said Sieur d'Andelot concluded me for dead, believing that I had suffered myself to be snapped about their artillery, or by a ship that lay upon the rivulet I passed over, but I was no such fool, for I call God to witness, and let him punish me according to my perjury, if of all that day I ever lost my understanding, and it was a great blessing that God was pleased to preserve it to me entire, for had I lost my judgment we had received a very great disgrace which we could neither have concealed nor excused, and I had been in great danger never to have been a Marshal of France. We had lost all our ensigns and those that carried them withal, which nevertheless God gave me the grace to save. When a man is once possessed with fear and that he loses his judgment, as all men in a fright do, he knows not what he does, and it is the principal thing you are to beg at the hands of Almighty God, to preserve your understanding entire, for what danger soever there may be, there is still one way or other to get off and perhaps to your honour; but when fear has once possessed your judgment, God ye good even! You think you are flying towards the poop when you are

[1] Joachim de Monluc, Sieur de Lioux (d. 1567), younger brother of Blaise.

running towards the prow, and for one enemy you think you have ten before your eyes, as drunkards do who see a thousand candles at once. Oh 'tis a wonderful advantage to a man of our trade when his danger does not deprive him of his sense, he may then take his opportunity and avoid both shame and ruin.

In the evening I went to the Dauphin for the word, because Monsieur de Taix himself was wounded and could not go, when so soon as I came into his presence, Monsieur d'Orléans, who always delighted to jest with me (as the Dauphin also himself sometimes would do), began to sing the camisado of Boulogne, and the assault of Cony [Coni][1] for the old soldiers of Piedmont, jeering and pointing at me with his finger, at which I began to be angry, and fell to cursing those who had been the cause. At which the Dauphin laughed and at last said to me, 'Monluc, Monluc, in plain truth, you captains can by no means excuse it that you have not carried yourselves very ill.' 'Which way, sir,' said I, 'can you conceive me to be any way in fault? If I knew myself to be guilty I would at this instant go and cause myself to be killed in the town, but in truth we are a company of coxcombs, to venture our lives in your service.' Whereupon he said 'No, no, I do not mean you, for you were the last captain that came out of the town, and above an hour after all the rest.' He gave me very well to understand, when he came to be King, that I had not failed of my duty, by the value he was ever pleased to put upon me; for when he went his expedition into Piedmont he sent an express courier to fetch me from my own house, to which I had retired myself by reason of a certain pique that Madame d'Estampes [d'Étampes] had conceived against me about the quarrel betwixt Messieurs de Chasteigneraye [La Châtaigneraie] and Jarnac.[2] A man has evermore one good office or another done him at court, and the mischief on't is, the women evermore rule the roost; but I shall not take upon me to be a reformer, Madame d'Étampes sent better men than myself packing from court who have made no boasts of it, but I wonder at our brave historians that they dare not tell the truth.

This was the success of the camisado of Boulogne; whereas had the camp followed after us they might all have quartered in the town and in four or five days (as I have already said) the higher town had been our own. Let anyone ask Monsieur de Téligny if he be the man who

[1] Bracketing the camisado with a previous failure at Coni, in Piedmont.

[2] The duel of La Châtaigneraie and Jarnac (July 1547) was celebrated. Monluc sided with the former and was banished the court by the King's mistress, the Duchess d'Étampes.

was taken prisoner there, and see whether or no I tell a lie. I do not know who was the cause that the Dauphin did not march, but I shall always affirm that he ought to have done it, and know also very well that it did not stick at him; but it were to enter into disputes to say any more of that business. Had they come, the English would not have known which way to turn them. I discovered them to be men of very little heart and believe them to be better at sea than by land.

The projected descent on England, July 1545. D'Annebaut failed to capture the Isle of Wight and retired to Normandy after some indecisive skirmishing in the Channel

The Dauphin, seeing the winter draw on (having left Monsieur le Marshal du Biez at Montreuil to bridle and keep Boulogne in awe), returned back to the King, who also had concluded a peace with the Emperor;[1] all this great preparation and those invincible forces, to our great good fortune, vanishing through the ill intelligence betwixt these two princes, I mean the Spaniard and the English. Evil befall him that will ever love the one or the other. Three months after I quitted my command of camp-master to go to defend a little estate that had been left me by an uncle of mine. I had much ado to obtain leave of the King to go, but in the end the Admiral wrought so effectually in my behalf that it was granted upon condition that I would promise him to take upon me the same employment in case the said Admiral should have the command of the army. He failed not of that command, nor thereupon to summon me upon my promise I had made him, but obtained a commission from the King (which he sent me) to be camp-master to fifty or threescore ensigns that his Majesty would set on foot for the English voyage. I brought the men accordingly to Havre de Grace [Le Havre], where I delivered them into the hands of Monsieur de Taix. We then put to sea. Our navy consisted of above two hundred and fifty sail and the most beautiful ships that ever eyes beheld, with their galleys. The ardent desire the King had to revenge himself on the King of England made him enter into a very vast expense, which in the end served to very little purpose, although we first landed and afterwards fought the English upon the sea, where many ships were sunk on both sides. When at our setting out I saw the great carrick (which was certainly the goodliest vessel in the world) burnt down to the water, I had no great opinion of our enterprise. But being that I

[1] The Peace of Crépy, September 1544.

for my particular performed nothing in that expedition worthy remembrance, and that moreover a perfect account of that naval engagement has been given by others,[1] I shall let it alone to give a narrative
of the conquest of the territory of Oye: and indeed our business lies
more properly by land than by water, where I do not know that our
nation has ever obtained any great victories.

The Marshal du Biez built the fort of Outreau to overawe Boulogne, and
captured another in the Terre d'Oye, the district from which the English
garrisons in Boulogne and Calais drew their supplies. Here Monluc decided
to test the 'mystery of the English'

Let me tell you captains, you ought not disdain to learn something of
me, who am the oldest captain in France and who have been in as
many battles, or more, as any captain of Europe, as you will judge at
the end of my book. Know therefore that the reasons which induced
me to attempt this assault[2] were these. First, because I had felt the
pulse of the English at my first arrival and found them a very easy
enemy. Secondly, because they had abandoned their fortifications,
which we gained, having the bastion that served them for a flanker.
Thirdly, because from the little eminence where I had made a halt
before I went down into the meadow, I had seen coming along the
plain on the inside toward Calais a great number of people coming
from thence and observed all the curtain to be full of men, by which
I saw it was high time to fall on; and for a fourth reason, because that
in the ditch next to the curtain there was very little water, and from
the said ditch to the said curtain it was but two good steps, where the
soldiers might stand well enough, and with a little help of their pikes
or halberds and the assistance of one another (the curtain being no
more than two fathoms high) we should carry the place. When
(captains) therefore your eye shall have discharged its office in discovering the number of your enemy and the strength of the place
where he is, and that you have tasted and found him apt to fly, charge
him whilst he is in the fear you have possessed him withal, for if you
give him time to recover his senses and to forget his fright, you will
be more often in danger of being beaten than likely to beat. Wherefore you ought evermore to pursue him in his fear without giving
him leisure to re-assume his courage, and carry always about you the

[1] In particular, by du Bellay.
[2] The attack on the fort in the Terre d'Oye, which Monluc describes, but is here omitted.

motto of Alexander the Great, which is: 'Defer not that till tomorrow thou canst do today, for many things fall out betwixt the lip and the cup', especially in war, and then it will be too late to say, 'I should never have thought it'. You shall execute many things in your heat which, if you give yourselves leisure to consider of, you will think of it thrice before you once attempt it. Push home then, venture, and do not give your enemies leisure to consult together, for one will encourage another.

Being returned to the fort of Outreau,[1] there was hardly a day passed that the English did not come to tickle us upon the descent towards the sea, and would commonly brave our people up to our very cannon, which was within ten or twelve paces of the fort: and we were all abused by what we had heard our predecessors say, that one Englishman would always beat two Frenchmen, and that the English would never run away nor never yield. I had retained something of the camisado of Boulogne and of the business of Oye, and therefore said one day to Monsieur de Taix that I would discover to him the mystery of the English, and wherefore they were reputed so hardy, which was that they all carried arms of little reach and therefore were necessitated to come up close to us to loose their arrows, which otherwise would do no execution. Whereas we who were accustomed to fire our arquebuses at a great distance, seeing the enemy use another manner of fight thought these near approaches of theirs very strange, imputing their running on at this confident rate to absolute bravery: but I will lay them an ambuscado and then you shall see if I am in the right or no, and whether a Gascon be not as good as an Englishman. In ancient time their fathers and ours were neighbours.

I then chose out sixscore men, arquebusiers and pikes, with some halberds amongst them, and lodged them in a hollow which the water had made, lying below on the right hand of the fort, and sent Captain Chaux [d'Echaux][2] at the time when it was low water straight to some little houses which were upon the banks of the river almost over against the town to skirmish with them, with instructions that so soon as he should see them pass the river he should begin to retire and give them leave to make a charge. Which he accordingly did, but it fortuned so that he was wounded in one of his arms with an arquebus

---

[1] If the contemporary English plan of Boulogne is accurate, the fort lay across the river Liane from the town, was pentagonal in shape and over 2,000 feet in circumference: B. M. Cotton Aug. I, suppt. 5.

[2] Jean d'Échauz, bastard son of a Navarrese noble.

shot, and the soldiers took him and carried him back to the fort so that the skirmish remained without a head. The English were soon aware of it and gave them a very brisk charge, driving them on fighting up to the very cannon. Seeing then our men so ill handled, I start up out of my ambuscado sooner than I should have done, running on full drive directly up to them, commanding the soldiers not to shoot till they came within the distance of their arrows. They were two or three hundred men, having some Italian arquebusiers amongst them, which made me heartily repent that I had made my ambuscado no stronger, but it was now past remedy, and so soon as they saw me coming towards them, they left the pursuit of the others and came to charge upon me. We marched straight up to them, and so soon as they were come up within arrow shot our arquebusiers gave their volley all at once and then clapped their hands to their swords, as I had commanded, and we ran on to come to blows. But so soon as we came within two or three pikes' length, they turned their backs with as great facility as any nation that ever I saw and we pursued them as far as the river close by the town, and there were four or five of our soldiers who followed them to the other side. I then made a halt at the ruins of the little houses, where I rallied my people together again, some of whom were left by the way behind, who were not able to run so fast as the rest.

Monsieur de Taix had seen all and was sallied out of the fort to relieve the artillery, to whom so soon as I came up to him I said: 'Look you, did I not tell you how it would be? We must either conclude that the English of former times were more valiant than those of this present age or that we are better men than our forefathers—I know not which of the two it is.' 'In good earnest,' said Monsieur de Taix, 'these people retreat in very great haste. I shall never again have so good an opinion of the English as I have had heretofore.' 'No sir,' said I, 'you must know that the English who anciently used to beat the French were half Gascons, for they married into Gascony, and so bred good soldiers; but now that race is worn out and they are no more the same men they were.'

From that time forwards our people had no more the same opinion nor the same fear of the English than before. Therefore (captains) as much as you can, keep your soldiers from apprehending an enemy, for if they once conceive an extraordinary opinion of their valour, they ever go on to fight in fear of being defeated. You are neither to despise your enemy, neither should your soldiers think them to be more valiant than themselves. Ever after this charge I observed our men always to go on more cheerfully to attack the English and came still up closer to them, and let anyone remember when the Marshal du Biez fought them betwixt the fort of Andelot [Hardelot] and the town, whether our people needed to be entreated to fall on.[1] The said Sieur du Biez there performed the part of a very valiant gentleman, for when his cavalry were all run off the field he came alone to put himself in the head of our battalion and alighted, taking a pike in his hand to go on to the fight, from whence he came off with very great honour. I myself was not there and therefore shall say nothing of it, for two or three months after our return out of the county of Oye I had asked leave of Monsieur de Taix to go to court. But the historians in the meantime are very unjust to conceal such brave actions, and that was a very remarkable one in this old cavalier.

Being at court I prevailed so far with the Admiral[2] that he procured me a dismission from the King, for as much as I had reassumed the office of camp-master upon no other terms but only to command in the first expedition that the Admiral should go upon, and having remained a month at court, attending the King in the quality of one of his gentlemen waiters (who was now grown old and melancholic and did not caress men as he had wont to do, only once he talked with me about the battle of Cérisoles, being at Fontenebleau [Fontainebleau]) I took my leave of his Majesty and never saw him after. I then returned into Gascony, from whence I never stirred till King Henry by the death of his father was become King, having all that while been oppressed with troubles and sickness. And that is the reason why I can give you no account of the surrender of Boulogne which the King of England, by the obstinacy of Francis the First, was constrained to quit for some consideration in money.[3] A little after he died and our King stayed but a very little behind him.[4] We must all die, but this surrender of Boulogne happened in the reign of King Henry, my good master, who succeeded his father.

Our new King having peace with the Emperor, and after the re-delivery of Boulogne being also friends with the King of England, it seemed that our arms were likely long to rust by the walls; and indeed, if these two princes sit still, France may be at rest.

[1] A later incident (January 1546) in the siege of Boulogne.
[2] Coligny.
[3] By treaty of March 1550 Boulogne was surrendered to the French for 400,000 crowns.
[4] Henry VIII died on 28 January, Francis I on 31 March 1547.

Part III   From Books III and IV

The Habsburg-Valois Wars,
1554–1559

Following his exploits before Boulogne, and the accession of the new King,
Henry II, who was his admirer, Monluc was given an independent command
in Piedmont in 1548. He remained there for most of the next six years,
serving with distinction under Marshal Brissac,[1] a commander he revered. He
was rewarded with the Governorship of Alba in 1553. Meanwhile the war
was extended by France to the north, with the seizure of the Lorraine
bishoprics, Metz, Toul and Verdun, in 1552, and the brilliant defence of the
first stronghold by the Duke of Guise in the winter following, against the
besieging army of Charles V; and in Italy with the French involvement in
Tuscany, where, as Monluc relates, Siena threw off its obedience to Spain
and Florence in 1552

Whilst the war was kept on foot in Piedmont, after the manner I have
before related, under the conduct of this great soldier, Monsieur de
Brissac, who there established so admirable a military discipline that
it might with good reason be said to be the best school of war in
Europe; they did not sleep in Picardy, Champagne, and Metz, which
was at this time besieged by the Emperor. There it was that the great
Duke of Guise acquired immortal glory. I was never more troubled at
anything in my whole life than that I had not the good fortune to see
this siege: but a man cannot be in so many places at once. The King,
who desired to discompose the Emperor's affairs in Italy, prevailed so
far by the practices and dexterity of some cardinals of his party and of
Monsieur de Thermes, that he made the inhabitants of Siena to revolt,
which is a very beautiful and important city in Tuscany, insomuch
that the Spanish garrison which was in it was driven out and the citadel
razed to the ground. So soon as these people had thus shaken off the
Spanish yoke, and saw themselves at liberty, having set up the ensigns
of France, they were not wanting to themselves in imploring succours
and assistance from the King, who accordingly gave the charge thereof

---

[1] For Brissac, see Appendix I, 'Cossé', Charles de.'

to Monsieur de Strossy [Strozzi] (the same who was afterwards Marshal),[1] who by the help and concurrence of the King's confederates and friends in those parts drew some forces into the field: being therein assisted by the Signors Cornelio Bentivolio [Bentivoglio],[2] Fregouse [Fregoso][3] and other Italians, with the Sieurs de Thermes and de Lansac [Lanssac].[4] Where, though he had all the

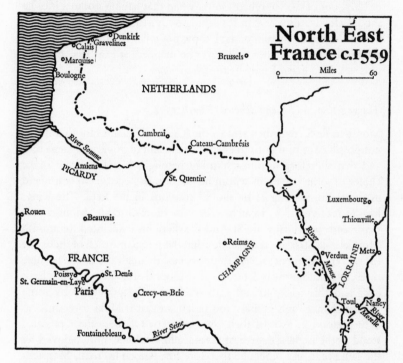

North East France c.1559

Miles

forces of the Emperor and the Great Duke of Florence to deal withal, he nevertheless carried himself with so much bravery and conduct, as to make head against the Marquis de Marignan[Marignano],[5] who

[1] For whom see Appendix I, 'Strozzi, Pietro'.

[2] Italian *condottiere* (d. 1585), who fought first for the Empire, then—from 1550—for France: aided Monluc in the defence of Siena.

[3] Aurelio Fregoso (d. 1581), Genoese *condottiere*, who fought in the service of France at this time, but later attached himself to the Duke of Florence.

[4] Louis de St Gelais, Sieur de Lanssac (*c.* 1512–89), courtier and statesman, Ambassador to England in 1551.

[5] For whom see Appendix I, 'Medici, Gianjacomo.'

prosecuted the war with might and main. Notwithstanding which Monsieur de Strozzi in despite of him took several little towns belonging to the state of Siena, the particulars whereof I shall not meddle withal, forasmuch as I was not there present: but, by what I have heard, he there performed several brave exploits; for the Emperor and the Duke of Florence desired nothing more than to drive the King out of Italy, out of the apprehension they had that having got in a foot he should afterwards screw in his whole body. But we never yet knew how to husband our conquests; I know not what we may do hereafter, though I fear that matter will never be mended, at least I see no signs of it yet. God grant I may be mistaken.

The government of Siena debated, March 1554

Monsieur de Strozzi then sent to the King to acquaint him that it was not possible for him both to keep the field and to govern in Siena too, and that therefore he most humbly besought his Majesty to make choice of some person in whom he might safely confide to command in the town, so long as he should continue in the field. The King, having received this dispatch, called for the Constable, Monsieur de Guise and the Marshal de St André, where he acquainted them with Monsieur de Strozzi's request, desiring them to name each of them one for this employment; for all things passed through the hands of these three, and nothing was determined without them. All our Kings have ever had this trick, to suffer themselves to be governed by some particular men, and perhaps too much, so that it looks sometimes as if they stood in awe of their own subjects. Of these the Constable stood in the highest degree of favour and was ever more beloved by the King than any other; he therefore first named his man, Monsieur de Guise another, and the Marshal a third. Which having done, the King said to them: 'You have none of you named Monluc.' To which Monsieur de Guise made answer, that it was out of his head, and the Marshal said the same; Monsieur de Guise moreover adding; 'If you name Monluc I have done, and shall speak no more of him I nominated before.' 'Nor I,' said the Marshal, who has since related to me the whole debate.

The Constable then stood up, and said, that I was by no means proper for this employment, as being too humourous, peevish and passionate; to which the King made answer, that he had ever observed and known me to be peevish and passionate upon the account of his service only, when I saw him not served so well as he ought to be, and that he had never heard I ever had a quarrel with anyone upon my own particular account. Monsieur de Guise and the Marshal said also the same, adding moreover that I had already been Governor both of Moncalieri and Alba without so much as any one man's opening his mouth to complain of my administration; and that also had I been a person of that temper the Marshal de Brissac would never have loved and favoured me at the rate he did, nor have reposed so great a confidence in me as he had ever done. The Constable hereupon answered very roundly again, and made good his former objection with great vehemency, and would by all means that the person he had nominated should stand: for he was impatient of being controverted, and more of being overruled; neither indeed did he ever much love me, nor any of his.[1] The Cardinal of Lorraine[2] was there present, who may better remember than I who it was that the Constable named: but (if I be not deceived) it was Boccal, who is since turned Huguenot. However, in the end the King would carry it, having Monsieur de Guise and the Marshal de St André on his side, and dispatched away a courier to the Marshal de Brissac to send me into Avignon, where accordingly I stayed expecting a gentleman his Majesty sent to me, who brought my dispatch to go presently away to Siena.

Now the Marshal had some days before given me leave to retire to my own house, by reason of a sickness I was fallen into, as I have said elsewhere; who had no mind to do it, as he himself confessed to me since; and has done me the honour to tell me that had he known of what importance the loss of me would have been to him, he would not have so commended me to the king as he had done, and that in his life he never repented anything so much as the letting me depart from him, telling me a great many things wherein he had not been so well served after my departure out of Piedmont. Monsieur de Cossé, President Birague and several others can witness how often they have heard him lament my absence, especially when matters did not succeed according to his desire. And if anyone will take the pains to consider what I performed while I was there under his command, he will find that what I say is very true, and that he had some reason to regret me. I was always at his feet, and at his head. I will not say nevertheless that anything would have been better done for my being there: but

---

[1] A reference to the longstanding antipathy between the Montmorency family and Monluc.

[2] Charles de Lorraine (1525–74), younger brother of the Duke of Guise.

however I must needs speak the truth, and there are those who can say more if they please.

He then wrote a letter to the King, and another to the Constable, wherein he sent his Majesty word, that he had made a very ill choice of me to command in Siena, for that I was one of the most cross-grained, choleric fellows in the whole world, and such a one that for half the time I had been with him he had been necessitated to suffer much from me, knowing my imperfections. That indeed I was very good for the maintaining of discipline and justice in an army, to command in the field, and to make the soldiers to fight: but that the humour of the Sienese considered, it would be fire to fire, which would be the only means to lose that state, which was to be preserved by gentleness and moderation. He moreover entreated the Constable to remonstrate as much to the King, and in the meantime dispatched a courier to me, who found me very sick, by whom he sent me word that the King would send me to Siena; but that, as a friend of mine, he advised me not to accept that employment, entreating me not to foresake him, to go serve elsewhere under another, and assuring me withal, that if any command happened to be vacant in Piedmont, that I had more mind to than I already had, I should have it; which were all artifices to detain me.

O that a wise lieutenant of a province ought to have an eye and to take heed of losing a man in whom he may absolutely confide, and whom he knows to be a man of valour, and ought to spare nothing that he may keep him; for oftentimes one man alone can do much. You must eat a great deal of salt with a man before you can rightly know him; and in the meantime you are deprived of him with whom you were thoroughly acquainted, in whom you reposed your trust, and of whose fidelity you have already had sufficient proof.

The said Marshal had moreover sent word to the King that I was in Gascony very sick, and in the morning as the letters were read, the Constable, who was mighty well pleased with the contents, said to the King: 'Did not I tell your Majesty as much; you find the Marshal to be of the same opinion, and no man living can know Monluc better than he who has so often seen him at work.' To which the King (who naturally loved me, and had ever done so after he had seen my behaviour at the camisado of Boulogne) replied that although all those of his Council should speak against me, yet should they prevail nothing by it; for it was his nature to love me, and that he would not alter his election let them all say what they would. Monsieur de Guise then spoke and said: 'Here is a letter very full of contradictions: for in the first place the Marshal de Brissac says that Monluc is cross-grained and choleric, and that he will never suit with the Sienese, but will ruin your service if you send him thither; and on the other side commends him for qualities that are required in a man of command, to whom the trust of great things is to be committed: for he speaks him to be a man of an exact discipline and great justice, and fit to make the soldiers fight in great enterprises and executions; and whoever saw a man endued with all these good qualities, that he had not a mixture of choler amongst them? Such as are indifferent whether things go well or ill may indeed be without passion, and as to the rest, since, sir, your Majesty has yourself made the election, I humbly conceive you ought not to revoke it.' The Marshal de St André spoke next and said: 'Sir, what the Marshal de Brissac complains of you may easily correct by writing to Monluc that yourself having made choice of his person above all others for this employment, he must for your sake as much as he can govern his passion, having to do with such a fickle-headed people as those of Siena.'

To which the King made answer that he did not fear but that after he had written me a letter, I would do as he should command me; and immediately thereupon dispatched away a courier to me to my own house by whom he sent me word, that although I should be sick, I must nevertheless put myself upon my way to go directly to Marseilles, where I should meet my dispatch and should there embark myself with the Germans that the Rincroq [Reckenrot][1] brought and ten companies of French foot, to which place he would also send me money for my journey, and that I must for a while leave my passion behind me in Gascony, and a little accommodate myself to the humour of that people.

The courier found me at Agen very sick, and under the physicians' hands, notwithstanding which I told him that in eight days I would begin my journey, which I did, and verily thought I should have died at Toulouse, from whence by the advice of the physicians I was to return back again, which I would not do: but caused myself to be hauled along as far as Montpellier, where I was again advised by the physicians to go no further, they assuring me that if I ventured to proceed on my journey I should never come alive to Marseilles. But whatever they could say, I was resolved to go on so long as life lasted, come on it what would. When just as I was going away there came

[1] Georges Reckenrot, German commander in French pay.

another courier from the King to hasten me, and from day to day I recovered my health in travelling. So that when I came to Marseilles I was without comparison much better than when I parted from my own house.

In plain truth the King my good master had reason to defend my cause, for my choler was never prejudicial to his service, it has indeed been sometimes prejudicial to myself and some others, who would not avoid nor comply with my humour. I never lost place, battle nor rencounter, nor ever was the occasion of losing any one of his subjects; my choler never so far transported me as to do anything prejudicial to his service, and if it be violent and prompt, it is the sooner gone. I have ever observed that such people are better to be employed than any other, for they have no malice in them, nor no dangerous reservations, and if they be more sudden they are also more valiant than those who by their moderation would appear to be more wise.

Monluc, as Governor, arrived at Siena in July 1554. The Italian condottiere, the Marquis of Marignano, commanded the forces of Spain and Florence sent to subdue the city. The attempts of Pietro Strozzi, the Florentine exile who now led the French army in Tuscany, to draw off the Imperialists ended disastrously at the battle of Marciano, and Marignano began his siege of the city in September. Monluc had not recovered from the illness which had earlier made him such a doubtful choice for the Governorship, and for a time his doctors despaired of his life. The prospect did not seem encouraging for the city or for himself. The garrison was a motley force of French, Germans and Italians; the city was divided into feuding political factions, not all favourable to France; and the hope of relief dwindled daily. Food rationing was introduced, and pleas for help sent to Paris and the Pope at Rome. In this posture Monluc awaited Marignano's attack

From this time forward I could do nothing worth speaking of until Christmas Eve [1554], saving that a little after the departure of the said Lécussan,[1] we again abated the soldiers' bread to eighteen ounces, and that of the city to fourteen, though all the while there were frequent skirmishes, and very handsomely fought on both sides. Upon Christmas Eve, about four of the clock in the afternoon, the Marquis of Marignano by one of his trumpets sent me half a stag, six capons, six

---

[1] François de Galard, Sieur de Lécussan (d. *c.* 1557), Gascon soldier, and neighbour of Monluc's.

partridges, six *borachios* of excellent wine and six loaves of bread, wherewith the next day to keep the feast. I did nothing wonder at this courtesy, because in the extremity of my sickness he had permitted my physicians to send men through his camp to fetch certain drugs from Florence, and had himself three or four times sent me a very excellent sort of birds, a little bigger than the *beccasiccos*[1] that are taken in Provence. He had also suffered a mule to enter the town, laden with Greek wine, which was sent me by the Cardinal of Armagnac,[2] my people having sent the Cardinal word that in the height of my sickness I talked of nothing but drinking a little Greek wine. Whereupon he so ordered the business, that the Cardinal de Medici[3] wrote to the Marquis his brother to suffer it to come to me, it being sent under pretence of making me a bath. The wine came at a time when I was at the last gasp, and so was not delivered to me; but the half of it divided amongst the big-bellied women of the town. Whilst Monsieur de Strozzi was there I gave him three or four bottles of it, the rest I drank as they do hippocras in the mornings. All these civilities I had received from the Marquis before, which made me nothing wonder at the present he sent me now: part of which I sent to the seigneury, part to the Reckenrot, and the rest I reserved for Signor Cornelio, the Count de Gayas [Caiazzo][4] and myself, because we commonly ate together. Such little civilities as these are very gentle and commendable, even betwixt the greatest enemies; if there be nothing particular betwixt them, as there was not betwixt us two. He served his master, and I served mine. He attacked me for his honour, and I defended myself for mine. He had a mind to acquire reputation, and so had I. 'Tis for Turks and Saracens to deny an indifferent courtesy even to an enemy: but then it must not be such a one, or of such importance as to break or damage your design.

But whilst the Marquis caressed me with his presents, which I only paid back in thanks, he was preparing for me another kind of feast; for the same night about an hour after midnight he with all his army gave a scalado to the citadel and to the fort Camollia.[5] 'Tis a strange

[1] Woodcock.

[2] Georges d'Armagnac (*c.* 1501–*c.* 1585), Cardinal (1544) and later Archbishop of Toulouse.

[3] Giovanni-Angelo Medici (1499–1565), famous churchman who became Pope (Pius IV) in 1559: brother of Marignano.

[4] Giangaleazzo di San Severino, Count of Caiazzo, Neapolitan commander.

[5] The citadel and this fort guarded the northern flank of the city.

thing that above a month before my mind gave me and seemed to presage that the Marquis would give me a scalado, and the Captain St Auban[1] would be cause of the loss of the fort. This was evermore running in my head, and that the Germans also would occasion the loss of the citadel, into which an ensign of that nation every night entered to keep guard there; and that was the reason why I placed an ensign of Sienese in guard over against the gate of the citadel. Signor Cornelio prevailed so far with the Reckenrot that he promised him that in case of an alarm, and that the enemy should offer an assault to the citadel, the German captain that he placed there every night upon the guard should from him have command to let in the Sienese to help to defend it, though I think he that night forgot so to do. Every night I went to see a company of French foot mount the guard in the fort Camollia, and another of Sienese betwixt the fort and the gate of the city under a great market house, which on the two sides was enclosed with a little trench; but in the front of it, which went directly to the fort, it was all plain with the pavement, and it might be from this court of guard to the fort threescore or fourscore paces, and as much to the gate of the city.

I placed this guard there for two reasons, whereof one was to relieve the fort if occasion should be, as the other company of Sienese was to do the citadel, and the other to watch that the enemy did not storm the wall of the city; forasmuch as on the left hand, at the going out of the town, the wall was very low and moreover a part thereof fallen down. I had several times before said to Signor Cornelio and to the Count de Caiazzo, seeing Captain St Auban's company enter into the fort, these words: 'Would you believe that it eternally runs in my mind that we shall lose this fort through the default of Captain St Auban and his company? I never see him enter into it that it does not put me into a fit of an ague out of the ill conceit I have of him.' I could never fancy him in my heart, because he never had twenty men of appearance in his company, for he valued a teston[2] more than the bravest man under the sun, and as to himself he would never stir from his lodging, for anything either I or any of his companions could say to him. I could have wished him far enough off, I had so strange an aversion to him. And these were the reasons why I ever fancied that this man would bring upon me some mischief or other.

[1] Gaspard Pape, Sieur de St Auban (d. 1567), French captain of foot.

[2] Coin, first minted by Louis XII.

Our fort of Camollia was environed with a ditch of a pike's length in wideness and as much in depth, and not much more on three sides; and in the front of it which butted directly upon the Sienese court of guard, nothing but a little rampart of six or seven foot high and no more, and about the middle of the rampart there was a little platform, where the soldiers had so much room only as to sustain themselves upon their knees. The enemy had another fort three times as big as ours and just opposite to it, within an hundred and fifty paces the one of the other. So that neither they nor we durst pop up a head without being hurt from that quarter, and in ours there was a little tower exactly over against theirs, where for greater security we had ever-more three or four soldiers which served us for sentinels and who got up into it by a little hand ladder, as they do into a pigeon-house. The said tower had been broke through on that side towards the enemy's fort and we had there placed barrels filled with earth, for the hole had been made by the artillery from their fort. Which fort of theirs Monsieur de Thermes had caused to be made, but when he went away it was not wholly finished.[1] Nevertheless when the Duke of Florence broke with the King, the Marquis in one night made a very long march, carrying a great number of pioneers along with him, and possessing himself of it (for there was no guard kept there) im-mediately put it into defence.

Now, as I have said before, at one of the clock in the night the Marquis at once gave me a scalado both to the citadel and the fort Camollia,[2] where by ill luck the company of St Auban was this night upon duty. The Marquis with the Spanish and German foot assaulted the citadel, where by good fortune they had but three ladders long enough, and at the very first so overcharged those three with men that one of them broke. Our Germans defended and the Sienese pre-sented themselves at the gate as they were appointed to do. But the captain of the Germans who had the command of the gate would by no means let them in. This dispute lasted for above half an hour, during which five or six of the enemy entered and forced the Germans, who began to turn their backs and fly. They then opened the gate to the Sienese, who ran to the head of the citadel, where the enemy began to enter, and met these five or six who were already entered, whom they cut in pieces, two of them being the Marquis his kinsmen, one

[1] De Thermes had assisted Siena in its revolt, but had left for Corsica in August 1553.

[2] In fact, in several other parts of the city as well.

whereof did not immediately die; and this cooled the courage of the rest who were upon the point to enter.

At the same time they gave a scalado to the fort Camollia. St Auban was in the city in bed at his ease, and his lieutenant called Comborcié [Combourcier][1] was at the fort, a young man of no experience, but that I think had he had good men in his company would have done his duty. They are both of them turned Huguenots since. So soon as the enemy presented their ladders by the three curtains, all his company betook them to their heels and the enemy consequently entered in; and of the four that were in the tower, three threw themselves headlong down and the fourth beat down the barrels from the hole and drew the enemy in. This rogue had been taken a few days before and had remained above ten days prisoner, and I do believe it was upon his account that the Marquis resolved upon this scalado; for he went away with them and we never saw him after.

Now Signor Cornelio and the Count de Caiazzo were lodged near unto the port Camollia, who immediately upon the alarm ran to the gate, where they found the greatest part of the company of the Sienese before it and the rest were firing at the enemy, who sallied out of the fort to fall upon them. Signor Cornelio then left the Count de Caiazzo at the gate and came running to give me the alarm, where he met me coming out of my lodging with two pages, each of them carrying two torches, and whom I immediately sent back, bidding him both he and the Count de Caiazzo to go out and of all things to take care that the Sienese did not forsake their court of guard, and to encourage them the best he could, for I would presently come out after him. He did as I bid him, and came in so opportune a season that he found all abandoned and gave the enemy a charge with the Sienese, and beat them back into the fort they had taken. The alarm was already throughout the whole city, and some ran to the citadel and others to the fort of Camollia.

As I arrived at the gate there came to me La Morlière and L'Espine, both on horseback, the one being muster-master and the other treasurer, whom I commanded the one to the Port San Marco and the other to Porto Nuovo, and that by the way as they went they should cry out, 'Victory, the enemy is repulsed.' Which I did, fearing lest some in the town might have intelligence with the enemy, who hearing this cry would not dare to discover themselves. In the meantime I

---

[1] Balthazar de Combourcier, Sieur de Monestier (d. 1583), French soldier.

was at the gate of the city, sending out the captains and French soldiers to succour Signor Cornelio, and when I saw there were enough gone out I commanded the lieutenant of Captain Lussan to stay at the gate and to shut the wicket so soon as ever I was out, and that in case I should be beaten back he should by no means open it but rather suffer us all to be killed without, and me in the first place. I then went out with my four torches and found Signor Cornelio, the Count de Caiazzo, and the other captains I had sent out, who had recovered the rampart and had placed the soldiers upon the little platform upon their knees, who shot at the enemy into the fort, and they again at ours, who could not put up their heads without being discovered, and on the other two sides the enemy assaulted and ours defended.

Now whilst I was putting the men out at the wicket St Auban slipped by without my seeing him. The gate into the fort which we had lost was contrived after the manner of a hole, having one step forwards and another on one side, waving and winding to and fro, and so strait that one man only could enter abreast. In this entry I found Captain Bourg, who was ensign to Captain Charry, Signor Cornelio, and the Count de Caiazzo close by him. Monsieur de Bassompierre,[1] master of the ordnance, was always with me, and one of his cannoneers. I saw very well that the fight was like to continue, and fearing lest our powder should fail us, bade Monsieur de Bassompierre dispatch away two of his cannoneers to fetch more, which he did, and I dare boldly say he was as much the cause of our safety as all our fighting, as you shall hear. Those that we fought withal were Italians, for the Spaniards and Germans stormed the citadel. I continually ran first to one and then to another, crying out to them 'Courage friends, courage comrades'. And presently on that side on the right hand of the gate, where the three forenamed stood, I spied St Auban, to whom (running to him and setting the point of my sword to his throat) I said 'Rogue! Son of a whore! Thou art the cause that we shall lose the city, which notwithstanding thou shalt never live to see, for I will at this instant kill thee if thou dost not immediately leap into the fort:' to which (sufficiently terrified) he made answer, 'Yes sir, I will leap in.' And then called to him Lussan, Blacons and Combas, who were his companions, saying to them, 'Come on comrades, second me, I pray leap in after me.' To which they made answer, 'Do thou leap and we will follow.' Whereupon I

1 Charles de Bassompierre, artillery commander, cited as still living when Monluc composed his memoirs.

said to him, 'Take thou no care, I will follow thee myself,' and we all set foot upon the platform with him.

And immediately after this first step, without any more delaying (for if he had he had died for it) he threw himself desperately in, having a target upon his arm, and his companions also, for he was no sooner in the air but the rest were also with him; and so all four leaped in together and it was within two steps of the entry that Bourg, Signor Cornelio and the Count de Caiazzo disputed. I then immediately made fifteen or twenty soldiers leap in after the four captains, and as all these were within, Bourg, Signor Cornelio and the Count de Caiazzo passed and entered into the fort. I caused the torches to be set upon the rampart that we might see and not kill one another, and myself entered by the same way Signor Cornelio had gone before me. Now neither pikes, halberds, nor arquebuses could serve us for any use here, for we were at it with swords and stilettos, with which we made them leap over the curtains by the same way they had entered, excepting those who were killed within.

There were yet however some remaining in the tower when Captain Charry came up to us, though but eight days before he had received an arquebus shot in his head and such a one as that thereupon we had given him for dead, notwithstanding there he was with his sword and target and a morion upon his head over the cap that covered his wound. A good heart will ever manifest itself, for though he was desperately hurt, yet would he have his share of the fight. I was at the foot of the ladder and had sent Signor Cornelio and the Count de Caiazzo out of the fort to encourage those who defended the flanks, bidding them take the one the one side and the other the other, as they did, and found work enough to do. I then took Captain Charry by the hand and said, 'Captain Charry, I have bred you up to die in some brave service for the King, you must mount the first.' Which said, he (who certainly a man of as much courage as ever any man had) without any more dispute began to climb the ladder, which could not be above ten or twelve staves, and he was to enter by a trap-door above, as I have said before. I had very good arquebusiers, whom I made continually to shoot at the hole of this trap-door, and put two of the said arquebusiers upon the ladder to follow after him. I had two torches with me (for the other two Signor Cornelio and the Count had taken along with them) by the light whereof we saw so clearly that the arquebusiers did no hurt to Captain Charry, who mounted step by step, still giving our arquebusiers time to fire, and so soon as he came to thrust up his head into the trap-door, they fired two arquebuses which pierced through his target and morion without touching his head. The arquebusier who followed next after him discharged his arquebus under his target, by which means Captain Charry advanced the last step, and so they all three leapt in the one after the other, where they killed three of the enemy and the rest leapt out at the hole. Those in the flanks were also beaten off, and so our fort was regained on every side.

Now the Marquis had given order to him that commanded at the scalado of the fort, which was the governor of their fort of Camollia, that in case he the Marquis should first enter by the citadel, that then he should come away to him with all his Italians, and if also he should first gain the fort, that then he would come with his Spaniards and Germans to relieve him. According to this agreement, so soon as the governor of the fort had gained ours, he presently sent to acquaint the Marquis with it. But there being several little valleys betwixt the citadel and the fort Camollia, the said Marquis could not come so soon as he would, though he had made so good haste that when we had thought all had been at an end we saw their whole camp coming upon us, having above an hundred and fifty torches with them; at which time by good fortune Bassompierre's two cannoneers returned with the powder, which in great haste we divided amongst the arquebusiers, for they had none left, and turning about I bade him send them again for more. At the same instant La Morlière and l'Espine returned to me, when I immediately sent back La Morlière to the gonfalonier of San Martino[1] to send me two hundred of the best arquebusiers he had and send them by the son of Misser Bernardin Bonnenseigne [Bernardino Buoninsegni], a young man that carried a colours in his regiment, full of courage, and of whom I had taken particular notice in several skirmishes, who accordingly came in all haste and found us at it with the whole camp. I then left Signor Cornelio and the Count de Caiazzo with the other captains to defend the fort and myself, Bassompierre, and the muster-master went along the flanks, doing nothing but run up and down from place to place to encourage our people. It might be about three hours after midnight when we rebegan the fight, and it lasted till the day took them off. They there committed one of the greatest pieces of folly that ever men did, for by the light of so many torches we saw them more plainly than if it had been broad day, whereas had they taken the advantage of the night and advanced with

[1] Each district of the city was commanded by a gonfalonier.

few lights, they had put us a great deal more hardly to it than they did. The two hundred Sienese arquebusiers that the son of Misser Bernardino brought did us notable service, as also did the powder that Bassompierre sent for, for we had use for it all before we parted, by reason of the long continuance of the fight, where it was well assaulted and better defended.

This was the issue of the fight, the greatest, and of the greatest duration without a battle wherein I have ever been, and where I believe God Almighty did as much assist me, if not more, preserving my judgment all the while entire, as at any time in my whole life. For had I failed in the least particle of command we had all been lost, and the city to boot, for on that side we had not fortified at all and all our confidence was in this fort. I protest to God that for at least three months after my hair stood an end, so often as I called to mind the danger we had been in. The enemy there lost six hundred men killed and wounded, as we were informed by prisoners we took, and we lost but an hundred and fifty in all both hurt and slain. That which made them lose so many was the light of the torches, which gave our men such aim that they could not miss, especially being within a pike's distance or two at the most of one another, which made a great incongruity in the Marquis, as I said before; for we having but little light, and they so much, we discovered them so plain as gave us a mighty advantage. So soon as it was fair light day we went to take a view of what dead we had in the fort amongst theirs, where I found my *valet de chambre* and my groom, who both leapt in after the captains; in my life I never had two better servants. Signor Cornelio and the Count de Caiazzo went likewise to visit the citadel, for I was no longer able to stand, being yet so weak with my great sickness that with a puff one might have blown me down; so that I wonder how I was ever able to take such pains. But God redoubled my forces in time of need; for in truth during all this great and tedious fight I never ceased running and skipping, now here, now there, without ever feeling myself weary, till there appeared no more an enemy to molest us. They came and gave me an account of all that had passed and there found a kinsman of the Marquis who was not yet dead, whom they caused to be carried to their lodging and his wounds dressed.

Marignano brings up cannon, January 1555

A little after, as we understood, there came a gentleman of the Emperor's bedchamber, who brought letters to the Duke of Florence and to the said Marquis [Marignano], wherein he writ them word that he thought it very strange this war should continue so long, and that he very well knew Siena was not a place to resist cannon, but that it was the Marquis his custom evermore to spin out a war in length. In answer whereunto the Marquis remonstrated that he had done all that in him possibly lay, and knew very well that artillery would not take the town, for I had valiant men within and the whole city were resolute to stand to me to the last, speaking more honourably of me than I deserved, commending my vigilancy and the provision I had made for my defence, so that he very well knew by the good order I had taken in the city he should but lose so much time by attempting to batter. Notwithstanding the gentleman being come from the Emperor to this effect, and having already spoken with the Duke of Florence, they together ordered it so that they made the Marquis at last resolve upon a battery. He had before omitted nothing that a good soldier ought to do, having cooped us close in without any hopes of relief, and yet he was accused of a design to protract the war. But it is the ordinary reward of a man's endeavour, when things do not succeed according to the appetite of such as talk of things at their ease. The desires of those we serve and fight for run a great deal faster than we are able to follow.

About the twentieth of January we had notice that the artillery set out of Florence, to the number of six or eight and twenty cannon or double culverin to come to the camp. The Sienese hearing this news were so curious as to send out a spy that they might be certain of the truth of this report, who at his return bringing them word back that the artillery was already come as far as Lucignano, it put the whole city into some apprehension and made them resolve the next day to assemble all the gentry and the chief of the city to the palace,[1] there to determine amongst themselves whether they should abide the assault or surrender upon composition. Now I was not to huff and vapour with these people, for they were stronger than I. I was therefore necessitated to win them by gentle remonstrances and civil persuasions, without the least heat or show of anger, and you may believe it was not without great violence to my own nature that I proceeded after this manner, contrary to my disposition and the image the Constable had represented of me to the King, as he had seen me in my younger and more precipitous age.

[1] The Palazzo Publico.

A prudent and staid governor, when he is amongst strange nations, must try as much as in him lies to conform himself to the humour of the people with whom he has to do. With the Germans and Swiss you must join in their carousals. With the Spaniards you must observe their starched face and formality, and pretend to be a little more religious and devout than you perhaps really are. With the Italians you must be discreet and circumspect, neither to offend them in themselves nor to court their wives. As for the Frenchman he is for anything. But so it was that God gave me the grace, who am a Gascon, sudden, choleric, wilful, and froward, so to deport myself with this jealous and mistrustful nation that not so much as any one citizen could ever complain of me.

Now as all the gentry and the heads of the corporation were going to the palace, Misser Hieronime Espano [Girolamo Spannocchi], a gentleman of Siena, a principal man in the city and one of the eight of the council of war, before he went to the palace came in all haste to speak with Signor Cornelio, where he told him that all the chief of the city were summoned to repair to the palace, and that it was to determine whether they ought to stand out a battery or to enter into capitulation with the Duke of Florence and the Marquis of Marignano, and that he had already heard that the major part of them had voted that they ought to condition and not to endure a battery and an assault, for fear they should come by the worse; that he was now going thither to them, wherefore he entreated him to give me notice of it. Hereupon Signor Cornelio came to me and found me ready to take horse to go view the guards. But so soon as he had told me the news we both went up into my chamber, where we long debated by what means we might divert this blow. And whilst we were in this deliberation came Signor Bartholomé Cavalcant [Bartolommeo Cavalcanti][1] who told me as much as I had heard before, and moreover that he thought the resolution was already taken throughout the whole city, and that he only went to the palace to cast in his lot, and that after the lots should once be cast it would be too late to speak.

Monluc prepares for his address to the Consistory

We were all three in a very great strait, they which way to advise me, and I was as much to seek what advice to take. In the end I resolved to

[1] (1503–62), Florentine exile, opponent of the Medici.

go to the palace and to take with me the Reckenrot and his captains, Signor Cornelio with his Italians, and Captain Combas with the French officers. Our Germans began to suffer much for want of wine, and their bread was very small, for as for flesh there was no more talk of any, unless of some horse or some ass that was exposed to sell in the butchery, and as for money there was no such thing in nature, for Monsieur de Strozzi had no possible means to send any in to us. All which considered, it put us into some fear lest the Germans should join with the city to enter into composition, which was the reason that I desired Signior Cornelio to go to the Reckenrot and entreat him from me to bear me company to the palace and to bring his captains along with him, and that he would in the meantime leave his lieutenants and ensigns every one in his own quarters, to the end there might be no surprise about the walls whilst we should be at the palace. I wished him also himself to do the same, and ordered Captain Combas to come likewise, which being done, I sent Bartolommeo in all haste to the palace, to try if he could secretly gain anyone to his party that might help to break this design. For I had an opinion that if I could but divert this one blow, I would deal with so many people afterwards that the blanks should be the greater number in the lottery, and so they all went out of my chamber without being further acquainted by me what I intended to do.

I was yet so extremely lean and worn with my late sickness, and the cold was at this time of the year so very great and sharp, that I was constrained to go continually with both my body and my head so wrapped and muffled up in furs that as they saw me go up and down the streets of the city, no-one had any hopes of my recovery, believing that my inwards were decayed and perished, and that I would fall down and die on a sudden. 'What shall we do,' said the ladies and the citizens' wives, 'what will become of us if our governor should die? We shall all be lost, for next after God our hope is in him; it is not possible he should escape.' I do verily believe that the prayers of those good women redeemed me out of the extremity and languishing weakness I was in, I mean that of my body; for as to the vigour of my mind and the quickness of my understanding, I never perceived any decay there. Having then before been accustomed to go so wrapped and muffled, and observing what moan the people made for me to see me in so lamentable a plight, I called for a pair of breeches of crimson velvet which I had brought from Alba, laid over with gold lace, finely cut and very neat, for I had made them at a time when I was forsooth in love. We had there leisure enough for those follies whilst we lay in garrison, and having little else to do it was fit to give the ladies some part of our time. I put on a doublet of the same, under which I had a shirt finely wrought with crimson silk and gold twist very rich (for in those days they wore the neckbands of their shirts a good way falling over the collar). I then took a buff collar, over which I put on the gorget of my arms, which was very finely gilt. I at that time wore gray and white in honour of a fair lady to whom I was a servant when I had leisure. I therefore put on a hat of gray silk of the German fashion with a great silver hatband and a plume of heron's feathers, thick set with silver spangles; the hats they wore in those days were not so broad as they wear them now. I then put on a short cassock of gray velvet garnished with little plaits of silver, at two fingers' distance from one another and lined with cloth of silver, all open betwixt the plaits, which I wore in Piedmont over my arms. Now I had yet two little bottles of Greek wine left of those had been sent me by the Cardinal of Armagnac, with which I wet my hands and with them rubbed my face till I had brought a little colour into my cheeks, and then drank a small draught with a little bit of bread, after which I looked myself in the glass. I swear to you I did not know myself, and methought I was yet in Piedmont and in love as heretofore. At which I could not forbear laughing, for methought I had got on a sudden quite another face.

The first that came to me with his captains was Signor Cornelio and the Count de Caiazzo, Monsieur de Bassompierre and the Count de Bisque [Vische], whom I had also sent for: who finding me dressed after this manner all fell a-laughing. I strutted up and down the room before them like fifteen Spaniards and yet had not strength enough to have killed a chicken, for I was so weak as nothing more. Combas and the French captains came also, and the whole farce tended to nothing but laughter for all the company. The last that came was Reckenrot and his captains, who seeing me in this posture laughed to that excess that he sobbed again, when pulling him by the arm I said to him, 'What, colonel, do you think me to be that Monluc that goes every day dying through the streets? No, no, you are mistaken, that fellow's dead, and I am another Monluc sprung up in his room.' His interpreter told him what I said, which made him laugh still more, and Signor Cornelio had already acquainted him with the reason why I had sent for him, and that it was necessary by one means or another to dispossess the Sienese of their fear.

Thus then we went all on horseback to the palace, where so soon as we were got up to the top of the stairs we found the great hall full of gentlemen and such other burghers of the city as were of the council. Within the great hall on the left hand there is a lesser room into which none were to enter but the captains of the people, the twelve counsellors, and the eight of the council of war, all which are called the Magistracy. Thus then I entered into the great hall, where I put off my hat to them but was known to nobody at first, they all believing me to be some gentleman sent by Monsieur de Strozzi into the city to command at the assault, by reason of my great weakness. I then entered into the little hall with all the colonels and captains after me, who kept at distance by the door whilst I went and sat down by the captain of the people in the place where those who represented the person of the King were used to sit, as I myself upon that account had often done. In going up with my hat in my hand, I smiled first upon one, and then upon another, they all wondering to see me, and two had already delivered their opinions when I began to speak to them in Italian.

Monluc's address to the Consistory—the leading magistrates—of Siena was not only in their native tongue but was a skilful appeal, full of apt references to the city's history, to the pride and loyalty of the citizens. This well-prepared exhortation, Monluc's fine clothes and apparently renewed good health, had a dramatic effect: he inspired the people to resist and persuaded them to lay aside temporarily civilian government in order to allow him to take all necessary steps for the further defence of the city

I then ordered in the first place that the city should be divided into eight parts, of which the eight of the council of war should have every one a part: that every one of the council of eight should appoint a person for whom he should himself be responsible to take a list of the quarter should be assigned him, how many men, women and children there were in that division, from twelve the males to sixty, and the females to fifty years of age, which were to carry baskets, barrels, shovels, picks and mattocks, and that each one of his own quarter should make captains of every trade, without mixing them together; that everyone should be commanded upon pain of death, so soon as ever their captain should send for them to come to the place appointed immediately to haste away, as also the women and children; that everyone should forthwith make provision of such things as were proper for his or her employment, and that the masters of men-servants and maids, or their mistresses, should be obliged speedily to take order that their men and maids be furnished with tools and utensils wherewith to labour at the work, for which they shall be appointed, upon pain of two hundred crowns, and the city to furnish the poor, who have not wherewith to buy them, at the expense of the public treasure; that the said deputies shall make their catalogues and shall go from house to house to register their people; and that so soon as the captains, every one in his own quarter, should cry 'Out, out', everyone, both men and women, should run to their tools and present themselves at the place to which the captain should lead or appoint them to come; and that the deputies should deliver in the lists of all, both men and women, they shall have found in their respective precincts to each of the eight of the council of war, quarter for quarter; that the old men and women above the forementioned ages shall remain in their masters' houses to get meat and to look to the house; that the said deputies should take a list of all the masons and carpenters who should be found in their quarter, which list they should also deliver to him of the eight of the council of war by whom they shall be deputed. And this was the order for the labourers and pioneers.

The order for those who bore arms was that the three gonfaloniers, namely of San Martino, of the City, and of Camollia, should forth-with take a view of all the companies, which were four and twenty, and examine every man's arms, if they were in good order for fight, and if not to make them presently to be repaired; that they should refine all the powder and cause great store of bullet and match to be made; that the three gonfaloniers should every one keep in his own quarter without stirring thence till one of the eight of war should come to give them order what to do; that the ancient gentlemen who were not able to bear arms nor to work should present themselves to solicit the pioneers of that quarter where their houses stood and to assist the captains of the said pioneers.

Now I had ever determined that if ever the enemy should come to assault us with artillery, to entrench myself at a good distance from the wall, where the battery should be made, to let them enter at pleasure, and made account to shut up the two ends of the trench, and at either end to plant four or five pieces of great cannon loaden with great chains, nails and pieces of iron. Behind the retirade I intended to place the muskets, together with the arquebusiers, and so soon as they should be entered in, to cause the artillery and small shot to fire all at once, and we at the two ends then to run in upon them with pikes and halberds, two-handed swords, short swords and targets. This I resolved upon as seeing it altogether impossible for the King to send us relief, by reason that he was engaged in so many places that it would not be possible for him to set on foot forces sufficient to raise the siege, neither by sea nor by land. And Monsieur de Strozzi had no means to relieve us, wherefore I would permit them to enter and make little defence, at the breach, to the end that I might give them battle in the town after they had passed the fury of our cannon and smaller shot. For to have defended the breach had in my opinion been a very easy matter, but then we could not have done the enemy so much mischief as by letting them enter the breach, which we would have pretended to quit only to draw them on to the fight.

For five or six days before the artillery came I every night sent out two peasants and a captain or a sergeant as sentinels perdues, which is a very good thing and of great safety, but take heed whom you send, for he may do you a very ill turn. So soon as the night came the captain set a peasant sentinel at some fifty or sixty paces distant from the wall, and either in a ditch or behind a hedge, with instructions that so soon as he should hear anything he should come back to the captain at the foot of the wall, which captain had in charge from me that immediately upon the peasant's speaking to him they should clap down upon all four and so creep the one after the other to the place where the peasant had heard the noise, or rather fall down upon their bellies close to the earth to discover if there were not three or four who came to view that place, and to observe if they did not lay their heads together to confer. For this is a certain sign that they came to view that place in order to the bringing up of artillery. To do which as it ought to be done, they ought to be no other than the master of the ordnance, the colonel or the camp-master of the infantry, or the engineer, the master carter, and a captain of pioneers, to the end that according to what shall be resolved upon by the master of the ordnance, the colonel, and cannoneer. The master carter may also take notice which way he may bring up artillery to the place, and the cannoneer ought to show the captain of the pioneers what is to be done for the esplanade or plaining of the way, according to the determination of the rest. And this is the discovery that is to be made by night, after you have discovered a little at distance by day, for if those within be an enemy of any spirit, they ought either by skirmishes or by their cannon to keep you from coming to discover at hand.

The captain had order to come give me a present account of what he and the peasants had heard or seen, and to leave the peasants still upon their perdue, and a soldier in his own place till his return. Three times the enemy was discovered after this manner, and immediately upon the notice, having also the list of the eight quarters and of the eight of war who commanded those quarters, I suddenly acquainted Signor Cornelio, who could presently tell me both the quarter against which it was and the gentleman of the eight of war that commanded it.

I had never discovered my intention to anyone but to Signor Cornelio only, who was a man of great wisdom and valour, and in whom I reposed a very great confidence. So soon as he knew that I meant to give them battle in the city, we did nothing of one whole day but walk the round both within and without, taking very good observation of all the places where the enemy could make a battery, and consequently by that knew where to make our retirade. And so soon as ever notice was given me by the captain who stood sentinel without the city, I presently advertised the commander of that quarter, and he his deputy, and his deputy the captain of the pioneers, so that in an hour's time you might have seen at least a thousand or twelve hundred persons beginning the retirade. Now I had ordered the city to make great provision of torches, so that those who had discovered were hardly returned to the Marquis but that they saw all that part within the town covered with torches and people, insomuch that by break of day we had very much advanced our trench, and in the morning sent back those to rest, calling in another quarter to the work till noon, and another from noon till night, and consequently others till midnight, and so till break of day, by which means in a little time we performed so great a work that we could by no means be surprised.

After this manner I still turned the defences of the town towards the Marquis his attempts, who lodged at the house of Guillot the Dreamer,[1] and Signor Hernandou de Selve [Fernando de Silva], brother to Signor Rigomès [Ruy Gomez][2] (who commanded the tercio near the little Osservanza[3], with whom I had some discourse

---

[1] 'A phrase signifying that a man is nonplussed.' Cotton's note.

[2] Ruy Gomez de Silva, Prince of Eboli, was chief minister of Philip II.

[3] The little convent of the Observants lay outside the walls of Siena, to the north-east of the city.

upon the public faith the Friday before we departed out of the city, betwixt their quarters and the fort Camollia), told me that the Marquis had some jealousy that some one of their council betrayed to me all their deliberations, seeing he had no sooner designed to batter any part but that we always fortified against that place. For by night the least noise is easily heard and so great a bustle cannot be concealed. And because he told me that he had compiled a book of the particularities of the siege of Siena, he entreated me to tell him by what means I so continually discovered their intentions, whereupon I told him the truth.

The bombardment of the city, January 1555

But to return to our subject, the Marquis in the end came and planted his artillery upon a little hill betwixt Port Oville [Porta Ovile] and the great Osservanza.[1] The choice of this place put me, who thought myself so cunning, almost to a nonplus, forasmuch as at Porta Ovile there is a very spacious antiport where the houses of the city do almost touch, having nothing but the street between, which made it impossible for me of a long time to make the necessary retirade, to do which I must be constrained to beat down above an hundred houses, which extremely troubled me. For it is to create so many enemies in our entrails, the poor citizen losing all patience to see his house pulled down before his eyes. I gave to the Count Vische the charge of terracing up this gate, for which use we took the earth out of the gardens and vacant places that lie a little on the left hand. O the rare example that is here, which I will commit to writing that it may serve for a mirror to all those who would conserve their liberty.

All these poor inhabitants, without discovering the least distaste or sorrow for the ruin of their houses, put themselves their own hands first to the work, everyone contending who should be most ready to pull down his own. There was never less than four thousand souls at labour, and I was showed by the gentlemen of Siena a great number of gentlewomen carrying of baskets of earth upon their heads. It shall never be (you ladies of Siena) that I will not immortalize your names so long as the book of Monluc shall live, for in truth you are worthy of immortal praise, if ever women were. At the beginning of the noble resolution these people took to defend their liberty, all the ladies of

---

[1] The Porta Ovile and the great church of the Observants—which must be distinguished from the little convent above—lay within the city, on the eastern side.

Siena divided themselves into three squadrons. The first was led by
Signora Forteguerra, who was herself clad in violet, as also all those
of her train, her attire being cut in the fashion of a nymph, short and
discovering her buskins. The second was la Signora Picolhuomini
[Piccolomini] attired in carnation satin, and her troop in the same
livery. The third was la Signora Livia Fausta, apparelled all in white,
as also her train, with her white ensign. In their ensigns they had very
fine devices, which I would give a good deal I could remember. These
three squadrons consisted of three thousand ladies, gentlewomen, and
citizens. Their arms were picks, shovels, baskets, and bavins, and in
this equipage they made their muster and went to begin the fortifications. Monsieur de Thermes, who has often told me this story (for I
was not then arrived at Siena), has assured me that in his life he never
saw so fine a sight. I have since seen their ensigns, and they had composed a song to the honour of France, for which I wish I had given the
best horse I have that I might insert it here.

And since I am upon the honour of these women, I will that those
who shall come after us admire the courage and virtue of a young
virgin of Siena who, though she was a poor man's daughter, deserves
notwithstanding to be ranked with those of the noblest families. I had
made a decree at the time when I was dictator, that no-one upon pain
of severe punishment should fail to go to the guard in his turn. This
young maid seeing a brother of hers who was concerned to be upon
duty not able to go, she took his morion and put it upon her head, his
breeches and a collar of buff and put them on, and with his halberd upon
her neck in this equipage mounted the guard, passing when the list
was read by her brother's name, and stood sentinel in turn without
being discovered, till the morning that it was fair light day, when she
was conducted home with great honour. In the afternoon Signor
Cornelio showed her to me.

But to return to our subject, it was not possible of all that day nor
the night following for the Count to perfect his terrace, nor we our
retirade, at which we wrought exceeding hard, leaving about fourscore paces to the Marquis, if he had a mind to enter there. We had
made a traverse by the Porta Ovile, where we had placed three great
culverins, laden as I have said before, at which place were Signor
Cornelio, the Count de Caiazzo, and three cannoneers, who were
there left by Monsieur Bassompierre. On the right hand upon an
eminence was the great Osservanza, betwixt which and the walls we
had planted five pieces of cannon rammed with the same, which the

said Bassompierre commanded in his own person. Yet both the one and the other were so well concealed that the enemy could discover nothing from the little hills about us. Well did they perceive that above at the Osservanza there were people, for they had evermore a clap at that, but we were all behind a trench we had cast up betwixt the Osservanza and the wall of the city, crouched and squat, so that we could not be seen. The soldiers were all before the houses, through which they had pierced several holes to come and go under cover. Behind the retirade, which was not much above the height of a man, they were also sheltered from being seen. Signor Cornelio was also under cover by reason that he lay in a low place and under the shelter of a very thick wall which joined to Porta Ovile.

The order of the fight was thus: Signor Cornelio had with him one ensign of Germans, two of French, four of Italians, and four of Sienese, having also the Count de Caiazzo to assist him; and with me at the Osservanza was Reckenrot with three companies of Germans, two of French, two of Italians, and four ensigns of Sienese. In all the two troops both of Signor Cornelio's and mine there was not so much as one arquebus, but pikes, halberds, and two-handed swords (and of those but few), swords and targets, all arms proper for close fight and the most furious and killing weapons of all other, for to stand popping and pelting with those small shot is but so much time lost. A man must close and grapple collar to collar if he mean to rid any work, which the soldier will never do so long as he has his firearms in his hands, but will be always fighting at distance.

All the night the enemy were placing gabions for six and twenty or seven and twenty pieces of ordnance, and by break of day they had planted twelve, as they would in that time have done all the rest had it not been that they had been necessitated to draw their cannon up to this mountain by strength of hand. The wall is good enough, which not long since by one of the two Popes Pius, who were of the house of Piccolomini, and of the order of the people, had caused to be made.[1] At break of day they began their battery within a foot or two of the bottom of the walls, at the distance of about an hundred paces; which they did to cut the wall by the bottom, making account the next day with the rest of the artillery in a short time to beat down the whole wall. But for all that the Count Vische ceased not continually to fill the antiport, leaving us flankers so that we could see all along the

[1] Aeneas Sylvius Piccolomini, Pope Pius II (1405–64), had had the wall rebuilt in order to accommodate the great church of the Observants.

breach. About noon they gave over their battery below and began to batter the middle of the wall, when so soon as I saw them begin to let in light I left Signor Cornelio, who continually went up and down from place to place, and took Monsieur de Bassompierre, with whom I went to the fort Camollia, from whence we could plainly see into the recoil of their cannon.

Monsieur de Bassompierre ran to fetch a cannon we had in the citadel, but as he went out to remove it the carriage broke, so that instead of it he brought a demi-cannon, which a Sienese the said Bassompierre had entertained in the quality of a cannoneer evermore shot in, and so well that he could hit with it as small a mark as if it had been an arquebus. He was assisted by some Italian and French soldiers of the citadel to bring it, whilst I was making ready a platform with the soldiers of the fort till my company of pioneers came, which I had sent for in all haste. And in less than an hour and a half we dispatched it, where I mounted my demi-cannon. I gave ten crowns to our Sienese that he might make some good shots with that piece here, as he had done several at the citadel before. The enemy had placed gabions on the flank of their battery towards us. Bassompierre and I went a little on the right hand and observed the bullet in the air like a hat on fire, flying very wide on the right hand, and the second as much on the left, which made me ready to eat my own flesh for rage. Monsieur de Bassompierre always assured me that he would presently take his level right and still went and came to and fro betwixt him and me. The third shot lighted upon the bottom of the gabions, and the fourth played directly into their artillery and there killed a great many of their men; whereupon all those that assisted fled behind a little house which was in the rear of their cannon. At which I ran and took him in my arms, and seeing him with his linstock ready to fire again, said to him, 'Fradel mio, da li da seno; per Dio, facio ti presente d'altri dieci scoudi, et d'un bichier de vino greco.'[1] I then left him the French captain, who had the guard of the fort, to furnish him continually with such things as he stood in need of, and Monsieur Bassompierre and I returned to our post.

There then advanced a German ensign to the enemy's battery, who came along by the other gabionade with his colours flying; and this might be about four of the clock in the afternoon. We could see him march from behind the Osservanza and was no sooner come to the

[1] 'My brother, let them have it; I'm giving you another ten *escudos* and a beaker of Greek wine.'

artillery but our piece fired and killed the ensign, upon which the Germans immediately fled away, retiring to the place from whence they came. And this Sienese made so many brave shots that he dismounted them six pieces of cannon, and their artillery remained totally abandoned till the beginning of the night without playing any more than two pieces of cannon that were covered with gabions and flanked towards the fort Camollia, which our artillery could not touch because they shot over by reason of the height of the gabions, and in the twilight they made seven or eight shots at the Osservanza where we were, and the houses adjoining, and of all night after shot no more.

We worked exceeding hard all night to finish our retirade, and the Count Vische was no less diligent at the antiport, so that two hours before day all was perfected and everyone settled in his post where he was to fight. That which made us make so much haste was that we heard a great noise at their artillery and thought they were bringing up the rest, which made me put out a man to discover their battery, who brought us word that they had cut above fourscore paces to the wall, within a span or two of the bottom, and that he believed in a few hours they would have beaten it totally down, which we did not much care for though they did, for we hoped to sell them their entry very dear. And about an hour before day they ceased their noise, which made us think that they only expected the break of day to give fire. I then mounted upon the wall, having Captain Charry always with me, who by main force would needs have me down when the day began to break, and soon after I perceived that at the windows of the gabions there was no artillery and that instead of planting more they had drawn off those there were. I then called out to Signor Cornelio that we were out of danger of an assault, and that the enemy had drawn off their cannon. At which news everyone began to come upon the wall, where the Sienese sufficiently rated the enemy in their language, saying, 'Coioni, marrani, venete qua: vi meteremo per terra vinti brassi di muri.'[1] They were constrained to stay three days at the foot of the mountain to repair their carriages, which the demi-cannon we had brought to fort Camollia had broken and spoiled them.

Now (as I have already said) the gentleman of the Emperor's bedchamber had all the while kept a great deal of clutter what cannon would do to the winning of the town. But after he had been an

---

[1] 'Fools, clods, come here: we'll knock you back twenty paces from the wall.'

eyewitness of all that has been related, and that the Marquis had remonstrated to him that the retirade and those other fortifications I made within was to let him enter and to give him battle in the city (for if I knew what he did, he was no less informed of my proceeding, there being evermore one traitor or another amongst all people), he then was of the same opinion with the Marquis and the other captains that the town was never to be taken by force; but that it was to be reduced to famine, and therefore thought it convenient that the artillery should be sent back to Florence. He then returned back to his master to give him an account of what he had seen, and that the Marquis could do no more than what he had already done. I do not know whether or no he acquainted the Emperor with the fright he had been in, which the Marquis himself gave me a relation of at my going out of Siena as he went along with me above two miles of my way: where he told me that at the time when their artillery was forsaken by reason of the havoc our demi-cannon made amongst them, he was close by the side of the little house in his litter, being then very lame of the gout, where his litter being set down upon the ground, this gentleman of the Emperor's was talking to him, having his hands upon the cover of the litter, and his head within it, whispering with the said Marquis; when our governor seeing the artillery abandoned, and everyone retired under the shelter of the little house, made a shot at it, with which a part of the wall, which was of brick, fell upon the litter, so that the said gentleman was by it beaten down upon the Marquis's legs, so astonished as nothing more. And the Marquis swore to me that in his life he was himself never in so much fear of being killed as at that time; that they drew the gentleman out from off his legs, and himself after with much ado, all the litter being full of the ruin and covering of the said house. And the said Marquis moreover told me that at the great fright he was in his gout left him, for the whole ruin fell at once upon him and upon the gentleman, who verily thought himself to be killed. I have often heard that the apprehension of death has cured many diseases. I know not if the Marquis his gout be returned since, but he assured me he had never had it after from that fright till the time I saw him. If it be returned or no I leave others to enquire.

The departure of the Germans

This might be about the middle of January, and not above eight days after we began to perceive that the Germans grew very impatient at the little bread they had, having no wine, which was the most insupportable of all. The Reckenrot himself, who was sickly, could no longer endure, there being nothing to be had unless it were a little horse flesh or a piece of an ass. Signor Cornelio and I then began to contrive which way we might get these Germans out of the city, and conceited that if they were gone we could yet keep the town above two months longer, whereas if they stayed we should be necessitated to surrender. We therefore concluded to send a man privately to Monsieur de Strozzi to remonstrate all this to him and to entreat him to send for them after the most plausible manner he could (which I also directed him how to do), and sent to him Captain Cosseil, who is now my ensign, very well instructed. It was with exceeding great difficulty that he was to pass, which that he might do we were to fight two courts of guard, by reason that the Marquis had already cast up a great number of trenches which came up close to the walls of the city on every side. Of these Captain Charry fought the one, and the Count de Caiazzo with a company of Italians the other; so that whilst they were fighting he got over the trench and recovered the rear of the camp with his guides, and two days after returned in company with an Italian gentleman called Captain Flaminio, who brought letters to the Reckenrot and to me also, wherein Monsieur de Strozzi writ to me to send the Reckenrot with his companies out to him, for that he intended to set on foot a flying army, having with him great store of Italian horse and foot, and that without some of those Transmontane sinews[1] he should never be able to relieve me and that he would protest against me if the city was lost. To the Reckenrot likewise he sent very obliging letters, having beforehand made Captain Flaminio very perfect in his lesson.

The Reckenrot upon receiving these orders broke out into very great complaints, saying that Monsieur de Strozzi reduced him to the greatest extremities and that it was impossible for him to get away without being defeated; but that he would however speak to his officers, which he did, and which begot a very great dispute amongst them. At length one of them in whom he reposed the greatest confidence and who served him in the quality of camp-master, remonstrated to him that he had much better hazard with his sword in his hand to make his way through the Marquis his camp than stay to die of famine, or by a capitulation to surrender himself to the enemy's discretion, which however in a few days he must of necessity do: for

[1] i.e. the Germans.

there was nothing left to eat and their soldiers began to murmur, insomuch that they evermore expected when a great part of them should go give themselves up to the enemy; which made them resolve to depart. The Reckenrot was not much to be blamed for his unwillingness, it being a very perilous journey, for at the very sallying out of the gate he was of necessity to fight several Spanish guards, and half a mile from thence another at a trench the enemy had cast up near unto a certain mill which was in his way. Upon their determination to depart, I gave express charge that no-one living should speak of this sally, causing the gates of the city to be close shut, and at the beginning of the night they all came with their baggage to the great place before Porta Nuova.

The Sienese, who understood nothing of all this, at the seeing the Germans in this marching posture began in all haste to repair to the palace in very great despair. I then caused three companies to sally out, two of French and one of Italians. The first whereof was led by Captain Charry, the second by Captain Blacons (who since died a Huguenot at Saintonge), and the third by the Count de Caiazzo. Captain Charry had order to fight the first court of guard, which was in a great street of the suburbs, the second was at the Augustins in the same street, and the third at Sainct-Laze [San Lazzaro].[1] They had in command from me never to give over till they had fought all the three courts of guards, and the Count de Caiazzo took the way on the outside of the suburbs on the right hand all along by the houses, still marching softly on to rally our men together as they should be separated and scattered by the fight. The tercio of Cecille [Sicily] lay at the Charterhouse, consisting of very good soldiers, and the Reckenrot at the going out of the gate took on the right hand, entering into a valley, and the Count de Caiazzo remained upon the eminence moving still softly on, which produced two effects for the relief of our people. The one as has been said by gathering our squandered men together, and the other to succour the Reckenrot also if he should stand in need. And so we began to open the gate, it being about one of the clock in the night.

Captain Charry marched out first (for it was he who always led the dance), Blacons after him, the Count de Caiazzo next, and then the Germans, who in a trice put themselves into the valley. We immediately heard the fight betwixt our French and the Spaniards. Captain Charry routed the two courts of guards, the one after the

[1] The suburb beyond Porta Nuova, now the Porta Romana, on the south side of the city.

other, and beat them up as far as that of San Lazzaro. Whereupon those of the Charterhouse came out to relieve their people, and came to the Augustins (where Blacons had made a halt expecting Captain Charry) and there clapped in betwixt them. Captain Charry having done his business, thought to return (hearing very well that they were fighting with Blacons), and met the enemy, which redoubled the fight. The Count de Caiazzo could not come to assist him by reason that I had expressly forbid him to engage in the fight till he should first be sure that the Germans were out of danger. But in the end he was constrained to do as the rest did, our two French companies being driven upon him. The fight continued above a long hour. Signor Cornelio and I were without the gate by the portcullis and nothing was open but the wicket, and there as the soldiers came one after another we put them in; when on a sudden we heard the fight coming towards us, some crying '*France*' and others '*Espagne*', when at last they all came up pell-mell together to the portcullis. We had torches within the gates and through the wicket saw a little light by which we drew the soldiers in. I must needs say there were very valiant men, both on the one side and the other, for not so much as either French or Italian ever once ran furiously upon us but still faced about at the portcullis, and never retired but step by step till we pulled them in. All the three captains were wounded, and we there lost, slain and wounded, above forty of the best soldiers we had, both French and Italians, and in the end we got in all the rest of our people. And because before the sally the Sienese were astonished at the departure of the Germans, I made Signor Cornelio to go about to the several guards and to the forts to reassure our men, for no-one knew that the Germans were to go away, and I myself went to the palace where I found all the senate in a very great distraction, to whom I spoke as followeth:

'I see well (gentlemen) that you have here assembled yourselves upon the occasion of the Germans' departure, and that you are entered into some apprehension and jealousy that by that means your city will be lost. But I must tell you, it is the conservation and not the loss of your city, for those six ensigns devoured more than the twelve of the Italians and French. On the other side, I know you must have heard that the said Germans already began to mutiny, being no longer able to endure. I also discovered well enough that even their captains were not like to govern them, themselves apprehending that they would go over to the enemy, and you yourselves have for five or six days last past heard the enemy call out to us at the very foot of our walls that we were lost and that our Germans would soon be with them. Yet did not this proceed from any default in their officers but from the impatience of the common soldiers, who were no longer able to suffer.

'Now (gentlemen) should you appear dejected upon their departure; the world would say that both your courage and ours depended only upon theirs, and so we should dishonour ourselves to honour them; to which I shall never give my consent. For you knew all the great fights that have happened in this siege have been performed by you, and us only, and they have never so much as sallied out of the town save only once, that in spite of me the Reckenrot would send out his people under the conduct of his nephew and his campmaster, and would accept of no-one of any other nation than his own, at which time you saw how soon and how easily they were beaten back, even into the ditch of the ravelin of Porta Nuova. So that if by good fortune I had not been there and had not made the Italian guard sally out to their rescue, not a man of them had come off alive. I will not disparage them, but they are much more proper for a battle than a siege. Why then (signors) should you be concerned at their departure?

'I will say one thing more to you, that although I had also sent away the twelve companies that remain with me in this town, I would yet undertake to defend your city, provided the captains stayed behind to relieve me. You must make your ensigns captains of the watch by turns, who shall have two nights of intermission, and ours shall have but one, and we must begin to contract our allowance of bread to fourteen ounces, and you of the city to ten. You must also put the useless mouths out of town and appoint six persons to take a list of their names tomorrow without further delay, and that without regard of persons, and speedily thrust them out of your city; by which expedient we shall make our bread last three months longer, which will be a sufficient time for the King wherein to relieve us, especially now that the spring is drawing on. Cease therefore your apprehensions, and on the contrary approve what I have done in order to your service. If I have done it without pre-acquainting the senate with my design, it was not out of any disrespect to them but to keep this departure secret, which was of very great consequence, as you yourselves may have observed, I having been constrained to put Monsieur de Strozzi upon the business to deliver myself from a people so entirely devoted to their bellies.'

The expulsion of the 'useless mouths'

The senate having heard my remonstrance, desired me to go to my repose and that they would consider of what I had said, rendering me very many thanks for the comfort and good counsel I had given them. In the morning my whole speech was divulged all over the city, and there was no more thought of fear amongst them; but they could not well agree amongst themselves about the unprofitable mouths, forasmuch as everyone was willing to favour his own relations and friends. Wherefore by ballot they created me their Dictator General for the space of a month, during which time neither the captain of the people nor the magistracy had any command at all, but I had the absolute authority and dignity, anciently belonging to the old dictators of Rome.[1] I thereupon created six commissaries to take a list of all the useless people, and afterwards delivered the roll to a knight of Malta, accompanied with five and twenty or thirty soldiers, to put them out of the town; which in three days after I had delivered in the list, was performed. A thing that had I not very good witness of, both of the Sienese, the King's officers, and the captains who were then present in Siena, I should not however have mentioned in this place lest the world should take me for a liar; but it is most perfectly true.

The list of these useless mouths I do assure you amounted to four thousand and four hundred people or more, which of all the miseries and desolations that I have ever seen was the greatest my eyes ever yet beheld or that I believe I shall ever see again. For the master was hereby necessitated to part with his servant who had served him long, the mistress with her maid, besides an infinite number of poor people who only lived by the sweat of their brows; which weeping and desolation continued for three days together. And these poor wretches were to go through the enemy, who still beat them back again towards the city, the whole camp continuing night and day in arms to that only end. So that they drove them up to the very foot of the walls that they might the sooner consume the little bread we had left, and to see if the city out of compassion to those miserable creatures would revolt. But that prevailed nothing, though they lay eight days in this condition where they had nothing to eat but herbs and grass, and above the one half of them perished, for the enemy killed them, and very few

---

[1] This transfer of power to the Governor occurred on 10 January 1555, before the bombardment of the city, not later, as Monluc here implies. See above p. 151.

escaped away. There were a great many maids and handsome women indeed, who found means to escape, the Spaniards by night stealing them into their quarters for their own provision. But it was unknown to the Marquis for it had otherwise been death; and some strong and vigorous men also forced their way and escaped by night. But all those did not amount to the fourth part and all the rest miserably perished. These are the effects of war. We must of necessity sometimes be cruel to frustrate the designs of an enemy. God had need to be merciful to men of our trade, who commit so many sins and are the causers of many miseries and mischiefs.[1]

You captains and governors of places, if you be not perfect already, learn these arts and stratagems. It is not all to be valiant and wise, you must also be circumspect and cunning. Had I entreated the Reckenrot to depart the city he would have been displeased and have reproached me that I sent him to the slaughter: but I proceeded more discreetly, serving myself with the authority of Monsieur de Strozzi, wherein I had no other end but to gain time to tire out my enemy and to give the King leisure to relieve us. But as I have said before, he employed his forces there where he had the most concern. 'Nearer is the skin than the shirt.' Never fear to discharge yourselves of useless mouths and bar your ears from all cries of the afflicted. Had I obeyed my own disposition I had done it three months sooner, which if I had I might peradventure have saved the town, or at least I had longer held my enemy in play, and I have a hundred times since repented me that I did not.

Monluc exposed an attempt by an Imperialist spy to exploit the political animosities in the city. But famine had set in and the capitulation could not long be delayed

Now after the Marquis saw himself disappointed of his expectation and that all his plots and stratagems came to nothing, he suffered us to rest in peace, not expecting to have us till we should be reduced to the last morsel of bread. And we began to enter into the month of March, when we were in the greatest necessity of all things: for of wine there had not been one drop in the whole city from the middle of February;

[1] This passage is a conflation of several separate incidents, which took place during the winter of 1554–5, and which are described in greater detail in Sozzini's *Diario* of the siege, *Archivio Storico Italiano*, vol. II.

we had eaten all the horses, asses, mules, cats and rats that were in the town. Cats sold for three and four crowns apiece, and a rat for a crown. And in all the whole city there was only remaining four old mares, so lean as nothing more, which turned the mills, two that I had, the controller La Morlière his, the treasurer L'Espine another, Signor Cornelio a little bay pad-nag that was blind with age, and Misser Girolamo Spannocchi a Turk of above twenty years old. These were all the horses and mares that were left in the city in this extremity, which was greater than I can represent it, and I do believe there is not in nature so dreadul a thing as famine.

We had from Rome some hopes sent us of succours and that the King was sending away the Marshal de Brissac to relieve us, which was the reason that we again lessened our bread to twelve ounces and the soldiers and citizens of the town to nine; whilst in the meantime by little and little we lost several inhabitants and soldiers, who fell down dead as they walked the streets, so that they died without sickness. At last the physicians found it out that it was the mallows they fed upon, that being an herb that does relax the stomach and obstructs digestion. Now we had no other herbs all along the walls of the city, they having been all eaten before, neither could we come by these without sallying out to skirmish, and then all the women and children of the town went out to gather them. But I saw I lost so many men in these skirmishes that I would no more permit anyone to sally out. Now to hear any more news of the Marshal [Strozzi] was henceforward impossible, for the trenches were brought up to the very gates of the city, which trenches the Marquis had also redoubled for fear we should sally out upon him in despair, and give him battle, as the Sienese in their ancient wars had formerly done as themselves report.[1]

In this condition we languished on till the 8th of April, that we had lost all manner of hopes of relief, and then it was that the seigneury entreated me not to take it ill if they began to think of their preservation. When seeing there was no other remedy, unless to eat one another, I could not deny them, cursing to the pit of hell all those who engage men of honour in places and then leave them in the lurch. Yet did I not herein intend to speak ill of the King, my good master, he loved me too well for that, but those who gave him ill counsels to the prejudice of his affairs; and I have ever observed more evil than good

[1] In July 1526, in the course of their war with Pope Clement VII.

counsellors about princes. They then sent out one of their people to
the Marquis to entreat of him a safe conduct for two of their senate,
whom they would send to him, which he granted, and they began to
capitulate. The Marquis himself did very much facilitate the treaty
and they began to enter into great confidence of him, for he very well
saw that to cause the city to be sacked and ruined would be no profit,
neither to the Emperor nor the Duke of Florence, and would only
benefit the soldier. And on the other side he feared lest if the Sienese
could obtain no good conditions, we should sally out upon him, *à la
désespérade*, having already lost above the third part of his men, who
were either dead through the length of the siege or run away, so that
he had almost no Italians, who were quartered at the fort San Marco.
And the Marquis had remained for above a month with no more than
six ensigns for the guard of his own person, all the rest being in the
trenches. Neither could he ever relieve them with more than ten
ensigns and those had only one night of intermission, and some such
guards there were that were not relieved in six days. To this condition
was he reduced without, as well as we within. Neither could he make
any use of his horse, no more than Monsieur de Strozzi could of the
cavalry he had, by reason that there was no manner of thing upon the
ground to give the horses to eat from Montalchin [Montalcino] to
Siena and from Siena to Florence.

I will now give an account of myself after what manner I lived. I
had no manner of advantage, no more than the meanest soldier, and
my bread weighed no more than twelve ounces, and of white bread
there was never above seven or eight made, whereof three were
brought to my quarters and the rest were saved for some captain that
was sick. Neither those of the city nor we from the end of February
to the 22nd of April ever ate above once a day; neither did I ever hear
so much as any one soldier complain, and I can assure you the remonstrances I often made to them served to very good purpose. For if they
would have gone over to the enemy's camp the Marquis would have
treated them very well; for the enemy very much esteemed our
Italian and French soldiers, and in the skirmishes that had happened
betwixt us had had very sufficient trial of their valour. I had bought
thirty hens and a cock to get me eggs, which Signor Cornelio, the
Count de Caiazzo and I ate, for we all three constantly ate together; at
noon in one place and in the evening at another, but towards the end
of March all these were eaten, the cock and all. 'Twas pity we had no
more; and so I remained without flesh and without eggs and had

nothing to eat but my little loaf, with a few peas boiled with a little bacon and mallows, and that but once a day only. The desire I had to acquire honour and to put this baffle upon the Emperor, so long to have held his army in play, made me find this so sweet that it was no trouble to me to fast: and this pitiful supper with a bit of bread was a feast to me, when returning from some skirmish I knew the enemy to be well drubbed, or that I knew them to suffer under the same necessities we did.

But to return to the capitulation: the Marquis sent to the Duke of Florence and Don Johan Manricou [Juan Manrique], who was ambassador from the Emperor to the Pope and resided at Florence by reason of the siege; whereupon the said Duke sending a safe conduct, the Sienese also sent to the Pope (which was Pope Julius, who died two or three days after)[1] from whom they received a very scurvy answer, he reproaching them with their obstinacy and commanding them to submit to the Duke of Florence his mercy without any condition. He was a terrible Pope; but the Duke proceeded after a more modest and courageous manner, as a prince ought to do who would gain the hearts of a people; and indeed he was one of the greatest politicians of our times. It behooved him so to be to establish his principality, in the time of two of the greatest and most ambitious princes that ever were, who had both of them a great mind to get footing in Italy. But the Spaniard was more subtle than we and this Duke managed his business very well; his name was Cosme [Cosimo de Medici] and I believe he is yet living.[2] In the meantime commissioners for eight days together went and came betwixt Florence and the camp.

Upon Monday night the capitulation was brought to Siena, and the morning before the Marquis had sent a trumpet to me entreating I would send two gentlemen out to him in whom I might confide, he having something to say to them that he desired I should know, and that he was come to San Lazzaro to that effect. I thereupon sent out to him Signor Cornelio and Captain Charry, who being come to him he there acquainted them with the terms of the capitulation, which would that night be brought to the city; and that amongst other things there was one article which expressed that the Sieur de Monluc with his Italian and French companies and all the officers of the King, should march out with bag and baggage, colours flying, drums

---

[1] Pope Julius III died on 25 March 1555.

[2] Cosimo, Grand Duke of Tuscany, died in 1574.

beating, with match lighted and bullet in mouth; but that this article would do me no good, forasmuch as we did not belong to the Sienese but to the King of France, and being we did not belong to them they consequently had no power to capitulate for us; that therefore I was myself to capitulate in the name of the King my master, which if I thought fit to do, he assured me I should have what conditions soever I would demand, and that his service to the Emperor excepted, he would do as much for me as for the Cardinal his brother; that he and I were two poor gentlemen, who by our arms were arrived to such degrees of honour that the greatest both of France and Italy would be glad to have our places; telling them withal he would there stay to expect my answer.

They found me at Porta Nuova walking with Messer Girolamo Spannocchi, where after I had received his message I bade them go back and tell him that I very well knew he had read the Roman history, wherein he might have taken notice that in the times of the ancient warlike Romans they had sent one of their colonies to inhabit Gascony, near to the Pyrenean Mountains, of which province I was a native, and that if he would not content himself that the Sienese had comprised me in their capitulation, I would at my coming out let him see that I was descended from those warlike Romans, who would rather have lost a thousand lives, could they have had so many to lose, than an inch of their honour; that I had rather the Sienese should capitulate for me than I for them, and that for my part the name of Monluc should never be found subscribed to a capitulation. They then returned to him, to whom having repeated my answer, he said to them in Italian, 'Che vol dir questo? mi pare che val iocar à la disperata. Altre volte io rese due forteresse con ragione, ne per questo ne fui mai ripreso de l'Imperatore, et no resta Su Maiesta a servir si di me.'[1] Signor Cornelio then told him that I was positive in this determination and would rather put all to the hazard of the sword than to the hazard of a capitulation. 'Well then', said he, 'recommend me to him and tell him I will let him see that I am his friend, and that he may march out in all assurance upon the capitulation of the Sienese, or after what manner he pleases himself.' And so they returned.

Oh comrades, you have here a fair example before you, when you shall find yourselves in such an affair, never to discover any fear, for

[1] 'What does this mean? It seems to me he's tilting at fortune. At other times I've quite rightly surrendered two fortresses, and I wasn't blamed for it by the Emperor, and his Majesty still allows me to serve him.'

nothing in the world so much startles an enemy as to see the chief with whom he has to do to be undaunted in all extremities, and that he gives him to understand he will rather run the hazard of a fight than a capitulation. Nothing so much puzzles him as that, besides the encouragement it gives to your own people. I was as much afraid as another, seeing myself so desperately engaged and no news of any relief, neither of victuals nor men. But ask anyone who is yet living whether they ever saw me any more dejected than the first day I came into the city. And at the last of all, when we were reduced to the extremest necessity of all things, I was more resolute to fight than before, which I believe conduced much to the obtaining of so good conditions both for the Sienese and for us, as we could have had had we capitulated the first day the enemy sat down before us.

The surrender of Siena, 21 April 1555

Before anyone of us stirred out of the town, I restored the citadel and the fort Camollia into the hands of the Sienese, where they put an ensign of the city in each, as I also made them to place an ensign at every gate of the city that stood open, which being done I returned to Porta Nuova. The Marquis had planted all his Spanish foot all along the street that leads to San Lazzaro, on both sides the street, his Germans were drawn up in battalia a little on the right hand in a camp, and at San Lazzaro was Signor Cabry [Gabrio Serbelloni] his nephew with fifty or threescore horse, which was all they could make (as I have said before) and three hundred Italian arquebusiers which they had drawn out of the forts of Camollia and San Marco, and was the convoy the Marquis had appointed to conduct us. Signor Cornelio then, and the Count de Caiazzo, armed at all points, with their pikes shouldered, went out side by side with a company of arquebusiers at their heels. After them went out two captains at the head of the pikes, amongst whom were a great company of corslets, and in the middle of the pikes the ensigns displayed and advanced, and in the rear of them the rest of the arquebusiers with two captains in their rear.

I had overnight sent to the Marquis that he would be so civil to the ancient women and children who were to go out with us, as to lend them forty or fifty of his carriage mules, which he did, and which before I went out I distributed amongst the Sienese, who put upon them the ancient women and some children in their laps. All the rest were on foot, where there were above an hundred virgins following their fathers and mothers, and women who carried cradles with infants in them upon their heads, and you might have seen several men leading their daughter in one hand and their wife in the other, and they were numbered to above eight hundred men, women and children. I had seen a sad parting at the turning out the useless mouths; but I saw as sad a one at the separation of those who went out with us and who remained behind. In my life I never saw so sad a farewell. So that although our soldiers had in their own persons suffered to the last extremes, yet did they infinitely regret this woeful parting and that they had not the power to defend the liberty of these people, and I more than all the rest, who could not without tears behold this misery and desolation of a people who had manifested themselves so devout for the conservation of their liberty and honour.

So soon as Signor Cornelio was gone out all the Italians followed, and the citizens in the rear of the Italians. Then at the head of our French went out St Auban and Lussan armed, with pikes upon their shoulders and a company of arquebusiers after them, two captains at the head of the pikes, with another company of arquebusiers led by Charry and Blacons, having each of them a halberd in his hand, and the ensigns in the middle of the pikes after the same manner the Italians had passed before. After these I went out armed, and Messer Girolamo Spannocchi side by side with me, for I was afraid they would have seized upon him, he having been a principal actor in the revolt of the city. He was mounted upon an old Turk and I upon another miserably lean and haggled out, notwithstanding which I set a good face on the matter and made the best mien I could. I left two Sienese ensigns at the gate, entreating them to clap to the gate immediately after me and not to open it till the Marquis himself came. The said Marquis rid up and down, and Signor Chiapin Vitello [Chiappino Vitelli] with him through all the files, to take care that no-one meddled with the Sienese, for as to our baggage, it was so little as it made no number.

The Spanish camp-masters then came to salute me, and all their captains. The camp-masters alighted not, but all the captains did and came to embrace my knee, after which they again mounted on horseback and accompanied me till we came to the Marquis and Signor Chiappino, which might be about 300 paces from the gate, where we embraced and they placed me betwixt them. After this manner we passed on discoursing all the way of the siege and the particularities had happened upon it, attributing much honour to us, the Marquis particularly saying that he had great obligation to me, for that besides he had learned several stratagems of war, I was the cause he had been cured of his gout, telling me the fear that both he and the Emperor's gentleman had been in, which did not pass without much laughter. Whereupon I told him that he had put me into a much greater fright the night of the scalado and yet that I was not for all that cured of my fever, adding moreover that he had done very ill to come upon me, as the Jews did to take Our Lord, for he brought along with him lanthorns and torches, which gave me a great advantage, to which he replied bowing his head (for he was a very courteous gentleman), 'Signor, un altra volta sero piu savio.'[1] I then told him that had he continued his battery, he would have had no very good bargain of us, for the Gascons were an obstinate people, but that they were flesh and bone as other men were and must eat.

With this and other discourse of the same nature we entertained ourselves till we were got a mile beyond San Lazzaro, and there the Marquis bade Signor Chiappino Vitelli to go to the head of our people and speak to Signor Gabrio, to take care there should be no disorder, and that if anyone offered to take anything from us, he should kill all such as should attempt it, and that he should give the same command to the captain of the three hundred arquebusiers. So soon as Signor Chiappino was gone from us, the Marquis embracing me in his arms said these words in as good French as I could have spoken myself. 'Adieu Monsieur de Monluc. I pray present my most humble service to the King, and assure him that I am his most humble and affectionate servant, as much (my honour safe) as any gentleman in Italy.' I then returned him thanks for the good inclination he had towards the King and the courtesies I had received at his hands, which I would proclaim in all places wherever I should come, and when it should ever lie in my power to do him service, would requite. He offered me the same and so we fell to embrace again. He had then no more than four or five horse with him, they being all behind in the same order he had left them, and so he returned back towards the city, and soon after Signor Chiappino Vitelli returned, where we also embraced and parted.

We then went to Arbierroute [Arbiarotta], a little village upon the Tresse [Tressa], or else the river itself is called Arbie [Arbia], and there we found eighteen asses loaden with bread which the Marquis had sent thither to distribute amongst us upon the way, of which one part

[1] 'Signor, another time I shall know better.'

I gave to the Sienese, another to the Italians, and the third to the French. To do which, as I passed through the Spaniards, I saw that the soldiers had also purposely brought bread along with them to give to our people. I dare boldly say, and that by the testimony of those who were then with me, that this bread saved the lives of two hundred persons, and there are many who will affirm that it saved the lives of four hundred, and yet could it not go so far that there was not above fifty who died that very day. For we had been from Wednesday till Sunday without eating any more than six ounces of biscuit a day a man; and upon the Thursday of two horses I had, I killed one, that would now be worth 900 crowns, he was then indeed very lean, which I divided amongst the Italian and French companies, causing all the oil to be taken out of the lamps in the churches, which I likewise divided amongst the soldiers, who with mallows and nettles boiled this flesh and oil, and so sustained themselves till Sunday morning, when not a man amongst us at our going out had eaten one bit of anything in the world.

The Marquis also caused four *borachios* of wine to be brought for me, together with five or six loaves of white bread, and so soon as we came to Arbiarotta we halted, and under some sallows that were by the riverside ate our bread. I gave two of my bottles of wine to the Sienese, the other two we drank ourselves, each one a little, and afterwards went on our way directly towards Montalcino, when so soon as we came to Bonconvent, Signor Gabrio made the foot convoy to return. But till he saw Monsieur de Strozzi, who came out with a party of horse to meet us, would himself never leave us, and then he bade me farewell, taking me in his arms, as he did Signor Cornelio, the Count de Caiazzo, and all our captains, for he was a very worthy gentleman and a brave soldier as any they had in their camp.

So soon as we came up to Monsieur de Strozzi, we embraced without being able either of us to utter one word; neither am I able to say which of us had his heart the most full of the remembrances of our fortunes. In this manner then, nothing but skin and bone, and more like ghosts than men, we arrived at Montalcino, which was upon Sunday, and all Monday and Tuesday we were shut up with the treasurers and comptrollers, to examine and state our accounts and to see what I had borrowed to lend the soldiers, where we found that the King was four months to us in arrear, and Monsieur de Strozzi gave me 500 crowns of his own money to carry me into France. I dare swear he had not half so much more left, for Signor Cornelio and I had been constrained to borrow 400 crowns to disengage his great order, which he had pawned to a Jew at the beginning when he came to Siena. I would afterwards have restored it to him, and namely at Thionville, though he would never receive it but laughed at me. And this was the end of the siege.

Monluc's heroic defence of Siena firmly established his reputation. He was appointed Governor of Moncalvo in Piedmont, and from 1555 to 1558 was involved in further campaigns there and in Tuscany. Early in 1558, however, his patron the Duke of Guise had taken Calais, and was now preparing for an assault upon the key Imperialist stronghold of Thionville on the Moselle. Monluc wished to join him for this exploit: in May he left Italy for the last time, and arrived at the court, then at Crécy-en-Brie

The same day that I went from Cressi [Crécy][1] back to Paris, Monsieur de Guise departed also to go to Metz to execute the enterprise of Tiomville [Thionville]. The King from the time of his return out of Italy had made choice of him for his Lieutenant General throughout his whole kingdom, so that before my coming I found that he had taken the town of Calais and sent back the English to the other side of the sea, together with Guines, and that he was now upon the siege of Thionville. Two days had not passed before the King sent for me to come to him to Crécy without giving me notice what it was about, and I heard that the next morning after I departed from thence the King had caused Monsieur d'Andelot to be arrested about some answer he had made him concerning religion. So soon as I was come the King sent for me into his chamber, where he had with him the Cardinal of Lorraine and two or three others (whom I have forgot, but I think the King of Navarre[2] and Monsieur de Montpensier[3] were there), and there the King told me that I must go to Metz to the Duke of Guise, there to command the foot, of which Monsieur d'Andelot was colonel.[4] I most humbly besought his Majesty not to make me to intermeddle with another man's command, which rather than I would do, I would go serve his Majesty under the Duke of Guise in the

[1] Crécy-en-Brie lies twenty-five miles to the east of Paris: see map, p. 133.

[2] For whom see Appendix I, 'Bourbon, Antoine de'.

[3] Louis II de Bourbon, Duke of Montpensier (1513–82).

[4] D'Andelot (see above, p. 122, n. 1) had been arrested on suspicion of Huguenotism in May 1558.

quality of a private soldier, or else would command his pioneers rather than take upon me this employment. The King then told me that Monsieur de Guise so soon as he had heard of d'Andelot's imprisonment had himself sent to demand me to exercise the said command.

Seeing then I could get nothing by excuses, I told his Majesty that I was not yet cured of a dysentery my disease had left me, and that this was a command which required health and disposition of body to perform it, which were neither of them in me. Whereupon his Majesty told me that he should think this command better discharged by me in a litter than by another in perfect health, and that he did not give it me to exercise for another but that he intended I should have it for ever. To which I made answer that I gave his Majesty most humble thanks for the honour he designed me herein, and made it my most humble request that he would not be displeased if I could not accept it. Whereupon his Majesty said to me these words: 'Let me entreat you to accept it for my sake,' and with that the Cardinal reproved me, saying 'You dispute it too long with his Majesty, 'tis too much contested with your master.' To which I replied that I did not dispute it out of any disaffection to his Majesty's service, nor that I was unwilling to serve under the Duke of Guise, I having upon my first coming to Paris laid out money to buy me some tents and other equipage in order to my attendance upon him, having engaged myself before at Rome so to do; but only upon the account of my incapacity in that posture of health wherein I then was. His Majesty then told me that there was no more to be said and that I must go, after which I had no more to say. And I fancy the King of Navarre and Monsieur de Montpensier both fell upon me to persuade me to accept of this command, forasmuch as I remember the King said to me: 'There is no more excuse, for you see all the world is against you.' And thereupon he commanded the Cardinal to order me another thousand crowns towards my equipage, which he presently did. I then returned to Paris, where I stayed but two days to provide myself of such things as I wanted, and so went away to the Duke of Guise to Metz.

I found him just mounting to horse to go to discover Thionville, but he would not suffer me to go along with him by reason of my long journey, and to speak the truth I was not very well; and the same night he returned and told me that if God would permit us to take that place, there was honour to be got. He was always wont when disposed to be merry to call me '*mouseigne*',[1] and smiling then said to me 'Courage, *mouseigne*, I hope we shall carry it.' And in the morning we departed, for he had all his tackle ready. I must needs say one thing with truth and without flattery, that he was one of the most diligent generals that I had served of eighteen under whom I had the honour to bear arms for his Majesty's service. And yet he had one fault, which was that he would write almost everything with his own hand and would not trust to any secretary he had. I will not say this was ill done, but it rendered him a little slow, and affairs of war require so prompt a diligence that a quarter of an hour's delay sometimes endangers the success of the greatest enterprise. One day I came from the trenches to demand of him four German ensigns to reinforce our guards, for we began to approach very near to the town; and because the artillery from the walls had forced him from his first quarter, he was lodged in a little low house which had one little chamber only, the window whereof was just over the door. I there met with Monsieur de Bourdillon,[2] who was since Marshal of France, whom I asked where the Duke was. He told me he was writing. 'The Devil,' said I, 'take all these writings for me, it seems he has a mind to save his secretaries a labour. 'Tis pity he was not a clerk of the Parlement of Paris, for he would have got more money than du Tillet[3] and all the rest of them put together.'

Monsieur Bourdillon was ready to die with laughing, because he knew (which I dreamt not on) that the Duke heard every word I said and therefore egged me on still to descant more upon this clerk; when presently Monsieur de Guise came out laughing and said, 'How now, *mouseigne*, what do you think I should have made a good clerk?' But in my life I was never so out of countenance, and was furiously angry with Monsieur de Bourdillon for having made me talk at that rate, though the Duke laughed at it only and gave me Count Rocquendolf [Roggendorf] with four ensigns. But to return to what I was saying of his diligence, there was not anyone who did not acknowledge him for one of the most vigilant and diligent generals of our times, and withal a man of so great judgment in deliberation that he having delivered his opinion and advice, a better was not to be expected. As to the rest, a prince so discreet, affable and familiar that there was not a man in his army who would not cheerfully run all hazards for the least word of

[1] The Gascon form of '*monseigneur*'.

[2] Imbert de la Platière, Seigneur de Bourdillon (*c.* 1500–67), Marshal of France in 1562.

[3] Jean du Tillet, Clerk of the Parlement of Paris.

his mouth; so great a dexterity he had in gaining hearts. Only his dispatches took up a little too much of his time, I think because he durst not trust his secretaries, a sort of men that do us a great deal of mischief and 'tis very rare to find out one that is faithful.

With Monluc commanding the French infantry, Guise began the siege of Thionville, June 1558

He besieged the town then on that side beyond the river, the river being between,[1] which he caused to be sounded to try if it was not very deep, by five or six soldiers that I brought with me. We were not above five or six with him, of which number were Monsieur de Bourdillon and Monsieur d'Estrée [d'Estrées],[2] and we found that some of the soldiers had water up to the codpiece and others to the girdle. I then told him that in case this was the weakest side, he ought not to defer making his battery, for I doubted not to make the soldiers pass over to the assault and that I myself would lead them the way. The night following we planted gabions upon the bank of the river, and in the morning by break of day the artillery began to thunder against the tower,[3] which was opened on the left hand towards a ravelin that flanked the said tower, as also was a little turret betwixt the great tower and the ravelin. This was all that could be done at that place.

The enemy planted ten or twelve great pieces of cannon just over against our artillery, and about eleven of the clock in the morning began to make a counter-battery, with which before two o'clock in the afternoon they had beaten all our gabions to pieces, excepting one and the half of another, behind which ten or a dozen of us that were there were squat with our bellies close to the ground. For all the soldiers and pioneers were constrained to quit the post and to go throw themselves behind another trench above sixscore paces behind us. So that durst the enemy have ventured over the water, they might have taken our artillery and at great ease have thrown them into the river. For the soldiers that were retired to the other trench could not have come up to relieve us but at the mercy of their cannon and smaller shot; forasmuch as the river was not above threescore and ten paces over and ran within four foot of the wall. Monsieur le Marquis

---

[1] i.e. to the east of Thionville, on the right bank of the Moselle.

[2] Antoine d'Estrées, Marquis de Coeuvres, later Grand Master of the Artillery.

[3] The Tour-aux-Puces, part of the defences of Thionville.

d'Elboeuf,[1] with fourteen or fifteen gentlemen of the Duke's train, never forsook me of all the while, and so we lay till dark night, that we planted new gabions and double the number, but it was all to no purpose, for we could do no good with our battery against the wall; forasmuch as they had cast up great terraces within so broad that two or three coaches might have gone upon them abreast both in that place and elsewhere quite round the town. In my life I never saw a fortress better fortified than that was.

Monsieur de Guise then called a council, where everyone was of opinion that he should draw off his artillery from that place and lodge all our infantry and Germans on the other side the river, and there to begin his trenches as near as he could to the wall. This being resolved upon, the said Duke caused a bridge in extreme diligence to be presently made, and we passed the river over it, though the planks were not as yet nailed, and encamped in a village about five or six hundred paces distant from the city, situate upon a plain, and so open that a bird could not stir without being seen.[2] And there they plied us with their cannon till they had not left a house standing in the whole village; insomuch that we were constrained to secure ourselves in the cellars under ground. I had pitched my pavilions very cunningly betwixt two walls, but they beat down both walls and pavilions; in my life I never saw a more furious counter-battery.

The night following the Marshal de Strozzi passed the river with Monsieur de Guise and we began to cast up our trenches along this plain, where we lay seven or eight days before we could approach within two hundred paces of the city by reason the nights were short, and by day they did so thunder the trenches that there was no working but by night. The Marshal never stirred from us, unless he went sometimes to his tents (which yet remained on the other side of the water) to shift his clothes, and that not above once in three days. He gave me leave to make the trenches according to my own fancy, for we had at first begun them a little too narrow through the wisdom of an engineer. At every twenty paces I made a back corner, or return, winding sometimes to the left hand and sometimes to the right, which I made so large that there was room for twelve or fifteen soldiers with their arquebuses and halberds. And this I did to the end that should the enemy gain the head of the trench and should leap into it, those in the back corner might fight them, they being much more masters of the

[1] René de Lorraine, Marquis d'Elbeuf (1536–66).
[2] The village of Manom on the left bank of the Moselle.

trench than they who were in the straight line, an invention that both the Marshal [Strozzi] and the Duke did very well approve of.[1]

Monsieur de Guise then told me that I must send to discover what effect our artillery had wrought against the tower and that I must do it by valiant persons. In order whereunto I took with me Captain Sarlabous the younger, Millac, St Estèphe, Cipierre and Captain Monluc my son, and went. So soon as we came near unto the tower we were to pass over certain little bridges the enemy had made, by which to pass over the marsh to the tower, and being come to the tower we found a palisade of posts as thick as a man's thigh, that from the tower went seven or eight paces into the river, and we were to go all along by the palisade in water to the end of it and afterwards on the other side of the palisade to return to the tower. We had made two soldiers bring two pikes along with us. I for my part did not go into the water but all the rest passed the palisade after this manner, and one after another viewed the breach that had been made in the tower, and they put a soldier into it with a pike and found that within the tower there was water up to the armpits; and being the river made a great noise at this place by reason of the palisade, their sentinels never heard us, though the tower was no more than four paces distant from the wall of the town.

This being done we returned and went to give Monsieur de Guise an account of what we had seen, who would not give credit to our discovery, but told me he was certain there was no palisade, and that people who came lately from thence had assured him to the contrary, and that therefore the night following we must discover it better. I was vexed to the blood at this answer but said no more to him but only this, that I conceived the testimony of those captains was sufficient, but seeing he was not satisfied with it, let somebody in the name of God discover it better. To which he made answer that he did not mean I should go myself. 'Neither', said I, 'do I intend it'. The Marshal [Strozzi] knew very well that I was angry, and said to the Sieur Adrian Baillon [Baglione] and to Count Theophile: 'I know Monluc is angry by his answer to the Duke of Guise, and you shall see if he do not go this night to discover after a terrible manner; for I know the complexion of the man.'

This night Monsieur de Guise detained the Marshal with him in his quarters. And so soon as it was night I took four hundred pikes, corslets all, and four hundred arquebusiers, and went to lay the corslets

1 On the use of places of arms see Introduction, p. 17.

upon their bellies upon the ground within a hundred paces of the gate of the city, and I with the four hundred arquebusiers marched directly to the palisade. The captains themselves who had discovered before were as angry at the answer Monsieur de Guise had given them as I, and themselves first passed the palisade. Now I believe the enemy had in the morning perceived that people had passed by the end of the palisade, for we there found a court of guard of twenty or five and twenty men, of which the most part were killed and the rest escaped into the rampire, where our people pursued and entered after them; but the door of the ravelin that went into the town was so narrow that one man only could pass at a time, which was the reason that our men stopped short, for the enemy defended the door. Nevertheless they made shift to dismount and tumble a bastard[1] from the ravelin on our side down to the ground, and being that by the tower our artillery from the other side of the water had beaten down part of the wall so that it was pretty low, we with some pikes that came along with us came to dispute it with them, where the fight continued for above a long hour. Monsieur de Guise, who saw all from the other side of the river, was stark mad at what he saw. But the Marshal who was with him laughed with Sieur Adrian and the Count de Theophile saying, 'Did I not tell you he would make one?'

I had made the soldiers to carry five or six hatchets along with them with which during the time of the fight I caused all the palisade to be cut and pulled up, so that we needed no more to wade the water at our return. Captain St Estèphe was there slain with the ensign of Cipierre and another ensign (but they had not their colours with them, for I had brought none), together with ten or twelve soldiers killed and wounded. Captain Sarlabous is yet living, and several others who can witness that had we taken with us five or six ladders seven or eight foot high only, we had entered the place, for they kept very ill guard on that side and in that place, relying upon the guard they had left without. So that it was a long time before they came to the defence of this post, whilst in the meantime five or six of our soldiers helping one another mounted upon the wall. Had we had ladders to reach from the top of the breach in the wall up to the terrace, I think fortune would have smiled upon us, for they say she favours the bold.

In the morning I sent Captain Sarlabous to give the Duke an account of what we had seen, for I would not go myself, being certain he was very angry. The Marshal was still with him, who laughing

[1] A bastard cannon, shorter in length of barrel than normally.

said, 'Would you have a breach better discovered than by giving an assault? This was a Gascon trick you were not aware of.' The thing that most troubled the Duke of Guise was that word would be sent to the King that we had given an assault and were repulsed, otherwise he had not cared so much. His incredulity and my despite were the loss of a great many good men.

When we had brought up our trench within fifty paces of the tower, one morning by break of day the Marshal would retire to his tent to shift himself, and I also would do the same. Now as our approaches came nearer to the town, I still made my back returns a little longer, to the end that two of them might receive a whole company. I had evermore an opinion that the enemy would make a sally upon us, but it would never sink into the Marshal's head, for he would always say, 'Would you have them such mad men as to make a sally to lose their soldiers, never any men of sense did such a ridiculous thing.' To which I made answer, 'Why should they not sally? For in the first place they are able from the walls to secure their men's retreat, on the other side they are in the town twelve ensigns of foot, four hundred Spaniards, choice men picked out of all the Spanish companies, and a good chief to head them, which is Joan Gaytan [Juan Gaetano], a man they esteem above all the captains they have, and a hundred horse besides, and the town would be sufficiently defended with half the forces they are within.' I could not for all this make him understand it. I know not why, for the reason of war I am sure was on my side.

This very morning I had placed Captain Lago the elder and his company in two of the long back returns on the right hand, whom I caused to enter before day, that the enemy might not perceive them, so that it was, as a man may say, a kind of ambuscado. The captains who mounted the guard had in charge that in case the enemy should make a sally and attack the head of the trenches, they should put themselves into the field and run to charge them in the flank, and those at the head of the trench had likewise order that in case they should attack the returns, they should likewise leap out of the trench to assault them in the flank also. We had every night four German ensigns quartered there where we began our trench, to assist us in time of need, but what regiment it was that was that night upon the guard I cannot remember; and before the Marshal and I were got to the end of the trenches it began to be fair broad day.

The Marshal trifled the time a little talking with a German captain and also to stay for a horse, which I had sent for to lend him to pass over the bridge to his tents, being at a stone cross close by the village. The horse I had lent him came, when, as my footman was alighting, on a sudden we heard a mighty noise and saw the enemy fighting with our men at the head of the trench and leaping headlong into the trenches, and had it not been for those back returns, had doubtless gained them from us. With them there sallied out also fifty or three-score horse. Captain Lago did there approve himself to be a valiant and a prudent man, for he cried to his lieutenant in the return behind him to run with his pikes charged full drive upon the horse, whilst he himself ran upon the enemy's flank, who were disputing the head of the trenches. Seeing this, I mounted upon the horse, whilst the Marshal remained at the cross, spectator of the whole action, nor ever stayed till I came up to our own men who were at it pell-mell with the enemy; who so soon as Lago came up to them would have retired, when our people leapt out of the trenches and flew upon them, and so we pursued them wounding and killing up to the very tower on the right hand.

I then presently sent back the horse to the Marshal, who found Monsieur de Guise and all the gentlemen that were quartered near him on horseback coming to relieve us. But he told them there was no need, for that he had seen all the fight and the victory was ours. As we retired from the pursuit, all the remainder of their arquebusiers were upon the walls and fired so round upon our retreat that it seemed as if it had been only a volley in compliment to us. I was alone on horse-back in the middle of our men, and therefore let anyone judge whether God did not by miracle preserve me in such a shower of arquebus shot, considering what a fair mark they had of me. The captains cried out to me to gallop off, though I would never leave them but came along with them to the edge of the trenches, where I alighted and presently delivered the horse to my lackey to carry him to the Marshal as I said before, and with the rest threw myself into the trenches, where I found a captain and a lieutenant of ours left dead upon the place. I do not remember their names (for they were French and I was but lately come to command in the army), with twelve or fourteen, what of theirs and ours dead in the trenches. And yet notwithstanding the brave volley they gave us from the walls, we had not above ten men hurt. And thus their sally did not so much endamage us by a great deal as it did themselves.

You may here captains take a good example concerning trenches and the order I took for the sally the enemy might make, with the advantage we had by it. Never believe that the defendants have need of men and therefore will be loath to attempt to force your trenches. 'Tis true if you sleep in them you will be surprised. Take notice also when you make your trenches to make them high and sloping and that they have back returns, or corners capable of lodging men, for they are as forts to repel an enemy. There was now no more talk of Monsieur de Guise his being angry with me, the Marshal and he holding no other discourse all dinner time but of the fight, and principally of the providence and circumspection wherewith I had proceeded, saying that it would be a hard thing ever to surprise me. And also in truth I walked whilst others slept, without fearing either heat or cold. I was inured to hardship, which all young gentlemen who will advance themselves by arms ought to study betimes and learn to suffer, that when they shall wax old it may not be altogether intolerable; but old age being once wholly come, Goodnight Godson.

Within two or three nights after we brought up our trench to the foot of the great tower. Whereupon Monsieur de Guise brought his miners to try if the tower was to be mined, and therefore fell to piercing the wall within two or three foot of the ground, when so soon as the enemy heard what we were about, they began to make casemates within the tower so that their casemates answered to our hole. We were three nights about piercing the wall; and at the same time that our miners were picking without, the enemy were picking within at their loopholes. Every night Monsieur de Guise sent us four gentlemen to help us to watch, and I remember that one night Monsieur de Monpezat [Montpezat][1] and Monsieur de Randan[2] came to lie there. So soon as the whole was almost through, Monsieur de Guise caused a cannon to be brought me to help to pierce the wall, for he knew very well that the picking we heard was about casemates, and that so soon as ever the wall should be pierced through, they would shoot at us from them. The day before the cannon was brought, the Marshal de Strozzi was gone to his tents on the other side the water to refresh himself and to shift both his shirt and his clothes, for we were all dirt.

Monsieur de Guise from the time that the miners began to work

---

[1] Melchior des Prez, Sieur de Montpezat (d. 1572), cavalry commander, later Ambassador to Germany.

[2] Charles de la Rochefoucauld, Comte de Randan (d. 1562), later Colonel-General of Infantry.

at the wall caused a great many pioneers to come and to begin a traverse of earth and bavins close adjoining to the tower, making them to leave a little path, at which they wrought so hard that as the hole was pierced, the traverse was also brought to perfection. The enemy had laid a great number of planks upon the tower in manner of a trench, and the night before we gave the assault, going up by the little path of the traverse and with the help of some ladders, we took away the planks of their trench from the top of the tower, which did us more harm than good. For when the planks were taken away the great platform which was close by the tower, there being only five or six paces betwixt them, so soon as any of us popped up a head, discovered us.

Now as I have already said the Marshal was only gone to shift himself, but Monsieur de Guise made him stay supper with him, and with great importunity kept him all that night, to his great misfortune. For Monsieur de Guise detained him the next morning to see where they should plant four culverins on that side where they were to play into the enemy's defences, when we should the next day give the assault. The Marshal several times begged of him to give him leave to return, telling him that should any business befall me that night, he should be extremely troubled if he should not be there. At last the said Marshal, to his great grief, was constrained to stay, and so much contrary to his mind that so soon as he was retired into his tent he asked the Sieur Adrian Baglione and Count Theophile if they had the word to pass through the Germans; for as for our people he did not care and could pass well enough without. They told him they had none, whereupon he said to them these words: 'It runs in my head that Monsieur de Monluc will this night have something to do, and that the enemy will come to attack him over the counterscarp of the ditch of the town, which should it so fall out, it would trouble me the longest day I have to live, that I was not there.'

To which they made answer that he ought not to fancy any such thing, for that I had placed a court of guard of four hundred men within twenty paces of the gate of the city, which they must of necessity fight withal before they could come to me. To which he replied, 'I know not what it is, but I am strangely possessed with an opinion that some misfortune will happen this night.' They endeavoured all they could to put this conceit out of his head, for the Sieur Adrian had no mind to repass the river and go to lie all night at the tower, he having been lately very sick and not yet perfectly recovered. For had they told him as they afterwards told me, that he might have passed through the German guards well enough without the word, being as well known to all the German officers as to those of our own nation, he would have gone, what promise soever he had made to the Duke of Guise to the contrary. But when the hour is come, I think God will have it so that death shall follow and 'tis to no purpose for a man to fly or to hide himself. He moreover said to them these words: 'Monsieur de Monluc is not yet well known to the King and Queen, although the King loves him very well; but if I escape from this siege I will make both the King and the Queen understand his worth.'[1] And the next day, when he was dead, the Sieur Adrian and Count Theophile told me that I had lost the best friend I had in the world, which I easily believed and do still believe it, and might well say that having lost the Duke of Ferrara[2] and him, I had lost the two best friends I had in Italy and France. He was killed the next day, as he was looking and consulting with Monsieur de Guise where to place the four culverins. Before dinner he had been looking long, but Monsieur de Guise would needs return again in the afternoon to consider of it better, having Monsieur de Salcedo with them. He was slain by a musket shot from a little bulwark that was at a corner of the town, pointing along by the river towards Metz. Thus when a man's hour is once come, he cannot avoid it. This poor lord had passed through above six thousand cannon and above fifty thousand arquebus shot which could not all kill him, and yet this accursed musket shot could do it at the distance of above five hundred paces, Monsieur de Guise being close by him. The King there lost a good servant, and as valiant a man died as any was in France.

Two hours after, Monsieur de Guise came to the tower, but gave express charge that no-one should speak a word of his death, when seeing the Sieur Adrian and Count Theophile I asked them where he was, to which they made answer that the last night he had not been very well but that tonight he would come to me. But perceiving Monsieur de Guise to be sad and all those who were with him very grave, my heart misgave me that something was amiss. When Monsieur de Guise being returned and having left Monsieur de Bourdillon with me in the Marshal's stead, I earnestly entreated him to tell me what was become of Monsieur de Strozzi; who made

[1] Strozzi was a favourite of the Queen, Catherine de Medici.

[2] Ercole II d'Este, Duke of Ferrara, had been aided by Monluc and had rewarded him handsomely. He died in October 1559.

answer, 'Why, I will tell you, and also if you know it not today, you will know it tomorrow.' And thereupon gave me the relation of his death, and how Monsieur de Guise had forbid them to tell me, fearing my grief would hinder me the next day from performing my duty in the fight. To which I replied that it was true, no man under Heaven was more afflicted for his death than I was, yet that I would endeavour to forget him for that night, and the day following, but it should be to lament him ever after whilst I had an hour to breathe. Count Theophile and the Sieur Adrian stayed with me all this night, during which we passed together our lamentations.

By break of day we began to play our cannon at the hole. Monsieur de Guise had caused an engine of planks[1] above a foot thick to be made to put before the cannon so soon as it had fired, to the end that the enemy from their loop-holes might not kill our cannoneers. At the foot of this engine there were two little wheels for it to move upon and it was drawn with a little cord which so covered the muzzle of the cannon that no arquebus shot could pierce it. After this manner we made twenty shot at this hole, which we broke through and made so wide that a man might easily pass through. But the cannon could do no hurt to their casemates, forasmuch as they were a little on the right hand and no man could approach the hole without being killed or wounded. Monsieur de Guise then sent me order that I should try to lodge three or four hundred men betwixt the tower and the ravelin and that he would to that purpose send me gabions and pioneers. He had caused mantelets to be made, to place from the great tower to the river, which might be some seven or eight paces, and from thence our arquebusiers shot at those who appeared upon the curtain; our ensigns planting themselves all along by the wall from the tower to the ravelin. Those upon the platform saw all along by the curtain, and ours who were by this ravelin on that side by the hole fired at them, whilst I made them shoot from behind the mantelets. Monsieur de Nevers,[2] the father of these three daughters now living, was come thither and stood by our traverse that was at the foot of the great tower, and Monsieur de Guise was on the other side of the river by the artillery. Poton, Seneschal of Agenois, commanded one of the four culverins, who made very brave shots and did us great service, for he played

[1] A mantelet. See Appendix II, Glossary of Military Terms.

[2] François de Clèves, Duke of Nevers (1516–62), Governor of Champagne: his three daughters, all living in 1570, married the Prince of Mantua, the Duke of Guise, and the Prince of Condé respectively.

continually upon the top of the curtain and the platform at those who showed themselves to shoot at our people below, and this continued four or five hours at least.

Monsieur de Guise then sent to me by Monsieur de Cipierre to try if we could by any means place the gabions he had sent me betwixt the wall and the hole, but all those who presented themselves to plant the gabions were either killed or hurt. I then bethought myself to put a hundred or sixscore pioneers into the water under the bank of the river, to cast up a trench all along by the waterside towards the ravelin. Monsieur de Cipierre saw the great difficulty and impossibility there was in executing the Duke's command, and found Captain La Bordezière [Bourdaisière] dead and his ensign wounded who died after. You could have seen nothing but wounded men carrying off to be dressed, and the mantelets shattered all to pieces with stones, so that we lay all open shooting at one another as one shoots at a mark. I had ordered our affairs pretty well, for I had placed most of the arque-busiers by hundreds, so that as one hundred had spent all their powder, another hundred came to supply their rooms, and still all the danger and mischief fell where I was; for as well the culverins that played from the other side of the river, as those men of ours that shot openly and without shelter, kept the enemy in such awe that not one durst pop up his head to shoot at our people who were under the wall below, but played continually upon us who were almost in a level right over against them.

Monsieur de Bourdillon then at the bidding of Monsieur de Nevers, came and caught me by the arms behind and hauled me above six paces backwards, saying, 'What will you do man, in the name of God, what do you intend to do, do you not see that if you be killed all this labour's lost, and that the soldiers will be discouraged?' To which, disengaging myself from him, I replied, 'And do you not also see, that if I be not with the soldiers, they will abandon this post and the enemy will kill all those that are under the wall? For then they will stand up at their ease and shoot plumb down upon them.' Monsieur de Nevers then called to me also from the other side of the hole to make me retire; which nevertheless I would not do, but said to Monsieur de Bourdillon these words: 'What God will do with me this day is already determined, I cannot avoid it, and if this place be appointed for my grave, it is in vain to shun my destiny.' And so, without saying any more to him, I returned back to the place from whence he had drawn me.

On a sudden I bethought myself of an enterprise, bidding Captain Volumat to take six arquebusiers and two halberds, and go place himself behind a canton of the wall that remained of the tower when it was beaten down, and there try if suddenly leaping out from behind this wall he could not throw himself headlong upon the casemates; a design grounded upon my belief that they could not be covered with anything but planks, for they made them after the same manner that we made the hole, or else that they were totally open. But be it how it would, I entreated him without dispute to throw himself upon them, assuring him that I would go make another captain fall on by the path of the traverse which led up to the top of the tower, and that both of them at the same time should throw themselves headlong upon the casemates. I then called to me a French captain (I do not remember his name) and said to him in the presence of Monsieur de Nevers and Monsieur de Bourdillon the same things I had said to Captain Volumat, and that so soon as ever he should be up, without pausing upon the matter, he should throw himself upon the casemates, desiring Monsieur de Nevers and Monsieur de Bourdillon to encourage the soldiers to follow this captain whilst I went to Captain Volumat to do the same. But so soon as ever this poor captain thrust up his head, he was killed by those of the great platform, and another after him, so that they fell dead betwixt the legs of Monsieur de Nevers and Monsieur de Bourdillon. I then cried out to Captain Volumat, being some fifteen paces from one another, that the captain who fell on by the traverse was already upon the top of the tower (to beget in him an emulation, which ordinarily sharpens the noblest courages). Whereupon the said Captain Volumat started up, for before he was kneeled down behind the canton, and ran up to the brink of the wall.

Now there was another wall betwixt the casemates and the corner of the tower, so that although he should leap into the first only he was never the nearer. Yet so it was that this very thing was cause of the winning of the place, for the casemates was all open and very low, so that so soon as ever they saw Captain Volumat upon the top making show as if he would leap in betwixt the two walls, they acquitted the casemates and fled away along by the curtain of the wall and the terrace, betwixt which and the wall five or six men might march abreast. And then a soldier of Captain Volumat's at two leaps was with me, telling me in great haste that the enemy had abandoned the casemate. Whereupon I immediately ran up to the side of the hole, and taking the soldier by the arm cried to him, 'Leap in, soldier, leap in,

and I will give thee twenty crowns.' But he told me flatly he would
not do it, for that he should certainly be killed, and thereupon
struggled with all the force he had to get away from me. My son
Captain Monluc, and those captains I named before, who always used
to bear me company, were behind me, at whom I began to swear and
curse that they did not help me to truss this gallant; when immediately
we thrust him in with his head forwards and made him bold in spite
of his teeth, and seeing they shot no more from the casemates we put
in two arquebusiers more, partly with their consent and partly by
force, first taking from them their flasks and their matches, for there
was water within up to the armpits.

And immediately after Captain Monluc leapt in, then the Captains
Cosseil, La Motte, Castel-Segrat, and the Aussillons, having all targets,
took the leap to save my son, and three or four arquebusiers after
them, when so soon as I saw they were nine or ten I cried out to them,
'Courage comrades, now show yourselves true Gascon soldiers and
fall upon the casemates.' Which they did, whilst the enemy upon the
terrace threw stones at their own people to make them return to the
casemates. And as Captain Monluc came to the door of the said casemates he met with the enemy, who would have re-entered into it but
an arquebusier of ours killed the chief of them, who was armed with
a mail covered over with green velvet, a gilt morion upon his head
and a damasked halberd in his hand. Two others were also killed by
hand and then our people leapt into the casemate and called out to me
through the hole, 'Succours, succours, we are in the casemate.'
Monsieur de Nevers then and Monsieur de Bourdillon helped me in
all haste to put more soldiers in. We took their flasks and their fire,
and so soon as they were in the water they took them again in their
hands and passed over throwing themselves into the casemates; and
ever after that time Monsieur de Nevers called me his Captain so long
as he lived, saying he had there served under me in the quality of a
private soldier.

We had there two captains of the garrison of Metz called le Baron
d'Anglure and Valenville [Vallainville], who at my request had obtained leave of Monsieur de Guise to be at the assault with five and
twenty arquebusiers each, whom I had all this while kept under the
traverse, so that as yet they had not spent one shot. I called them and
they were with me at a leap and threw themselves into the hole, and
their soldiers followed after, when as fast as they entered I made them
run to the door of the casemate and to enter into it. The door was

little and very low and the enemy durst not deliver their shot plumb down, because our men who were all along by the wall would see them as soon as they put up their heads, as also would those who were there where I had been. But they tumbled down a great quantity of stones, for all which our people desisted not from going in and out of the casemate as occasion required. And as the soldiers of the Baron d'Anglure and Vallainville entered the casemate, I made those come out who had gained it before, the place not being capable to contain above forty or fifty persons.

Now as God would have it, and to our great good fortune, the defendants could not agree amongst themselves about the defence of the casemates; for the Spaniards who were in the town would keep them but the Flemings would not suffer it, and the governor would that some of his own company should defend them. For which he lay a long time in prison, and the King of Spain would have put him to death, the Spaniards accusing him that he had put in corrupted people purposely to lose the place. The governor defended himself, saying that he had seen Juan Gaetano and his Spaniards behave themselves so ill that he durst not trust them with the defence of the casemate, and so they accused one another. All which we knew from the Constable and the Marshal de St André at their return out of prison, who left this governor still a prisoner. I have in my time observed the Spaniards to be severe punishers of those who by cowardice or treachery have lost or surrendered places, and it were well and prudently done if all princes would punish such as commit so important offences, at least by degradation from arms, which is worse then death. But then they ought to be censured without prejudice or passion; for I have known a man accused by another who could not himself have done better.

But to return to our siege, Monsieur de Guise being with the culverins and making them continually to shoot at the enemy's defences, perceived that the soldiers of the trenches run straight up to the tower (which were the two captains, Anglure and Vallainville, that I had called up to me) and Lunebourg (Colonel of a regiment of Germans, who was at the farthest end of the trench, to whom I had sent to send me a hundred of his arquebusiers in all haste, for ours had spent all their powder) came also running himself with the hundred arquebusiers and a hundred pikes to me to the tower; whom Monsieur de Guise seeing to run after this manner, and seeing the others that were by the tower run to the hole, he cried out (as they told me afterwards) 'O good God the tower is taken, do you not see how everyone

runs to the place?' Which having said he immediately mounted a bay
curtal[1] he had ready by him and ran full speed to pass the bridge,
galloping all the way till he came to the trenches.

So soon as I saw that Anglure and Vallainville were in the tower I
spoke to a gentleman that stood by, and said: 'Run to Monsieur de
Guise and carry him news that the tower is taken, and that now I
think he will take Thionville, which till now I did never believe.' The
gentleman ran as fast as he could and met him just as he was entering
the trenches, where he said to him, 'Sir, Monsieur de Monluc sends
you word that the tower is taken,' who still galloping on made
answer, 'I have seen all my friend, I have seen all,' and some fifty or
threescore paces from the tower alighted, and leaving his horse came
running to us on foot: when so soon as he came, I began to smile upon
him and said, 'O sir, I now think you will take Thionville. *Mas bous
hazets trop bon mercat de nostre pet et de bost mouseigne'.*[2] Whereupon he
threw his arms about my neck and said, 'I now see, *mouseigne*, that the
old proverb is true, that a good horse will never tire.'

Now Lunebourg was already got in, and fifteen or sixteen Germans,
and the rest were entering in file, when Monsieur de Guise also put
himself into it and by the little door entered the casemate, and so soon
as he was in called to me through a loophole that I should put him
some pioneers into the tower to beat down the casemates and that I
should see that no more soldiers entered, they being already so many
that they began to be crowded. I then put pioneers into the tower, who
presently fell to breaking the wall of the casemate, when the Germans
seeing the rascals lazy at their work, themselves took the picks and fell
to cutting the wall. Monsieur de Guise then sent out Lunebourg to
look that no more entered into the tower, telling him that he would
see that they should ply their work in the casemates, as they also did;
and so well that in less than half an hour all the casemates were overturned into the water that was in the tower, the ruins whereof drank
it all up, and then we had room enough and everyone entered that
would. And then Monsieur de Guise came out as he also made the
Germans to do, and to return to their post, and then I drew off
Captain Sarlabous and all his companions who was along by the
curtain and under the ravelin and put them into the trenches.

Now so soon as the enemy saw the tower lost, they shot no more
so smartly as before and we very well perceived them to be down in

[1] Short-tailed horse.

[2] Gascon: 'But you sell our skin and your *mouseigne* too cheaply.'

the mouth. The English miners the Duke of Guise had had never stirred from me of all this while, and Monsieur de Guise before he came out of the tower had consulted with them whereabouts to begin the mines, and found that it was under the great platform, marking the places where they were to be made, and so went back with Monsieur de Guise, who said to me, '*Mouseigne*, I will gallop home to my quarters to send the King word of the taking of the tower, and assure yourself Monsieur de Monluc, I will not conceal from him the brave service you have performed at this siege. I will send the miners back to you at night, and I pray appoint some gentlemen to be continually with them that by them they may send you word what they want.' And so he went away to dispatch a courier to the King, for these great ones think the time long if news do not fly.

His Majesty had the day before made them read the prophesies of Nostradamus[1] and found for the next day 'Good news for the King'. People may say that these are fopperies and idle things, but I have seen many of his predictions come to pass. The tower was taken betwixt four and five o'clock in the afternoon, and we had disputed it from ten of the clock in the morning, so that we made account the fight lasted betwixt six and seven hours. This fight and that of the fort Camollia at Siena were the longest and the most dangerous wherein battle or no battle I have ever been, for upon my word it was very hot and many were left dead upon the place.

In the beginning of the night the miners came and I myself went with them to see them begin. Of all night long I never slept, because seeing them ply their work so well I would not that anything should be wanting, but immediately be brought them, that they might not lose a quarter of an hour for want of materials. So that by break of day they had perfected two mines and charged them with powder ready to be sprung, and the third they made account would be perfected by ten of the clock: wherein my presence served not a little to the advancement of the work, neither indeed had I any more mind to sleep than to dance.

Monsieur de Nevers and Monsieur de Bourdillon were gone back overnight with Monsieur de Guise and returned the next day by sunrise; and at eight of the clock the said Sieur de Nevers caused his dinner to be brought. When, as we were eating upon three drumheads, upon which his people had laid the cloth, sitting upon three

---

[1] Michael Nostradamus (1503–66), celebrated astrologer, published part of his series of predictions, the *Centuries*, in this year (1558).

others, we had scarce drank each of us a draught of wine, the sentinels came to tell me that a trumpet from a canton of the town sounded a parley. Whereupon I started up and delivering the drum I sat upon to his master, bade him go answer the parley. The drum presently returned and brought me word that the trumpet entreated me, knowing I commanded there, to send word to Monsieur de Guise that they desired to parley; which so soon as Monsieur de Nevers and Monsieur de Bourdillon heard they gave over eating, and mounting to horse galloped away to the Duke's quarters, to carry him the news. The Duke then sent away a trumpet of his own, by whom they sent word that if Monsieur de Guise would please to send four gentlemen to parley, they would deliver him four others in hostage. Whereupon the Duke sent thither Monsieur de La Brosse, Monsieur de Bourdillon or else Monsieur de Tavannes, Esclabolle [d'Esclavolles], and another, but whom I have forgot. They capitulated to march out with what money they could carry about them, and (not to lie) I remember nothing of the other articles. As indeed I never used much to trouble myself with these scribble-scrawls, having enough to do to provide that nobody might be unseasonably slain during the time of the treaty, as it oft falls out.

But the next day they marched out, and I dare boldly say that of four parts three were wounded, and almost all in the head, which was done when they stood up to shoot at us there where I had planted my arquebusiers. For they could not shoot at those who were under the wall but they must discover themselves from the girdle upwards, and all their harm came from those of ours who were under the ravelin and those I commanded where we shot point-blank. The same night that the capitulation was signed, Monsieur de Guise dispatched away Monsieur de La Fresne, who before he went came to take his leave of me on horseback, asking me if I would command him any service to the King, to which I made answer that he himself had seen how all things had passed, and that I had so much confidence in Monsieur de Guise that he would not conceal my service from the King; who thereupon told me that he had express charge to give his Majesty a particular relation of the fight and that amongst other things, the Duke had commanded him to tell the King that three men had been the cause of the taking of Thionville, of which I was one, and that his Majesty ought to acknowledge my service. And I perceived afterwards that he had done me right to the King, for he brought me back letters from His Majesty full of very obliging expressions, of which one among the rest was, that he would never forget the service I had done him. I shall not I hope deprive other men of their due honour, relating what I did myself. I believe the historians who write of none but princes and great persons will speak enough, and pass over in silence those of a more moderate stature.

Thionville had fallen on 22 June 1558. Shortly afterwards Monluc captured Arlon, a small town close by, while his commander slept. Following these successes the army, 40,000 strong, is reviewed by Henry II at Pierrepont on a hot and dusty August day, and Monluc provides dinner for the Duke of Guise and the Duke of Saxony

Monsieur de Guise who had given order that no-one should disturb him but let him that night sleep his fill, knew nothing of all this till break of day; that asking if the artillery had begun to play they told him the town was already taken, from about midnight, and the artillery returned back to its place: which made him make the sign of the cross, saying 'This is quick work,' when presently making himself ready and mounting to horse he came up to us. Now by misfortune the fire had taken in two or three houses by reason of some powder that was found in them, which in removing thence accidentally took fire and burnt four or five soldiers, so that the town being almost full of flax ready dressed for spinning and the wind very high, no so good means could be used but that above half the town was reduced to ashes, by reason whereof the soldiers did not get so much as otherwise they had done.

The next day Monsieur de Guise marched away with all his army and never stayed till he came to Pierrepont,[1] where himself and all the gentlemen of his train lodged in the town, which was very large, whilst we encamped without on both sides the river; and there it was that the Swiss came to us, and John William Duke of Saxony, who brought a great and very brave troop of reiters along with him and, if I mistake not, a regiment of Germans also. The King himself likewise came and lay at Marché [Marchais], a house belonging to the Cardinal of Lorraine, which altogether made up the greatest and the bravest army that I think ever King of France had, for when the King would see them all drawn into battalia, they took up above a league and a

---

[1] Aisne, arrondisement of Laon: on the river La Souche. In this area the Guise family were dominant.

half in length, and when the van began to march to go back to the rear and to return back to the front took up three hours' time.

Two hours before day Messieurs de Bourdillon and de Tavannes, field marshals, came to the place assigned for the rendezvouz, where as we came they still drew us up, and before all the army was in battalia it was above eight hours and was excessively hot. Monsieur de Guise came himself by break of day and helped to put the army into battalia. I with my French foot was placed betwixt the Swiss and a battalion of Germans, where as Monsieur de Guise passed by the head of our battalion he said, 'Would to God we had some good fellow here with a bottle of wine and a crust of bread, that I might drink a glass or two, for I shall not have time to go dine at Pierrepont and be back again before the King comes.' Whereupon I said to him, 'Sir, will you please to dine with me at my tents?' (which was not above an arquebus shot off) 'I will give you very good French and Gascon wine and a whole covey of partridges.' 'Yes *mouseigne*,' said he, 'but they will be garlic and onions.' To which I made answer that they should neither be the one nor the other, but that I would give him as good a dinner as if he was in his own quarters, and wine as cool as he could desire, and moreover Gascon wine, and admirable good water. 'Are you in earnest *mouseigne*?' said he. 'Yes upon my faith am I,' said I. 'Why then', said he, 'I would willingly come, but I cannot leave the Duke of Saxony.' 'Why sir,' said I, 'in the name of God bring the Duke of Saxony and who you please.' 'Aye, but,' said he, 'the Duke will not come without his captains.' 'Why,' said I, 'bring his captains too, I have belly-timber for you all.' Now I had overnight promised Messieurs de Bourdillon and de Tavannes to treat them at dinner, after they had drawn the army up in battalia. But they could not come by reason that part of the cavalry, who were quartered a great way off, were not yet come up; and on the other side, I had one of the best providores in the army.

Monsieur de Guise then went to find out the Duke of Saxony and his captains and I sent in all haste to my steward to get all things ready. My people had made a cellar in the earth where the wine and the water was as cool as ice; and by good fortune I had got a great many partridges, quails, turkeys, leverets and all that could be desired wherewith to make a noble feast, with baked meats and tarts. For I knew that Messieurs de Bourdillon and de Tavannes would not come alone and I had a mind to entertain them very well, they being both of them very good friends of mine. They were so well treated that Monsieur de Guise asking the Duke of Saxony by his interpreter what he thought of the French colonel, and whether or no he had not treated them well and given them good wine, the Duke made answer that if the King himself had treated them, he could not have done it better, nor have given them better nor cooler wine. The Duke of Saxony's captains spared it not but drank freely to our French captains that I had brought along with me, neither though Messieurs de Bourdillon and de Tavannes had also come had I been surprised, for next to the Duke de Guise his own table, there was not one in the whole army longer or better furnished than mine: a way that I have always used in what command soever I had been, being willing thereby to honour the employments I have had from my masters, to increase my expense; and have always observed such as have lived after this manner to be in greater reputation and better followed than others; for such a gentleman may be, and of a good family, that sometimes knows not where to dine, and knowing where a good table is kept will be glad to be there, who if he follow you at your table will follow you anywhere else, if he have never so little good blood or breeding in him.

But to return to my guests; so soon as they rose from table Monsieur de Guise asked me what laundress I had that kept my table linen so white, to which I made answer that they were two men I had that did it. 'Believe me,' said he, 'you are served like a prince;' and thereupon entertained the Duke of Saxony upon that subject, speaking better things of me than I deserved. Whereupon I took occasion to tell him that he would do well to persuade the King to give me money to buy silver vessel, that another time, when he and the Duke of Saxony would do me the honour to come eat in my pavilions, I might serve them according to their quality. Monsieur de Guise told the Duke of Saxony what I said, who made answer that he would tell the King; when being about to mount to horse to return to the camp, word was brought that the King was upon his way from Marchais and coming to the camp. Whereupon they two went out to meet him and we returned everyone to his place, all of us I assure you very well drunk and our pates full. About a quarter of a league from the battalions they met the King, where his Majesty asked them if they had dined, to which Monsieur de Guise made answer that they had, and as well as they had done of a year before. 'Why,' said his Majesty (seeing them come from the battalions), 'you did not dine at Pierrepont?' 'No Sir,' said Monsieur de Guise, 'neither can your Majesty guess where we dined, nor by whom so well entertained.' 'I pray by whom?' said the

King. 'Marry Sir,' replied Monsieur de Guise, 'by Monluc.' 'I believe then,' said the King, 'he feasted you with his own country diet, garlic and onions, and wine as warm as milk.' Whereupon Monsieur de Guise up and told him how I had entertained them, when the King asking the Duke of Saxony by his interpreter if it were true, the Duke made answer that if his Majesty himself had treated them, they could not have had better meat nor cooler wine; and that since I was so good a fellow, his Majesty might do well to give me money to buy plate, nothing having been wanting but that, and that Monsieur de Guise and he had both promised me to make that request to his Majesty in my behalf; which the King promised them to do, and that since I was so honourable in my expense he would give me means to do it more than hitherto he had ever done.

Part IV   From Books V, VI and VII

The French Religious Wars, 1562–1570

The long-drawn-out Habsburg-Valois Wars, in which Monluc had won fame, honour and wealth, were ended by the Peace of Cateau-Cambrésis, 1559. Peace, and the deaths, in quick succession, of his 'good master' Henry II, and Henry's son Francis II, left Monluc exposed to his enemies. He pays court to the Queen Mother, Catherine de Medici, and returns to Gascony in 1560, where he observes the growth of Huguenotism

King Francis being dead at Orléans,[1] where I then was, I went to wait upon the Queen Mother, who although she was very ill, nevertheless did me the honour to command that they should permit me to enter into her chamber. I had taken notice of the practices set on foot, which did by no means please me, and especially those of the estates then sitting,[2] by which I saw we should not long continue in peace, and that was it which made me resolve to retire from court that I might not be hooked in, either by one faction or another; especially considering that I had been made guilty that way before (contrary to all truth, as God be my help), which was the reason that taking leave of her Majesty, and not thinking it fit to trouble her with much discourse in her indisposition, I said to her these words: 'Madam, I am going into Gascony with a determination to do you most humble and faithful service all the days of my life, which I most humbly beseech your Majesty to believe, and if anything fall out considerable enough to engage you to call your servants about you, I promise you and give you my faith, I will never take other side than that of your Majesty's and my lords' your children; but for that will be on horseback so soon as ever your Majesty shall please to command me.'

[1] Francis II died on 5 December 1560, and was succeeded by the ten-year-old Charles IX.

[2] The Estates-General met at Orléans, 13 December 1560, expressed conflicting views on the religious dispute, and was prorogued on 31 January 1561.

The very night of the same day on which King Francis died, I had given her the same assurance, for which she now did me the honour to return me thanks; when Madame de Cursol [Crussol], who stood at her bedshead, said to her, 'Madame, you ought not to let him go, your Majesty having no servants more faithful than those of the family of Monluc.' To which I made answer, 'Madame, you shall never be without Monlucs, for you have three yet remaining, which are my two brothers and my son, who with myself will die at your feet, for your Majesty's service.' For which her Majesty returned me many thanks. She who had a great deal of understanding, and who has given very ample testimony of it to the world, saw very well that having so many affairs upon her hands during the minority of her children, she should have use for all the servants she had, and may herself remember what she said to me, wherein if I have failed to execute her commands it was because I did not understand them. And so I took my leave of her Majesty; Madame de Crussol followed me to the middle of the room, where she took her leave of me, and Madame de Curton did the same, and thus I returned to my own house.

Some months after my return home, I had news brought me from all sides of the strange language and most audacious speeches the ministers of the new faith impudently uttered, even against the royal authority. I was moreover told that they imposed taxes upon the people, made captains and listed soldiers, keeping their assemblies in the houses of several lords of the country who were of this new religion; which was the first beginning and cause of all those mischiefs and massacres they have since exercised upon one another. I saw the evil daily to increase but saw no-one who appeared on the King's behalf to oppose it. I heard also that the greatest part of the officers of the treasury were of this religion (the nature of man being greedy of novelty), and the worst of all and from whence proceeded all the mischief, was that those of the long robe, the men of justice in the parlements and senechalseys, and other judges, abandoned the ancient religion and that of the King to embrace the new one. I met also with strange names of elders, deacons, consistories, synods and colloquies, having never before breakfasted of such viands. I heard that the elders had bulls' pizzles by them called *Iohanots*, with which they misused and very cruelly beat the poor peasants if they went not to their conventicles; the people being so totally abandoned by justice that if anyone went to complain, they received nothing but injury instead of redress, and not a sergeant that durst attempt to execute anything in the behalf of the Catholics but for the Huguenots only (for so they were called, though I know not why), the rest of the judges and officers who were Catholics being so overawed that they durst not have commanded so much as an information to be made for fear of their lives.

All these things together were presages to me of what I have since seen come to pass, and returning from another house of mine to that of Estillac, I found the town of La Plume besieged by three or four hundred men. I had my son Captain Monluc with me, whom I sent with all sorts of fair language (for I had no more than ten or twelve horse in my company) to try to persuade them to desist. Wherein he prevailed so far that he overcame the Brimonts, the principal heads of this enterprise (which was undertaken to rescue two prisoners of their religion, that the magistrates of La Plume had for some disorders committed). My son having promised them that if they would retire I would cause them to be delivered, they took his word and drew off from before the town. The next day accordingly I went to speak with the officers of the said city, to whom having remonstrated that for these two prisoners they ought not to suffer a sedition to be set on foot, they brought them out to me and let them go.

Monsieur de Burie,[1] who at this time in the absence of the King of Navarre commanded in Guienne, was at Bourdeaux, where he had as much work cutting out for him as in any other part of the province, but I did not hear that he made any great stir and I believe he was very much astonished. For my part I had command of nothing but my own company; nevertheless I would once take upon me to meddle at the request of the court presidial and the consuls of Agen, about the concern of a minister the magistrates had committed to prison, which set the whole city in commotion one against another; whereupon the consuls came to entreat me to come to Agen, for that otherwise the inhabitants would cut one another's throats. Which I accordingly did, where upon my coming the Huguenots were of themselves possessed with so great a terror that some of them hid themselves in cellars and others leapt over the walls, not that I gave them any occasion so to do, for I had as yet done them no harm. Neither did I do any more now but only take the minister out of a house to deliver him into the hands of justice. But these people have ever feared my name in Guienne, as they have that of Monsieur de Guise in France. But how little soever

[1] For whom see Appendix I, 'Coucys, Charles de.'

the thing I did was, the King of Navarre took it so highly ill at my hands that he mortally hated me for it and wrote to the King that I had dispossessed him of his lieutenancy, entreating to know if his Majesty had given me authority so to do, whilst in the meantime he meditated his revenge at what price soever. This happened in the time when King Francis was yet living; for in those times these new people began their innovations. Monsieur de Guise sent me word by my son Captain Monluc that I should use all the means I could to restore myself to his favour, for although the King was satisfied with what I had done, he could not nevertheless make any show of it, it being requisite for him to proceed after this manner. This letter might very well have been the cause of my ruin, for without this private advice from Monsieur de Guise I had never reconciled myself to the King of Navarre, as having much rather have chosen to have stood upon my guard and in my own defence than to have any tampering with the King of Navarre in anything but what should be by his Majesty's command. But I conceived I could not err in following the advice of Monsieur de Guise, for he absolutely governed all things at court.[1]

Monluc is sent into Guienne, December 1561

But to return to my first subject, having heard and seen all these affairs and novelties which still much more disclosed themselves after my return, and after the death of the King (for they now explained themselves in downright terms) than before; I deliberated to return to court, no more to stir from the Queen and her children, but to die at their feet in opposition to all such as should present themselves against them, according to the promise I had made to the Queen, and put myself upon my way in order to this resolution. The court was then at Sainct Germain-en-Laye [St Germain]. I stayed but two days at Paris, and at my coming to St Germain found not one person of the House of Guise, nor any other but the Queen, the King of Navarre, the Prince of Condé, and the Cardinal of Ferrara;[2] where I was very

---

[1] The Duke of Guise and the Cardinal of Lorraine were the most influential figures at the court of Francis II.

[2] The death of Francis II had been immediately followed by the temporary eclipse of the Guise interest, and the rise of Catherine and the Bourbons (Navarre and Condé). Ippolito d'Este, Cardinal of Ferrara (1509–72), brother of Monluc's friend the Duke of Ferrara, was the papal representative at the Colloquy of Poissy, September–October 1561.

well received by her Majesty and by them all. The Queen and the King of Navarre, drawing me apart, enquired of me how affairs stood in Guienne; to which I made answer that they were not yet very ill but that I feared they would every day grow worse and worse, telling them withal the reasons why I conceived that it would not be long before they would break into open arms. I stayed there but five days, in which time news came that the Huguenots were risen at Marmande[1] and had killed all the religious of the Order of St Francis and burnt their monastery. Immediately came other news of the massacre the Catholics had made of the Huguenots at Cahours [Cahors],[2] with that of Grenade near unto Toulouse. After that came news of the death of Monsieur de Fumel, barbarously massacred by his own tenants who were Huguenots; which troubled the Queen more than all the rest, and then it was that her Majesty saw that what I had prophesied to her, that they would not long abstain from arms, was very true.

They were six days before they could resolve at which end to begin to extinguish this fire. The King of Navarre would that the Queen should write to Monsieur de Burie to take order in those affairs. But the Queen said that if none but he put their hands to the work, there would be no great matters done, by which she implied some jealousy of him; and I know what she said to me. A little thing will serve to render us suspected. I perceived also that the King of Navarre was not so kind to me as formerly, which I believe proceeded from my own behaviour, I being not so observant to him as at other times and never stirring from the Queen. In the end they resolved to send me into Guienne with a commission to raise horse and foot, and to fall upon all such as should appear in arms. I defended myself the best I could from this employment, knowing very well that it was not a work done, but a work that was only about to begin, and such as required a great master to execute it as it ought to be; and therefore remained at this bout constant not to take it upon me.

The next morning the Queen and the King of Navarre sent for me, and the Queen had in the interval commanded Monsieur de Valence my brother[3] to persuade me to accept of this commission, so that when I came before them, after several remonstrances they made me, I was constrained to accept of it, provided that Monsieur de Burie

---

[1] Marmande, on the Garonne, between Bordeaux and Agen: see map, p. 33.

[2] 16 November 1561.

[3] Jean de Monluc, Bishop of Valence, at this time played a leading part in the Colloquy of Poissy.

might be joined in the commission, for I would have him have his part of the cake. But the Queen would by no means hear of it, alleging but too many reasons (princes may say what they please), till in the end I was forced to tell her Majesty plainly that in case he was not comprehended in the commission, he being the King's lieutenant as he was, would underhand strew so many traverses and difficulties in my way that I should never effect anything to the purpose; which at last they allowed to be a sufficient reason and let it pass according to my own desire. The same commission they gave me for Guienne, they also gave Monsieur de Crussol[1] for the province of Languedoc, giving us both in charge that which of us soever should first have dispatched our own business, should go help his fellow if he should stand in need. Monsieur de Crussol was no more of this new religion than I, and without all doubt afterward turned to it more out of some discontent than for any devotion, for he was no great divine, no more than I was. But I have known many turn to this religion out of spite who have afterwards very much repented. We both of us together took our leaves of the Queen and the King of Navarre, and went to Paris, and Monsieur de Valence with us. I demanded two counsellors of that part of France to sit upon life and death (fearing that those of the country would do no good, being that some of them would incline to the Catholics and others to the Huguenots), and had given me two of the damndest rogues in the whole kingdom, one whereof was Compain, a counsellor of the great council, and the other Girard, lieutenant to the Prevost d'Hostel, who have since gained no better a reputation than they had before. I repented me that I had demanded them; but I thought I did well in it, and so I came into Gascony in all diligence.

I found Monsieur de Burie at Bourdeaux, where I delivered him the patent, and where all the city was divided against one another, and the Parlement also, because the Huguenots would that they might preach openly in the city, alleging that by the conference at Poissy it was permitted them so to do; and the Catholics affirmed the contrary. So that Monsieur de Burie and I had for a whole day together enough to do to keep them from falling together by the ears; and thereupon agreed to raise some men, and that so soon as our commissioners should be come, we would march directly to Fumel, our patent expressing that we should begin there. Now the power of raising forces and of

---

[1] Antoine de Crussol (1528–73), Comte de Crussol, leiutenant-general in Dauphiné, Languedoc and Provence.

commanding them was in me, wherefore we concluded together to raise two hundred arquebusiers and a hundred *argoulets*,[1] the command of which I gave to the younger Tilladet, the same who is now Lord of Saint-Orens.

I had scarce been four or five days in my house Estillac, when a minister called La Barrelle came to me in the behalf of their churches, telling me that the churches were exceeding glad of my coming and the authority the Queen had given me, being now assured to obtain justice against those that had massacred their brethren. To which I made answer that he might be confident all such as should appear in fault should be certainly punished. He then told me that he had in commission from the churches to make me a handsome present and such a one as therewith I should have reason to be well satisfied. I told him that there was no need of any presents to me, forasmuch as my integrity would oblige me to do my duty, and that for all the presents in the world I was never to be made to do anything contrary to it. He then told me that the Catholics had declared they would never endure to have justice executed upon them, and that therefore he had in commission from all the churches to present me with four thousand foot in good equipage and paid. This word began to put me into fury and made me angrily demand of him: 'What men, and of what nation must those four thousand foot be?' To which he made answer: 'Of this very country, and of the churches.' Whereupon I asked him if he had power to present the King's subjects and to put men into the field without the command of the King or the Queen, who was at this time regent of the kingdom and so declared by the estates held at Orléans. 'O you confounded rogues,' said I, 'I see very well what you aim at, it is to set divisions in the kingdom, and 'tis you ministers that are the authors of this godly work, under colour of the Gospel.' And thereupon fell to swearing, and seizing him by the collar said these words: 'I know not, rascal, what should hinder me that I do not myself hang thee at this window, for I have with my own hands strangled twenty honester men than thou.' Who then trembling, said to me, 'Sir I beseech you let me go to Monsieur de Burie, for I have order from the churches to go speak with him, and be not offended with me, who only come to deliver a message; neither do we do it for any other end but only to defend ourselves.' Whereupon I bade him go and be hanged to all the devils in hell, both he and all the rest of his fellow ministers; and so he departed from me, as sufficiently frighted

[1] Light horse.

as ever he was in his life. This action got me a very ill repute amongst the ministers, for it was no less than high treason to touch one of them.

Nevertheless a few days after came another minister called Boernormant [Boisnormand], alias La Pierre, sent in the behalf of their churches (as he said) to entreat me to accept the present and offer that Barrelle had made me, saying that it was not for the intention I imagined, and that without costing the King so much as a *liard*,[1] I might render equal justice both to the one party and the other. At this I was almost ready to lose all manner of patience, and with great vehemency reproached him with the levying of money and the listing of men, but he denied it all. Whereupon I said to him: 'But what if I prove to you that no longer since than yesterday, you listed men at La Plume, what will you say?' To which he made answer that if it was so, it was more than he knew. Now he had a soldier with him that had formerly been in my company in Piedmont, called Autièges, which made me turn to him saying, 'Will you, Captain Autièges, deny that you yesterday listed men at La Plume?' To which, seeing himself caught, he made answer that indeed the church of Nérac had made him their captain. Whereupon I began to say, 'What the devil churches are those that make captains?' and fell to reproach him with the good usage and respect I had showed him when he was in my company; forbidding them ever again to come to me with the like errand, which if they did I should not have the patience to forbear laying hands upon them; and so they departed.

An incident at St Mézard, and the first execution of Huguenots, February 1562

Now there was a village two leagues from Estillac called Sainct Mezard [St Mézard], the greatest part whereof belonged to the Sieur de Rouillac, a gentleman of eight or ten thousand *livres* a year. Four or five days before I came thither, the Huguenots his tenants were risen up against him because he offered to hinder them from breaking open the church and taking away the chalices, and kept him four and twenty hours besieged in his own house. So that had it not been for a brother of his called Monsieur de Saint-Aignan and some other gentlemen his neighbours who came in to his relief, they had certainly cut his throat, as also those of d'Astefort [Astaffort] would have done to the Sieurs de Cuq and de la Montjoye, so that already there began

1 Copper coin of little value.

to be open war against the gentry. I privately got two hangmen (which they have since called my lackeys because they were very often at my heels) and sent to Monsieur de Fontenilles, my son-in-law (who carried my cornet and was at Beaumont-de-Lomaigne, where he lay with all my company in garrison), that he should come away upon Thursday in the beginning of the night, and by break of day be at the said St Mézard, there to seize of those persons whose names I had sent him in writing and whereof the principal was nephew to the advocate of the King and Queen of Navarre at Lectoure, called Verdier.

Now the said advocate was he that fomented all the sedition, and I had private word sent me that he would come that very Thursday to St Mézard, for he had some estate there. I was resolved to begin with this fellow's head, forasmuch as having advertised the King of Navarre at court that the said Verdier and other of his officers at Lectoure were the principal incendiaries of rebellion, and having writ as much to the Queen [Catherine de Medici] of the King's officers, she had writ back that I should begin with those people first, and the King of Navarre had writ in his letter that if I hanged the King's officers on the lower branches of a tree, I should hang his on the uppermost of all.[1] But Verdier came not, which was well for him, for if he had I had branched him.

Monsieur de Fontenilles performed a very long march and came by break of day to St Mézard, where at his first coming he took the nephew of the Verdier and two others and a deacon. The rest escaped away, there being not anyone who knew the houses, for there was not so much as any one man at arms or archer who had any knowledge of the place. A gentleman called Monsieur de Corde, who lived at the said place, had sent me word that when in the presence of the consuls he had remonstrated to them that they did ill and that the King would be highly displeased with their doings, they made answer: 'What King? We are the kings, he that you speak of is a little turdy roylet; we'll whip his breech and set him to a trade, to teach him to get his living as others do.' Neither was it only there that they talked at this precious rate, but it was common discourse in every place. I was ready to burst with indignation at it and saw very well that all this language tended to what had been told me by Lieutenant du Franc, which in sum, was to make another king.

I had agreed with Monsieur de Saint-Orens that he should also

[1] The King of Navarre was now (1562) a follower of the Catholic *Triumvirs*, to the displeasure of his wife.

take me five or six of Astaffort, and especially one Captain Morellet the chief ringleader of them all, and that if he could take him and those I named to him, he should with good words bring them to me to St Mézard the same day that I performed the execution, which was upon a Friday, which nevertheless that day he could not do but he snapped them the Sunday following and brought them prisoners to Villeneuve.

So soon as I came to St Mézard, Monsieur de Fontenilles presented the three prisoners and the deacon, all bound in the churchyard, in which there was yet remaining the foot of a cross of stone they had broken that might be about some two foot high. I presently called Monsieur de Corde and the consuls, bidding them upon pain of death to deliver truly what words they heard these fellows speak against the King. The consuls were afraid and durst say nothing; whereupon I told the said Sieur de Corde that it belonged to him to speak first and therefore bid him speak, upon which he maintained to their faces that they had spoken the forementioned words, and then the consuls told the truth and justified the same the Sieur de Corde had done. I had my two hangmen behind me very well equipped with their tackle, and especially with a very sharp axe, when flying in great fury upon this Verdier, I took him by the collar saying to him, 'O thou confounded rogue! Durst thou defile thy wicked tongue against the Majesty of the King and Sovereign?' To which he replied, 'Ah sir, have mercy upon a poor sinner.' At which more enraged than before, I said to him 'Thou ungracious rascal, wouldst thou have me to have mercy upon thee, who hadst no reverence nor respect for thy King,' and with that pushed him rudely to the ground, so that his neck fell exactly upon the piece of the cross, crying to the hangman, 'Strike villain,' which he did, and so nimbly that my word and the blow were the one as soon as the other, which fetched off his head and moreover above another half foot of the cross. The other two I caused to be hanged upon an elm that was close by, and being the deacon was but eighteen years old I would not put him to death, as also that he might carry the news to his brethren; but caused him nevertheless to be so well whipped by the hangman that, as I was told, he died within ten or twelve days after. This was the first execution I did at my coming from my own house without sentence or writing; for in such matters, I have heard, men must begin with execution, and if everyone that had the charge of provinces had done the same, they had put out the fire that has since consumed all. However, this served to stop the mouths of several seditious persons who durst no more speak of the King but with respect; but in great privacy and with greater circumspection carried on their practices and designs.

The state of Guienne, 1562

I do not think it is to be found in history that ever such rogueries, cheats and machinations were invented or practised in any kingdom of the world. And had the Queen delayed sending me with this commission but three months only, all the people had been constrained to turn to this religion or have lost their lives, for everyone was so terrified with the severity that by the judges was exercised upon the Catholics that there was no other way left them but either to abandon their habitations, to lose their lives, or to turn to that party. The ministers publicly preached that if they would come over to their religion, they should neither pay duty to the gentry nor taxes to the King, but what should be appointed by them. Others preached that kings could have no power but what stood with the liking and consent of the people: and others, that the gentry were no better men than they, and in effect, when the gentlemen's bailiffs went to demand rent of the tenants, they made answer that they must show them in the Bible whether they ought to pay or no, and that if their predecessors had been slaves and coxcombs they would be none.

This insolence grew so high that some of the gentry began so far to give way to its fury as to enter into composition with their tenants, entreating them to let them live in safety in their houses and to enjoy their own demesnes, and as to rents and chiefs they would not ask them any. No-one was so bold as to dare to go out a-hunting, for they came and killed their hounds and greyhounds in the field before their faces, and no-one durst say wrong they did, for fear of their lives; but if anyone meddled with any of them, all their churches were presently made acquainted with it and within four or five hours you had been dispatched out of the world, or enforced to hide yourself in some of the confederates' houses or in Toulouse, there being no safety in any other place. And this was the miserable condition to which Guienne was reduced. The particularities whereof I am necessitated to insist upon, to let you see whether or no the King had not reason to honour me with that glorious title of Conservator of Guienne, and whether it was not necessary to fall to work in good earnest, for had

I proceeded with mildness and moderation as Monsieur de Burie did, we had been lost. He promised them great matters; but I performed nothing, knowing very well that it was only to deceive us and by degrees to get places into their hands. To be short, these upstart Christians would give us the law and there was not a little minister amongst them who did not lord it as if he had been a bishop; and these were the hopeful beginnings of this fine religion and the manner after which she instructed men to live.

As Lieutenant in Guienne from 1563 Monluc faced many difficulties, but by and large he preserved peace and order in the province. When the new war broke out in 1567 Monluc was ordered to attack the Huguenot stronghold of La Rochelle, and the islands off the west coast of France

In this interval Monsieur de Pons[1] had reduced the isles of Oléron and Alvert [Arvert],[2] for they are for the most part his own, and Captain La Gombaudière was in them, having his house there, and commanded as well in Arvert and Oléron. There only then remained the isle of Ré, where they had erected a fort near unto a church and several others at the places of landing. I caused five hundred arquebusiers to be chosen out of all our companies, with all the captains, lieutenants, and ensigns, the one half of Mongauzy the elder's company excepted, who stayed ashore to command those that were left behind, making my nephew de Leberon with the said five hundred to embark at the port of Brouage. Guillet, the King's receiver in those parts, took great pains to victual and prepare the vessels, whom the Queen of Navarre put to death in the late troubles, but I could never learn for what. I ever knew him to be a good servant of the King's and believe his diligence upon this occasion of our men's putting to sea did him more harm than good and perhaps might be the cause of his death, for the Queen of Navarre did by no means love those people.

My said nephew was a day and a night hindered by foul weather from landing, as also the enemy defended the landing places from the forts they had made. But in the end he bethought him in the night to send away all the lesser boats he had brought along with him full of soldiers, to land amongst the rocks on the back of the island where the enemy kept no guard; who so soon as part of them were got on shore, the enemy discovering the stratagem ran to that part and fought

[1] Antoine de Pons, Comte de Marennes (d. 1586), Governor of Saintonge.
[2] Arvert, a promontory south of La Rochelle, is divided from the mainland by rivers.

them, but ours remained masters of the place. My nephew who was the one that was engaged in the fight thereupon presently dispatched a skiff to the captains and soldiers who were aboard the greater vessels to bid them come away; which being suddenly done, so soon as they were all landed they marched directly to the great fort by the church, a long league and a half from thence, which they assaulted on two or three sides at once. So that they carried the place, putting all they found within it to the sword, whilst the rest who guarded the landings put themselves into little boats and fled away towards Rochelle. Monsieur de Pons and I were on the sea-shore, and seeing the boats sail towards Rochelle we imagined them to be the people, inhabitants of the island, who escaped away and that our people had gotten the victory. And two days after my said nephew sent me an account of the whole action, which sooner he could not do, the wind being so contrary that they could not possibly get to Marennes, where the aforesaid Sieur and I lay; upon which news we called back my said nephew, leaving two foot companies in the isle.

I then left Monsieur de Pons at Marennes and went away to St Jean, where Monsieur de Jarnac came to me to take order for all things necessary for me in order to the siege. I caused great provision of victuals to be made ready, wherein the providore of the late Monsieur de Burie was very assisting to me, for he was of that country.

In the meantime I still expected to hear from the King but could never obtain the favour of one syllable, neither did any of my messengers ever return; and in truth there was a very great danger by the way, the enemy being possessed of all the great roads by which they were to return into Saintonge. The first that came was Dagron, who brought news that the peace was as good as concluded and that the King would suddenly send me word what I was to do. I think that having seen the Prince and the Admiral with their forces at the gates of Paris, ready to fight a battle, and afterwards at liberty to overrun all France, they more thought of that than they considered the affairs of Guienne.[1]

This was the success of my expedition into Saintonge; and seeing I have been reproached that for three years I had done nothing considerable, I could wish that such as propose enterprises to the King would be as prompt to provide things necessary for such designs as they are ready to give assignments that signify nothing, like those they

[1] The Huguenot forces of the Prince of Condé and Admiral Coligny, together with German reinforcements, marched on Paris in January 1568.

sent me, and then perhaps some good might be done. But as they order it, a man must be a God to work miracles.

The Peace of Longjumeau ended this second civil war, March 1568

A few days after the King sent me the peace to cause it to be proclaimed at Bourdeaux, commanding me to disband the foot and to dismiss them every man to his own house; which I accordingly did and sent the proclamation to the court of Parlement and the jurats to cause it to be published. But for my own part I would not be present at it, knowing very well that it was only a truce to get breath and a peace to gain time to provide themselves better for a war to come, and not intended to be kept. For the King, who had been taken unprovided, I was confident would never put up the affront had been put upon him, who though he was very young, was notwithstanding a prince of great spirit and that bore this audacious enterprise with very great impatience, as I have since been told by some who were then about him. He gave sufficient testimony of a generous courage and truly worthy of a king, when he put himself in the head of the Swiss to escape to Paris; and do you think, gentlemen, you who were the leaders of those mutinous troops, that he will ever forget that insolence? You would hardly endure it from your equal, what then would you do with a servant? For my part I never saw nor ever read of so strange a thing, which made me always think it would stick in the King's stomach. The Prince and the Admiral committed a great oversight in this peace; for they had by much the better of the game and might doubtless have carried Chartres, so that those who mediated and procured this accommodation performed a very signal service for the King and kingdom.

This was all I did in the second troubles, and methinks it was no contemptible service to send the King a recruit of eleven or twelve hundred horse, thirty ensigns of foot, and to preserve for him the province of Guienne, conquer him the Isles, and not to be wanting on my part that I did not try my fortune at Rochelle and send him all the money the rebels had amassed together in that part of his kingdom. But I must do miracles forsooth, those who are about the King's person have ever done me one good office or another, and on my conscience would his Majesty hearken to them now that I have nothing at all to do, they would find out one thing or another to lay to my charge. For the customs of the court must not be lost, which is to do all ill offices and invent slanders against those who have a desire to do well. Was I near them I could quickly give some of them their answer, but the distance is too great betwixt Gascony and Paris. Besides I have lost my children, and 'an old beast has no resource'.

Monluc's advice to the King on the strategic importance of La Rochelle and command of the sea

Before I departed from Bourdeaux I in the morning assembled the attorney general, the General de Gourgues, Captain Verre [Berre], and my nephew the Sieur de Leberon, to whom I would communicate what I had fancied with myself upon the news that daily came from court of the diffidence and discontent the Prince of Condé was in, and what I should do if I were in his place. In which discourse they may remember I told them that if the Prince could pass he would infallibly come into Saintonge, having Rochelle and almost all the country at his devotion; that the Isles when they should see forces in Saintonge and at Rochelle, and Monsieur de La Rochefoucauld so near them, would presently revolt, and that then the said Prince and the Huguenots would resolutely turn all their designs this way; for in France Rouen was no longer theirs, which being gone they had not one port town at their devotion, and that it would be in them a ridiculous and a senseless thing to begin a third war without first having a sea-port in their power. Now they could not possibly make choice of one of greater advantage to them than that of Rochelle, on which depends that of Brouage, which is absolutely the fairest and the most commodious haven in all the kingdom. For being there they might have succours out of Germany, Flanders, England, Scotland, Brittany and Normandy, all of them countries abounding in people of their own religion, so that in truth should the King give them their choice to canton themselves in any port of the kingdom, they could not possibly choose a more advantageous nor a more commodious place.

They all approved of my discourse as being near the truth, which I had framed in the night as I lay considering the state of our affairs, for so I used to pass part of the time in bed; and this waking fancy of mine seemed to presage almost as much disaster and misfortune as the dreams I had dreamt of King Henry and King Charles.

Having entertained them with this discourse, I then proceeded to tell them that it would be convenient to find out some fit remedies against the evil before it should arrive; for to communicate this

conceit to their Majesties without proposing at the same time some
way to frustrate the enemy's designs, were, I thought, to make them
neglect my intelligence and to slight my advice. We therefore fell to
considering that to prevent the mishaps which seemed to threaten us
there was no other way than by making forts upon the sea, and
betimes to secure the ports, which with four ships and as many
shallops to lie at Che-de-bois [Chef-de-Baie], la Pallice, and the mouth
of the harbour at Brouage,[1] might sufficiently be provided for; and
that the ports being once our own, neither English nor any other of
their party could or would attempt to come into their assistance,
knowing they were to land at places where they are almost always
certain to meet with very tempestuous weather; and that seamen will
never venture out to sea to go to any place unless they are first sure of
a free and a secure harbour to lie in; and on the other side, that our
ships lying about the Isles would so awe the inhabitants that they
would never dare to revolt, and our men-of-war would so keep
Rochelle as it were besieged, that it must of necessity in a little time
either wholly submit to the King's devotion or at least contain themselves quiet, without attempting anything of commotion. All which
being remonstrated to them we unanimously concluded that I ought
to send an account thereof to the King and Queen.

*The peace was of short duration, and civil war broke out again in October
1568. Monluc was ordered by the King to lead an expedition into Béarn, to
punish the Queen of Navarre: and in July 1570 he laid siege to her fortress
of Rabastens, in the foothills of the Pyrenees*

The fifth day of the siege, the 23rd of July, in the year 1570, upon a
Sunday about two of the clock in the afternoon, I resolved to give an
assault, the order whereof was after the manner following: that
Monsieur de Saint-Orens, field marshal, should lead the companies
one after the other up to the breach, which that he might the better
do without confusion, I ordered all the companies to be drawn by four
and four together out of the town; which upon pain of death were not
to stir from their places till Monsieur de Saint-Orens should come to
fetch them, who was to stay three quarters of an hour betwixt every
leading up, and in that manner to conduct all the companies one after
another. And it was also ordered that the two captains who were upon
the guard by the breach, which were Lartigue and Sollés of Béarn

[1] Ports close to La Rochelle.

should go on first to the assault. As I was setting down this order one came in haste to tell me that the two cannons that battered the flank and that had been removed in the night were forsaken, and not a man durst show himself upon the battery by reason the artillery itself had ruined all the gabions.

I therefore left it to Messieurs de Gondrin and de Saint-Orens to conclude the order of the fight, that is to say, that the companies should go on successively one after another, which was to be set down in writing, and myself ran on the outside to the hole of the wall, where I found only ten or twelve pioneers squat with their bellies close to the ground. For Tibauville, the commissary of the artillery, who had the charge of those two pieces of cannon, had been constrained to quit them, and even Monsieur de Bazillac himself. Seeing then this disorder I bethought myself of a great number of bavins I had the day before caused to be brought into the town and said to the gentlemen who were with me these words: 'I have heard, and always observed, that there is no labour nor danger that gentlemen will ever refuse. Follow me therefore I beseech you, and do as you shall see me do.'

They did not stay to be entreated and so we went in great haste directly to the bavins that were within the town, and lay in the middle of a street there where not a man durst abide, and there I took a bavin and laid it upon my shoulder, as also every gentleman took one and there were a great many who carried two apiece. After which manner we returned out of the town by the same way we entered in, and thus I marched before them till we came to the hole. By the way as we were going I had given order that they should bring me four or five halberdiers, which at my return I found already arrived at the hole and made them enter into it. We threw them the bavins into the hole, which they took with the points of their halberds, and ran to throw them upon the gabions to raise them. I dare be bold to affirm with truth that we were not above a quarter of an hour about this work, and so soon as ever the cannon was covered Tibauville and the other cannoneers returned into the battery, where they began to shoot with greater fury than of all the days before, every clap almost overtaking another, everyone assisting them with great cheerfulness. If, captains, you shall do the same, and yourselves first put your hands to the work, you will make everyone follow your example, very shame will push and force them on; and when the service is hot in any place, if the chief do not go in person or at least some eminent man, the rest will go very lamely on and murmur when a man sends them to slaughter.

And if you covet honour, you must sometimes tempt danger as much as the meanest soldier under your command.

I will deprive no man of his due honour, for I think I have assisted at as many batteries as any man this day alive and must needs say this, that I never saw commissaries of the artillery more diligent and adventurous than both Fredeville and Tibauville showed themselves during the whole five days that the battery continued, in my whole life. For they themselves both levelled and fired, though they had as good cannoneers as ever I saw handle linstock in my days. And I dare be bold to say that of a thousand cannon shot we made against this place not ten failed of their effect or were spent in vain.

In the morning I sent for Monsieur de Gohas, who was at Vic-Bigorre, and the captains who were set to have an eye to Montamat,[1] and the succours expected by him, writing to him to come away that he might be with me at the assault by reason that Captain Paulliac, colonel of the infantry, was so dangerously wounded that we had no hopes of his life. He received his shot at the time when I went over-night to carry Messieurs de Leberon and de Montaut to cut off the great counterscarp, which shot went quite through his body. My son Fabien was also shot in the chin, and two soldiers close by my side.

I there committed a very great error, for I went in the evening before it was dark and I believe they were aware that we intended to cut the counterscarp, for all their arquebusiers were run together to that place; and the reason why I committed this error was that having computed with myself how many hours the night was long, I found that it was not above seven hours or thereabouts. And on the other side I saw that in half an hour I should lose all that I had done if the counterscarp was not pulled down by break of day, and in that case I should think fit to give an assault that day, they would be so strongly rampired and fortified that with as many more cannon shot as I had made against the place it would be a matter of very great difficulty to enter. This was the reason why I made so much haste to go and begin the work, that I might have it perfected by break of day; where I recommended the care of it to Messieurs de Leberon and de Montaut and the two captains upon the guard, by telling them that in their diligence our victory wholly consisted. And in truth they slept not, as I have already said, for by break of day the artillery began to play and the counterscarp was wholly pulled down.

[1] Guillaume d'Astarac, Baron de Montamat (d. 1572), the Queen of Navarre's general in Béarn.

O comrades, you who shall go to besiege places, you cannot but confess that both here and in several other places my enterprises and victories have succeeded more from my vigilancy and prompt execution than my valour, and I on my part am willing to confess that there were in the camp braver men than I. But no-one can be a coward that has these three things, for from these three all the combats and victories proceed and all valiant men choose to follow captains that are provided with these three qualities. And on the other side he cannot be called hardy, let his heart be never so good, if he be tardy, backward and slow in execution. For before he has fixed his resolution he has been so long deliberating about it that the enemy is advertised of what he intends to do and consequently is provided to prevent his design, but if he be quick he shall even surprise himself. So that there is no great confidence to be reposed in a chief that is not endued with these three qualities: vigilancy, promptitude and valour.

If a man examine all the great warriors that have ever been he will find that they had all those qualities. Alexander did not in vain bear the device I have mentioned before.[1] Examine Caesar's *Commentaries* and all the authors that have writ of him, you will find that in his life he fought two and fifty battles without ever losing any, saving that of Dirache [Dyrrachium]. But within thirty days he had a sufficient revenge against Pompey, for he won a great battle and defeated him. You will not find that in these two and fifty battles he ever fought three times in his own person, that is, with his own hand, though he was always present there; by which you will understand that all his victories were the effects of his conduct, for being diligent, vigilant, and a prompt executer of his designs.

But for all this, these qualities are rarely found, and I believe we Gascons are better provided of them than any other people of France, or perhaps of Europe, and many good and great captains have gone out of it within these fifty years. I shall not compare myself to them, but this I will say of myself, because it is true, that my master never lost anything by my sloth or remissness. The enemy thought me a league off when I came to beat up his quarters. And if diligence be required in all exploits of war, it is much more in a siege, for a very little thing will serve to overthrow a great design. If you press your enemy you redouble his fear, he will not know where he is nor have leisure to recollect himself. Be sure to wake whilst others sleep, and never leave your enemy without something to do.

[1] See above, p. 129.

I shall now return to the assault. Our order being set down, I went and placed myself at the gate of the town near unto the breach, where I had all the gentlemen with me, of which there might be six or seven score and still more came up to us, for Monsieur de La Chappelle-Louzières, who came from Quercy, brought a great troop of gentlemen along with him. I shall here relate one thing of my own presage, which is perfectly true, that it was impossible for all the friends I had to dispossess me of an opinion I had that I should in this assault be killed or wounded by a shot in some part of my head: and out of that conceit was once half in a mind not to go to the assault, knowing very well that my death would at this time be of ill consequence, if not to the enterprise in hand, yet to the general design upon that country. This fancy therefore still running in my head the morning before the assault was to be given, I said to Monsieur de Las, the King's Advocate at Agen, who was of our council, these words. 'Monsieur de Las, there are some who have exclaimed and do yet cry out that I am very rich. You know of all the money I have to a *denier,* for by my will, to which you are a witness, you are sufficiently informed of my estate. But seeing the world are not otherwise to be persuaded but I have a great deal of money and that consequently if by accident I should die in this assault, they would demand of my wife four times as much as I am worth, I have here brought a particular of all the money I have at this day in the whole world, as well abroad at interest as at home in the custody of my wife. The account is of my steward Baratte's drawing and signed by my own hand. You are my friend, I beseech you therefore if I die that you and the Councillor Monsieur de Nort will transfer your love and friendship to my wife and my two daughters and that you will have a care of them, especially Charlotte-Catherine, who had the honour to be christened by the King and the Queen his mother.'[1] Which having said, I delivered the scroll into his hands and very well perceived that he had much ado to refrain from weeping. By this you may judge if I had not the misfortune that befell me before my eyes. I have no familiar spirit, but few misfortunes have befallen me in the whole course of my life that my mind has not first presaged. I still endeavoured to put it out of my fancy, resigning all things to the good will of God, who disposes of us as seems best to his own wisdom, neither did I ever do otherwise, whatever the Huguenots my enemies have said or written to the contrary against me.

[1] Monluc's eldest daughter by his second marriage was christened at Agen in 1565, in the presence of Catherine de Medici and Charles IX.

So soon as two of the clock, the hour prefixed for the assault, was come, I caused eight or ten bottles of wine, that Madame de Panjas had sent me, to be brought out, which I gave the gentlemen, saying, 'Let us drink comrades. For it must now soon be seen which of us has been nursed with the best milk. God grant that another day we may drink together; but if our last hour be come, we cannot frustrate the decrees of fate.' So soon as they had all drunk and encouraged one another, I made them a short remonstrance in these words, saying, 'Friends and companions, we are now ready to fall on to the assault and every man is to show the best he can do. The men who are in this place are of those who with the Count de Mongommery [Montgomery][1] destroyed your churches and ruined your houses. You must make them disgorge what they have swallowed of your estates. If we carry the place and put them all to the sword, you will have a good bargain of the rest of Béarn. Believe me they will never dare to stand against you. Go on then in the name of God, and I will immediately follow.' Which being said I caused the assault to be sounded and the two captains immediately fell on; where some of their soldiers and ensigns did not behave themselves very well. Seeing then that those were not likely to enter, Monsieur de Saint-Orens marched up with four ensigns more and brought them up to the breach, which did no better than the former. For they stopped four or five paces short of the counterscarp, by which means our cannon was nothing hindered from playing into the breach, which made those within duck down behind it.

I then presently perceived that somebody else and other kind of men than the foot must put their hands to the work: which made me presently forget the conceit I had of being killed or wounded, and said to the gentlemen these words: 'Comrades, nobody knows how to fight but the *noblesse* and we are to expect no victory but by our own hands. Let us go then, I will lead you the way and let you see that a good horse will never be idle. Follow boldly and go on without fear, for we cannot wish for a more honourable death. We defer the time too long, let us fall on.' I then took Monsieur de Gohas by the hand, to whom I said, 'Monsieur de Gohas, I will that you and I fight together. I pray therefore let us not part; and if I be killed or wounded, never take notice of me but leave me there and push forward, that the

---

[1] Gabriel de Montgomery, Sieur de Lorges (*c.* 1530–74), Captain of the Scots Guard at the court of Henry II, was the man who mortally wounded the King in the tournament of June 1559. He fled the court and later joined the Huguenots, relieving Béarn in 1569.

victory however may remain to the King.' And so we went on as cheerfully as ever I saw men go on to an assault in my life, and looking twice behind me saw that the gentlemen almost touched one another, they came up so close.

There was a large plain of an hundred and fifty paces over or more, all open, over which we were to march to come up to the breach, which as we passed over, the enemy fired with great fury upon us all the way and I had six gentlemen shot close by me. One of which was the Sieur de Besolles; his shot was in his arm and so great a one that he had like to have died of his wound. The Viscount de Labatut was another, and his was in his leg. I cannot tell the names of the rest because I did not know them. Monsieur de Gohas had brought seven or eight along with him and amongst the rest Captain Savaillan the elder, of which three were slain and the said Captain Savaillan wounded with an arquebus shot quite through the face. There were also hurt one Captain du Plex, another Captain La Bastide, both kinsmen of mine about Villeneuve, who had always served under Monsieur de Brissac, one Captain Rantoy of Damazan, and Captain Sollés of Béarn, who had before been wounded with the thrust of a pike in the eye.

There were two little chambers about a pike height or more from the ground, which chambers the enemy so defended both above and below that not a man of ours could put up his head without being seen. However, our people began to assault them with a great shower of stones which they poured in upon them, and they also shot at us, but ours throwing downwards had the advantage of this kind of fight. Now I had caused three or four ladders to be brought to the edge of the graffe, and as I turned about to call for two of them to be brought to me, an arquebus shot clapped into my face from the corner of a barricade joining to the tower, where I do not think there could be four arquebusiers, for all the rest of the barricade had been beaten down by our two cannon that played upon the flank. I was immediately all over blood, for it gushed out at my mouth, nose and eyes. Whereupon Monsieur de Gohas would have caught me in his arms, thinking I would fall, but I said, 'Let me alone, I shall not fall, follow your point.'

Upon this shot of mine almost all the soldiers and the gentlemen began to lose courage and to retire, which made me cry out to them, though I could scarce speak by reason of the torrent of blood that pasht out at my mouth and nose: 'Whither will you go? Will you be terrified for me? Do not flinch nor forsake the fight, for I have no hurt, and let everyone return to his place,' in the meantime hiding the blood in the best manner I could: and to Monsieur de Gohas I said, 'Monsieur de Gohas, take care I beseech you that the soldiers be not discouraged, and renew the assault.' I could no longer stay there, for I began to faint, and therefore said to the gentlemen, 'I will go get myself dressed, but if you love me, let no-one follow but revenge me.' Which having said I took a gentleman by the hand, I cannot tell his name for I could scarce see him, and returned by the same way I came; where by the way I found a little horse of a soldier's upon which by the gentleman's assistance I mounted as well as I could, and after that manner was conducted to my lodging, where I found a chirurgeon of Monsieur de Gohas called Maître Simon, who dressed me and with his fingers (so wide were the orifices of the wound) pulled out the bones from my two cheeks and cut away a great deal of flesh from my face, which was all bruised and torn.

Monsieur de Gramon [Gramont][1] was upon a little eminence hard by, looking on at his ease, who being of this new religion, though he had never borne arms against the King, had no mind to meddle amongst us. He was aware how upon my hurt all the soldiers were disheartened and said to those who were with him, 'There is some eminent person slain; see how the soldiers are discouraged. I am afraid it is Monsieur de Monluc,' and therefore said to one of his gentlemen, called Monsieur de Sart [Sarp], 'Go run and see who it is, and if it be he, and that he is not dead, tell him that I entreat him to give me leave to come and see him.' The said Sieur de Sarp is a Catholic, who accordingly came, and at his entering into the town he heard that it was I that was hurt, and coming to my lodging found my people weeping for me and me tumbled upon a pallet upon the ground; where he told me that Monsieur de Gramont begged leave that he might come to see me. To which I made answer that there was no unkindness betwixt Monsieur de Gramont and me, and that if he pleased to come he would find that he had as many friends in our camp, and peradventure more than in that of their religion. He was no sooner gone from me but Monsieur de Madaillan my lieutenant, who had marched on the one hand of me when I went on to the assault, as Monsieur de Gohas did on the other, came to see if I was dead and said to me: 'Sir, cheer up your spirits and rejoice, we have entered the castle and the

[1] Antonoine d'Aure, Sieur de Gramont (d. 1576), one of the Huguenot leaders in Béarn.

soldiers are laying about them, who put all to the sword, and assure yourself we will revenge your wound.' I then said to him, 'Praised be God that I see the victory ours before I die. I now care not for death. I beseech you return back, and as you have ever been my friend, so now do me that act of friendship not to suffer so much as one man to escape with life.' Whereupon he immediately returned and all my servants went along with him, so that I had nobody left with me but two pages, Monsieur de Las and the chirurgeon.

They would fain have saved the minister and the governor, whose name was Captain Ladoue, to have hanged them before my lodging, but the soldiers took them from those who had them in their custody, whom they had also like to have killed for offering to save them, and cut them in a thousand pieces. They made also fifty or threescore to leap from the high tower into the moat, which were there all drowned. There were two only saved who were hid and such there were who offered four thousand crowns to save their lives, but not a man of ours would hearken to any ransom; and most of the women were killed who also did us a great deal of mischief with throwing stones. There was found within a Spanish merchant whom the enemy had kept prisoner there, and another Catholic merchant also, who were both saved; and these were all that were left alive of the men that we found in the place, namely the two that someone helped away and the two Catholic merchants. Do not think, you who shall read this book, that I caused this slaughter to be made so much out of revenge for the wound I had received as to strike terror into the country, that they might not dare to make head against our army. And in my opinion all soldiers in the beginning of a conquest ought to proceed after that manner with such as are so impudent as to abide cannon. He must bar his ears to all capitulations and composition if he do not see great difficulties in his enterprise, and that his enemy have put him to great trouble in making a breach. And as severity (call it cruelty if you please) is requisite in case of a resolute opposition, so on the other side mercy is very commendable and fit if you see that they in good time surrender to your discretion.

Monsieur de Gramont then came to visit me and found me in a very ill condition, for I had much ado to speak to him by reason of the great quantity of blood that issued from my mouth. Monsieur de Gohas also immediately after him came back from the fight to see me, saying, 'Take comfort Monsieur, and cheer up, upon my word we have sufficiently revenged you, for there is not one man left alive.'

He thereupon knew Monsieur de Gramont and saluted him, who after they had embraced, entreated him to carry him to the castle, which he did, where Monsieur de Gramont found the taking of it exceeding strange, saying he could never have believed this place had been near so strong, and that had I attacked Navarreins it would have been more easily taken. He would then needs see all the removes I had made of the cannon, which having seen, he said it had not been requisite that we should have omitted anything of the battery. About an hour after he returned, where he offered me a house of his hard by and all other things in his power, and has since told me that at that time, and in the condition he then saw me, he never thought I could have lived till the next day and believed he had taken his leave of me for ever. All that day and all that night I bled continually, and the next morning sent to entreat all the captains to come and see me, which they did.

Monluc's disablement at Rabastens was immediately followed by the conclusion of the Peace of St Germain (August 1570). Monluc was dismissed from the lieutenancy of Guienne and so was provided with the opportunity to write his memoirs, which he here concludes with some reflections on his long career in arms and with appeals to King Charles IX and to the Duke of Anjou, the future Henry III, for justice against his detractors

Behold here (fellows in arms) you who shall read my life, the end of the wars in which I have served five and fifty years together, that I had the honour to be in command for the kings my masters. From which services, that I might not forget them, I brought away seven arquebus shots for a memorandum, and several other wounds besides, there being not a limb in all my body that has escaped, my right arm only excepted. But I have by these wounds purchased a renown throughout Europe and my name is known in the remotest kingdom, which I esteem more than all the riches in the world; and by the grace of God, who has ever been assisting to me, I will carry this reputation along with me to my grave. This is a marvellous contentment to me when I think upon it and call to mind how I am step by step arrived to this degree of honour, and through so many dangers am come to enjoy the short repose that remains to me in this world, in the calm and privacy of my own house, that I may have leisure to ask God forgiveness for the sins I have committed.

Oh if his mercy was not infinitely great, in how dangerous a condition were all those that bear arms, especially that are in command; for the necessity of war forces us in despite of our own inclinations to commit a thousand mischiefs and to make no more account of the lives of men than of a chicken: to which the complaints and outcries of the people, whom we are constrained in despite of us every day to swallow up and devour, and the widows and the fatherless that we every day do make load us with all the curses and execrations misery and affliction can help them to invent, which by importuning the Almighty and daily imploring the assistance of the saints, 'tis to be feared lie some of them heavy upon our heads. But doubtless kings shall yet have a sadder account to make than we, for they make us commit those evils (as I told the King in discourse at Toulouse) and there is no mischief whereof they are not the cause; for seeing they will make wars, they should at least pay those who venture their lives to execute their passions, that they may not commit so many mischiefs as they do.

I think myself then exceedingly happy in that God has given me leisure to think of the sins I have committed, or rather that the necessity of war has enforced me to commit. For I am not naturally addicted to mischief; above all I have ever been an enemy to the vice of impurity and a sworn adversary to all disloyalty and treason.[1] I know very well and confess that my passion has made me say and do things for which I now cry '*Mea culpa*', but 'tis now too late to redress them, and I have one that lies heavier upon my heart than all the rest. But had I proceeded otherwise everyone would have flirted me on the nose, and the least consul of a village would have clapped to his gates against me had I not always had the cannon at my heels, for everyone had a mind to lord it. God knows how fit I was to endure such affronts, but all's done and past; my hand was ever as prompt as my tongue and it was but a word and a blow. I could have wished, could I have persuaded myself to it, never to have worn a sword by my side, but my nature was quite otherwise, which made me carry for my device '*Deo duce, ferro comite*'.[2]

One thing I can truly say of myself, that never any King's lieutenant had more commiseration of the ruin of the people than I in all places where ever I came. But it is impossible to discharge those commands without doing mischief, unless the King had his coffers crammed with

[1] A somewhat idealized view of his conduct, in the light of his secret dealings with Philip II: see Introduction, p. 7.

[2] 'With God leading, and a friendly sword.'

gold to pay his armies, and yet it would be much to do. I know not if those that succeed me will do better, but I do not believe it. All the Catholics of Guienne can witness, if I did not always spare the people; for I appeal from the Huguenots, I have done them too much mischief to give me any good testimony; and yet I have not done them enough, nor so much as I would. My good will was not wanting. Neither do I care for their speaking ill of me, for they will say as much or more of their kings.

But before I put an end to this book of mine, which my name will cause to be read by many, I shall desire all such as shall take the pains to read these *Commentaries* not to think me so ingrate that I do not acknowledge, after God, to hold all I have of estate and preferment of the kings my masters, especially of my good master King Henry, whom God absolve. And if I have in some places of my book said that wounds were the recompense of my service, it is not at all intended to reproach them with the blood I have lost in their quarrels. On the contrary I think the blood of my sons who died in their service very well employed. God gave them to me, and he took them from me. I have lost three in their service: Marc Anthony my eldest, Bertrand (to whom I gave the name of Peyrot—which is one of our Gascon names—by reason that Bertrand did not please me) and Fabien, Seigneur de Montesquieu.[1]

God gave me also three others. For of my second son I had Blaise, and of my youngest Adrian and Blaise, whom God preserve, that they may be serviceable to their kings and country, without dishonouring their race; that they may well study my book and so imitate my life, that, if possible, they may surpass their grandsire. And I beseech your Majesty[2] be mindful of them. I have left them, amongst my papers, the letter your Majesty was pleased to write to me from Vilecoustrets [Villers-Cotterets] dated the 3rd of December 1570, which contains these words: 'Assure yourself that I shall ever be mindful of your many and great services, for which if you shall in your own person fall short of a worthy recompense, your posterity shall reap the fruits of your merit; as also they are such and have so well behaved themselves in my service that they have of themselves very well deserved my acknowledgment, and that I should do for them what I shall be very ready to do whenever an opportunity shall present itself.' Sir, this

---

[1] Marc Anthony was killed before Ostia, near Rome, in 1556; Bertrand in 1566 on the island of Madeira; and Fabien at Nogaro, in Béarn, in 1573.

[2] Charles IX.

is your Majesty's promise, and a King should never say or promise anything but he will perform.

I do not then by any means reproach my masters; and I ought also to be satisfied, though I am not rich, that a poor cadet of Gascony is arrived at the highest dignities of the kingdom. I see several at this day who murmur and repine at their majesties, and for the most part those who have done little or nothing make the greatest complaints. In others who have really deserved something it is a little more pardonable; all that we have, of what degree soever we are, we hold it of the kings our masters. So many great princes, lords, captains, and soldiers, both living and dead, owe to the king the honours they have received, and their names shall live by the employments they have received from the kings they served, and were not only enterred with those honourable titles but have moreover honoured those who are descended of them, and mention will be made of their virtue whilst any records of honour remain in the world. I have listed a good number in my book and have myself had soldiers under my command, who have been no better in their extraction than the sons of poor labouring men, who have lived and died in a reputation as great and high as they had been the sons of lords, through their own virtue and the esteem the kings and their lieutenants had of them. When my son Marc Anthony was carried dead to Rome, the Pope and all the cardinals, the senate and all the people of Rome, paid as much honour to his hearse as if he had been a prince of the blood. And what was the cause of all this but only his own valour, my reputation, and my King, who had made me what I was? So that the name of Marc Anthony is again to be found in the Roman annals.[1]

When I first entered into arms out of my pageship in the House of Lorraine, there was no other discourse but of the great Gonsalvo, called the Great Captain.[2] How great an honour was it to him (which also will last for ever) to be crowned with so many victories? I have heard it told that King Lewis and King Ferdinand being together, I know not at what place but it was somewhere where they had appointed an interview,[3] these two great princes being sat at table together, our King entreated the King of Spain to give leave that Gonsalvo might

---

[1] His death was widely mourned. A Latin epitaph by George Buchanan, the great Scottish humanist and tutor of James VI and I, is reproduced in the 'Tombeau de Monluc' at the end of the first edition of the *Commentaries*.

[2] Gonsalvo de Cordoba (1443–1515), the renowned Spanish general.

[3] Louis XII met Ferdinand of Aragon at Savona, near Genoa, in 1507.

dine with them; which he accordingly did, whilst men of far greater quality than he stood waiting by. So considerable had the King his master's favour and his own valour made him. This was the honour he received from the King of France, who in recompense for his having deprived him of the kingdom of Naples put a weighty chain of gold about his neck. I have heard Monsieur de Lautrec say that he never took so much delight in looking upon any man as upon that same. O how fair an example is this for those who intend to advance themselves by arms! When I went the second time into Italy,[1] as I passed through the streets of Rome, everyone ran to the windows to see him that had defended Siena, which was a greater satisfaction to me than all the riches of the earth. I could produce several examples of Frenchmen, of very mean extraction, who have by arms arrived at very great preferments, but out of respect to their posterity I shall forbear, but it was the bounty of their kings that so advanced them for the recompense of their brave services.

It is then just that we confess we could be nothing without their bounty and favour; if we serve them, 'tis out of obedience to the commandment of God and we ought not to try to obtain rewards by importunities and reproaches. And if anyone be ill rewarded, the fault is not in our kings but in them who are about them that do not acquaint them who have served well or ill (for there are many of both sorts), to the end that his Majesty's largesse should be rightly placed. And there is nothing that goes so much to the heart of a brave and loyal subject as to see the King heap honours and rewards upon such as have served him ill. I am sure it is that that has vexed me more than any disappointment of my own. I have often heard some men say, the King or the Queen have done this and that for such a one, why should they not do as much for me? The King has pardoned such a one such an offence, why does he not also pardon me? I know also that their Majesties have said, 'They will no more commit such oversights, we must wink at this one fault,' but it was the next day to begin the same again.

However a man ought never to be vexed with his prince. The honour of such men lies in a very contemptible place, since they more value a reward or a benefit than their own reputation or renown, and are so ready to take snuff if they fail of their expectation. And moreover (as I have already said) they are commonly men that have never struck three strokes with a sword and yet will vapour what dangers

[1] In September 1556.

they have passed and what hardships they have endured. If a man should strip them naked, one might see many a proper fellow that has not so much as one scar in all his body. Such men, if they have borne arms any while, are very fortunate, and at the Day of Judgment if they go into Paradise, will carry all their blood along with them without having lost one dram of their own or having shed one drop of any other's here upon earth.

Since I have spoken of others, I will now say something of myself. Some perhaps after I am dead will talk of me as I talk of others. I confess that I am very much obliged to the kings I have served, especially to Henry my good master, as I have often said before: and I had now been no more than a private gentleman, had it not been for their bounty and the opportunities they gave me to acquire that reputation I have in the world, which I value above all the treasure the earth contains, having immortalized the name of Monluc. And although during the long time that I have borne arms, I have acquired but very little wealth, yet has no-one ever heard me complain of the kings my masters. Marry, I have spoken loudly of those about them when in these late troubles I was calumniated by them, as if I could have done all things with nothing. Believe me the wounds I have received have administered more comfort than affliction to me, and one thing I am sure of, that when I am dead they can hardly say that at the Resurrection I shall carry all the blood, bones and veins I brought with me into the world from my mother's womb along with me into Paradise. As for riches I have enough.

I do really believe that there is never a little pedlar in the world who, having trotted, run and moiled as I have done, but would have enriched himself to a merchant. And there is never a treasurer nor a receiver (let him be as honest as he would) in the kingdom that had had so much money pass through his hands as has done through mine, but more would have stuck to his fingers. I have been seven or eight times captain of foot, which is none of the worst commands for getting of money; and I have known several captains in my time who have enriched themselves merely out of their soldiers' pay. I was not so ignorant nor so raw a soldier, neither did I want dexterity, but that I could have done the feat as well as they; neither was it any such hard matter to learn, for with a good quarter-master and some few other little helps the business had been done. I have since been three times camp-master, in which employment God knows I might have had skip-jacks enough to have made muster and intelligence enough with the commissaries.[1] I could have discovered when anything was to be got as soon or sooner than any man in the army, I had nose good enough. I was after governor of a place where I could have had four-score or a hundred men at my devotion to have passed muster, as *messieurs les gouverneurs* know well how to do. By which means, having been so long in these commands as I have been and made so many musters as I have done in my life, with a little good husbandry, Good God! What a mountain of gold might I have had! I never think of it but it makes me wonder at my own honesty that could resist so many temptations.

I was moreover the King's lieutenant in Siena, and another time at Montalcino; where I had ways enough to have lined my pockets as others in the like commands have done; for it had been no more but to have had intelligence with three or four merchants who should have affirmed that the corn of the garrison had been bought by them and taken up upon their credit, and it had been done. God knows what profits are made of these magazines! I could then have made demands upon the account of borrowing, and have deputed some who would have been ready to have taken the employment upon them, to have brought in a hundred or two hundred thousand francs in debentures. But instead of this his Majesty owed us five pays when we came out of Siena, whereof I found means to acquit him of three so soon as we came to Montalcino.

I have been his Majesty's lieutenant in this province of Guienne and have been much up and down abroad in the world, but never saw any country equal to it, either in riches or convenience of living. And having such an employment, I could have had intelligence with the receiver of the province (those kind of men desire no better) and have stuffed my own coffers; for what upon musters, garrisons, and equipages of the artillery, I could have made infinite advantages. How many impositions might I have laid upon the country? For the King had given me power to do it, which would have turned to my particular benefit. For although his Majesty in that commission doubt-less intended those levies for his own service, I could, if I would have

[1] It was common practice at the time to pass non-soldiers—*passe-volants*—in the musters and so pocket a proportion of the pay earmarked for the soldiery on the basis of the muster rolls.

put the charge upon him, have converted a great part of them to my own proper use. I could if I would have fired towns and have sent a Will o' the wisp up and down to the towns and villages to whisper the principal inhabitants in the ear, that they must either give me money to free them, or that otherwise I would cause them to be undone and come quarter soldiers upon them who should eat them to the very bones; for they know men of our trade are seldom weary of ill doing. I could also have sent to tell the Huguenots, who lived at home under the protection of the edict, that unless they greased me in the fist, I would cause them all to be ruined and pulled in pieces, and what would they not have given me to have secured their lives and estates? For they did not greatly confide in me, hearing how I had handled them before. But instead of making use of such artifices of these to enrich myself, I let the captains and *gendarmes* and others who served the King, and asked it of me, take all, reserving very little or nothing to my own benefit. And even that which I had at Clairac I took by the King's permission. Let others therefore rest content.

If God would please to let me be once cured of this great arquebus shot in the face, I think yet that should the war break out again I should be one to mount to horse; and I think it is not far off, for so long as there are two religions, France will evermore be in division and trouble. It cannot otherwise be, and the worst on't is, 'tis a war that will not be ended of a long time. Other quarrels are easily composed, but that for religion has no end. And although the martial sort of men are not very devout, they however side, and being once engaged stick to their party. In the posture that affairs now stand, I do not think we are at an end. However, I have this satisfaction in myself, that I have to my utmost opposed it and done my best endeavour to settle the peace of the kingdom. Would to God that all those who have been in command had connived no more than I. But we must let God work his own will. After he has sufficiently scourged us for our sins he will burn the rod.

And now, you lords and captains, who shall do me the honour to read my book, let me beseech you not to read it with prejudice but believe that I have delivered the truth, without depriving anyone of his due and merited honour. I make no question but that some will bring some things that I have here related into dispute to see if they can catch me tripping in point of truth; forasmuch as they will find that God has never more accompanied the fortune of any man, for the employments I have gone through than he did mine. But let me assure such, that I have omitted an infinite number of passages and particularities by reason that I never committed anything to writing nor ever kept any memorial, as never suspecting myself to become a writer of books. I ever thought myself unfit for that employment, but in the time of my last hurt and during my sicknesses I have dictated this that I leave you; to the end that my name may not be buried in oblivion, nor so many other gallant men whom I have seen perform so many and so brave exploits. For the historians write only of kings and princes. How many brave gentlemen have I here set down of whom these people make no mention, no more than if they had never been? He who has writ the battle of Cérisoles, though he does name me, yet it is but slightly and *in transitu* only;[1] and yet I can honestly boast that I had a good hand in that victory, as also at Boulogne and Thionville. Which they take no notice of at all, no more than of the valour and gallant behaviour of a great number of your fathers and kindred whose names you will find here.

Fellows in arms, how many and how great things shall you perform if you put your whole trust in God and set honour continually before your eyes; discoursing with yourselves that if it be determined you shall end your days in a breach 'tis to much purpose to stay behind in the graffe. '*Un bel morir*' (says the Italian) '*tuta la vita honora.*'[2] 'Tis to die like a beast for a man to leave no memory behind him. Never go about to deprive another man of his honour, nor ever set avarice and ambition in your prospect; for you will find that it will all come to nought and end in misery and disgrace. I do not say this that I have any mind to play the preacher, but merely out of respect to truth. How many are there in the world who are yet living and whom I shall forbear to name, that have had the reputation of valiant men and yet have been very unfortunate in their undertakings? Believe me the hand of God was in this, and though they might implore his divine aid, their devotion was not right, which made the Almighty adverse to them.

If therefore you would have God to be assisting to you, you must strip yourselves of ambition, avarice, and rancour, and be full of the love and loyalty we all owe to our prince. And in so doing although his quarrel should not be just, God will not for all that withdraw his assistance from you; for it is not for us to ask our King if his cause

---

[1] A reference to the *Memoirs* of du Bellay.
[2] 'A brave death illustrates a man's whole life.' Cotton's note.

be good or evil, but only to obey him. And if you are not rewarded for the services you have performed, you will not be grieved at your being neglected, by reason it was not your intention nor design to fight upon the score of ambition and greatness, nor out of a thirst of riches; but upon the account of fidelity and duty that God has commanded you to bear to your prince and sovereign. You will rejoice to find yourselves esteemed and beloved by all the world, which is the greatest treasure a man of honour ought to covet. For great estates and high titles perish with the body, but a good reputation and renown are immortal as the soul. I now see myself drawing towards my end and languishing in my bed towards my dissolution, and 'tis a great consolation to me that in spite of death my name shall live and flourish, not only in Gascony but moreover in foreign nations.

This then is the end of my book, and of thus far of my life, which if God shall please longer to continue to me, some other may write the rest, if ever I shall again be in place, where I shall perform anything worthy of myself; which nevertheless I do not hope for, finding myself so infinitely decayed that I never again expect to be able to bear arms. I have however this obligation to the arquebus shot, which has pierced through and shattered my face, that it has been the occasion of writing these *Commentaries*, which I have an opinion will continue when I am dead and gone. I entreat all those who shall read them, not to look upon them as proceeding from the pen of an historian, but of an old soldier and a Gascon, who has writ his own life truly and in the rough style of a soldier. All such as bear arms may take example by it and acknowledge that from God alone proceed the successes or the misfortunes of men. And seeing we ought to have recourse to him alone, let us beseech him to assist and advise us in all our afflictions, for in this world there is nothing else, of which the great ones have their share as well as the meanest of us all. Wherein he manifesteth his own greatness, in that neither King nor prince are exempted from his correcting hand, and who stand not continually in need of him and his divine assistance.

Do not disdain, you who desire to follow arms, instead of reading *Amadis de Gaule* and *Launcelot du Lake*,[1] to spend sometimes an hour in reading what I have done, and in taking notice of what I have been, in this treatise that I leave behind me. By which means you shall learn to know yourselves and betimes to form yourselves to be soldiers and captains; for you must first learn to obey that you may afterwards

[1] Romantic tales of chivalry, popular in the sixteenth century.

know how to command. This is not for silk-worms and spruce courtiers to do, nor for those that are in love with their ease, but for such as by the ways of virtue and at the price of their lives will endeavour to immortalize their names, as I hope, in despite of envy, I have done that of Monluc.

Appendix I
Biographical notes

ALBON, JACQUES D', SIEUR DE ST ANDRÉ (*c.* 1512–1562). One of the chief Councillors, as he was a long-standing favourite, of Henry II, becoming Marshal of France in 1547 and Ambassador to England in 1551. He served with d'Enghien (*q.v.*) in the Piedmont campaigns of 1543–44, and was taken prisoner at the defeat of St Quentin in 1557. He was one of the authors of the Peace of Cateau-Cambrésis, 1559. As with Montmorency, his position was endangered by the death of Henry II, but he allied with the Guises and Montmorency to form the *Triumvirs*, to protect Catholic interests against the Protestants dominant at court in 1561. He was killed at the battle of Dreux, 1562. His interests and abilities were mainly in the military sphere, and he was on the whole friendly to Monluc, supporting his nomination as Governor of Siena in 1554.

ALBRET, JEANNE D', QUEEN OF NAVARRE (1528–1572). Only daughter and heiress of Henry II of Navarre and Margaret d'Angoulême, sister of Francis I, she married Antoine de Bourbon (*q.v.*) in 1548; their son was Henry of Navarre, later Henry IV. She and—for a time—her husband acted as the patrons of the Reformed churches in Béarn and Gascony after 1560. Monluc attempted to gain their friendship, but failed. She was outraged by his high-handed conduct in Guienne as royal Lieutenant and intrigued against him. She consented to the marriage of her son Henry to Margaret of Valois, sister of the King, Charles IX, in 1572.

ANNEBAUT, CLAUDE D', BARON DE RETZ (d. 1552). Military commander and chief minister of Francis I. He was created Marshal of France, 1538, Governor in Piedmont, 1539, in which capacity he successfully defended Turin against the Imperialists, and Admiral in 1544. He led the abortive descent on England in the following year. Monluc fought alongside d'Annebaut at the siege of Perpignan, 1542. He was accounted brave and honest, but was not a capable general.

AVALOS, ALFONSO D', MARQUIS DEL VASTO (1502–1546). Castilian gentleman and Imperialist commander, sometime Governor of

Milan. He aided in the conversion of Andrea Doria to the Emperor in 1528, and was Lieutenant General of the armies of Charles V which opposed the French forces under d'Enghien in Piedmont in 1543. He was defeated and wounded at the battle of Cérisoles in the year following. Monluc considered him a wily politician as well as an able commander.

BOURBON, ANTOINE DE, KING OF NAVARRE (1518–1562). The nephew of the Constable Bourbon, who had rebelled against Francis I, and brother of Louis, Prince of Condé, the Huguenot leader, Bourbon was first prince of the blood. He helped to recover the position of his family, weakened by the Constable's disgrace, by his marriage to the heiress of the kingdom of Navarre, Jeanne (*q.v.*). He fought in Picardy and Piedmont, gaining a reputation as 'a brave soldier and an incapable commander'. He was a more uncertain convert to the Huguenot cause than his forceful wife. He became Lieutenant General of France in 1560, and sided with the Catholic *Triumvirs* in 1562. He was killed besieging the Huguenot garrison of Rouen.

BOURBON-VENDÔME, FRANÇOIS DE, COMTE D'ENGHIEN (1519–1546). Younger brother of the above, he was appointed to the command of the French armies in Piedmont at the age of twenty-four, and won the crushing victory of Cérisoles in April 1544. He was killed at La Roche-Guyon two years later. Although he possessed, according to Monluc, 'an infinite number of shining 'qualities' [90], he showed himself hesitant, inexperienced and ill-advised for much of the Cérisoles campaign.

COLIGNY, GASPARD DE, SEIGNEUR DE CHÂTILLON (1519–1572). Soldier, and head of one of the great houses of France, he was a prominent convert to the Huguenot cause. He served under d'Enghien in Piedmont, 1544, and—like Monluc—was knighted at Cérisoles. Made Admiral of France in 1552, he defended St Quentin in 1557. In the civil wars he fought alongside Condé, and was defeated at Moncontour (1569). He was assassinated in the massacre of St Bartholomew.

COSSÉ, CHARLES DE, COMTE DE BRISSAC (*c.* 1505–1564). Took part, as did Monluc, in the ill-fated expedition to Naples in 1528, and was commander in Roussillon in 1542, where Monluc served under him. He became the protégé of the King's mistress, Diane de Poitiers; in 1547 he was named Grand Master of the Artillery on the fall of Taix (*q.v.*), and in 1550 Marshal of France. General in

Piedmont from that year, he employed Monluc on several missions, wished the King to reward him, and was reluctant to release him for Siena. Brissac established in Piedmont, said Monluc, 'the best school of war in Europe' [132]. One of his last successes was the recapture of Le Havre from the English in 1563.

COUCYS, CHARLES DE, SIEUR DE BURIE (1492–1565). Gentleman of the Chamber in the royal household and courtier, he had some military experience before his appointment as Lieutenant of Guienne, 1543, a post he occupied till his death. He was aged, dilatory and timorous when Monluc was added to the lieutenancy in order to strengthen the crown in the province. His proceedings against the Huguenots after 1559 were half-hearted, and he was suspected of leanings towards their cause. His death gave Monluc more complete power than formerly.

FOIX, ODET DE, VICOMTE DE LAUTREC (c. 1481–1528). Of a famous military family whose territory lay on the borders of Spain, brother of Lescun. Marshal of France, 1511, and Governor of Guienne, 1515, he was appointed Governor of the Duchy of Milan from 1516 and defended it until his defeat at Bicocca in 1522. He commanded the forces opposing the Spanish invasion around Bayonne, 1523, where Monluc saw action. He led the expedition to Naples, 1527–28, which ended in disaster and his own death. Monluc respected his generalship, and the loss of his patronage was a blow to Monluc's chance of advancement.

LA BARTHE, PAUL DE, SIEUR DE THERMES (1482–1562). French commander in Piedmont and Picardy. He was Governor of Savigliano in 1543 when Monluc joined him there for the relief of Mondovi, and he shared in some of Monluc's exploits. He was in command of a major part of the French cavalry at the battle of Cérisoles. He defended Parma against the Imperialists in 1550, aided the Sienese in their rebellion, and seconded Strozzi (q.v.) in Tuscany (1553). He was created Marshal of France in 1558, the year of his great defeat at the hands of Egmont at Gravelines.

LORRAINE, FRANÇOIS DE, SECOND DUKE OF GUISE (1519–1563). Nephew of Antoine, Duke of Lorraine, he represented the powerful Guise interest at court. He patronized Monluc, whom he had observed on the campaign in Picardy in 1544–45, and pressed the King to send Monluc to Siena, and later to appoint him Colonel-General of Infantry. Guise made his military reputation with the defence of Metz against Charles V, 1552–53; then consolidated it with the capture of Calais from the English in 1558. He asked Monluc to join him for the siege of Thionville which followed. The Guise party gained predominance under Francis II, husband of their kinswoman, Mary Queen of Scots, but lost it on his death. They recovered influence when the Duke, one of the *Triumvirs*, perpetrated the massacre of Vassy and marched on Paris, 1562. He was assassinated in the following year as he was besieging the Huguenot stronghold of Orléans.

MEDICI, GIANJACOMO, MARQUIS OF MARIGNANO (1498–1555). Brother of Pope Pius IV. An Italian *condottiere*, in the service of Charles V from 1528. He held high command in the Imperialist armies at the siege of Luxembourg, 1543, and at Metz, 1552. He commanded the forces which besieged Siena, held by Monluc, in 1554–55, defeating Strozzi at Marciano and eventually compelling the surrender of the city in April 1555. He had a high regard for Monluc's generalship of the defence. He died at Milan later in the same year.

MONLUC, JEAN DE, BISHOP OF VALENCE (*c.* 1500–1579). Diplomat and churchman, brother of Blaise, he was employed by Francis I to negotiate an alliance with the Algerian corsair, Barbarossa II, and with the Sultan Suleiman himself, in 1536. Turkish aid was to be of notable assistance to the French thereafter. Monluc was also successful in reconciling Venice to the policies Francis was pursuing (1542), and he became well-known for his powers of oratory and his mastery of languages. He served Pope Paul III, and became Bishop of Valence in 1553. He was an important moderating influence at the Colloquy of Poissy, 1561, and was suspected of leanings to the Huguenots. Condemned by the Inquisition at Rome, he was protected by Catherine de Medici. He was Ambassador to Poland in 1572 and negotiated the offer of the Polish crown to the Duke of Anjou, later Henry III.

MONTMORENCY, ANNE DE, CONSTABLE OF FRANCE (1493–1567). Head of a family of great influence, he won fame at Marignano, Bicocca and Pavia. He became Constable in 1538, but was banished the court in 1541 as leader of the peace party. Henry II restored him to favour, and his opposition to the advancement of Monluc— identified with Guise and the war party—was of great importance to the latter's career for over ten years. In 1552 he led the army which took the Lorraine bishoprics; he was defeated and captured at St Quentin in 1557. He was much criticized for his part in the

Peace of Cateau-Cambrésis. A *Triumvir* in 1561, he took a prominent part in the civil wars; he was captured at Dreux and was mortally wounded at St Denis, 1567.

MONTMORENCY, HENRY DE, MARQUIS OF DAMVILLE (1534–1614). The younger son of the Constable, Anne de Montmorency, he was appointed the Governor of Languedoc in 1563, where he quarrelled with Monluc, then Lieutenant of Guienne, and contributed to his fall. He was made Marshal of France in 1566, and helped to create a strong faction in his support in southern France. He sided with the later Henry IV in the War of the Three Henries, and was created Constable of France in 1593.

STROZZI, PIETRO (1510–1558). Florentine *condottiere*, who came of a well-known banking family of great wealth. He was a cousin of Catherine de Medici, and an implacable enemy of Cosimo de Medici, Duke of Florence. He was active in the service of France, first in Italy, then, after 1541, in France itself, and became Chamberlain to the King. He took part in the siege of Luxembourg, 1543, was appointed Colonel-General of the Infantry, 1547, then General of the Galleys. He was in command of the army sent to relieve Siena, and suffered defeat at Marciano in 1554. He was killed by a musket shot at the siege of Thionville. Monluc recognized him as one of his masters in the art of war.

TAIX, JEAN DE (*d.* 1553). Courtier and soldier, he was sent as Ambassador to England in 1538, and in 1543 was named Colonel-General of French Infantry in succession to Brissac. He commanded in Piedmont and Picardy (1544), and promoted Monluc, who had served him well: he was the latter's commander at the battle of Cérisoles. He became Governor of Loches, 1546, Captain of *Gendarmes*, and was appointed Grand Master of the Artillery, 1547; but was shortly afterwards displaced by Brissac in a court intrigue. Monluc uses Taix's fall as an example of the evil influence of women at court. He was mortally wounded at the siege of Hesdin in 1553.

Appendix II
Glossary of Military Terms

AMBUSCADO—ambush

ARQUEBUS—the earliest form of personal firearm, shorter and lighter than the later musket, and in use for most of Monluc's career

BASTION—the projecting part of a fortified line, usually with two faces and two flanks

BATTALION—not, as today, a division of a regiment (both units were unknown at this period) but a large body of foot, 4,000–5,000 strong, commanded by a colonel

BATTLE—the centre body of any army drawn up in order of battle (in battalia); the main section of any force

BAVIN OR FASCINE—a faggot or cylindrical bundle of brushwood, used in defensive works and also to fill up the ditch in an attack

CANNON, DEMI-CANNON, CULVERIN—types of artillery, large, medium and medium long-range

CAMISADO—a sortie or surprise assault, usually made at night when the attackers covered their armour with dark shirts or camisades

CASEMATE—a vaulted chamber built in the thickness of the ramparts of a fortress, with embrasures for its defence

CORSLET—piece of armour covering the body; soldier so armed

COURT OF GUARD—sentry post; guard position or guardroom

COUNTERSCARP—the outer wall or slope of the ditch, which supports the covered way; often extended, as in the *Commentaries*, to include the covered way and the glacis

COVERED WAY—the platform running round the outer rim of the ditch, usually defended by a palisade and commanding the approach up the glacis

CURTAIN—the plain wall of a fortified place

FALCHION—a broad sword with curving blade; a sword of any kind

GABION—a basket, often 6 ft high and 4 ft wide, filled with earth and used to form temporary parapets, particularly in gun emplacements; gabionade—a parapet so formed

GLACIS—the parapet of the covered way, normally constructed as a gently sloping bank to the field beyond

GRAFFE—a trench serving as a fortification; a dry or wet ditch; a foss or moat

LINSTOCK—a gunner's forked stick, used to hold the lighted match

MANTELET—a large wooden protective shield, carried upright on two wheels, which pioneers used to protect themselves from enemy fire

MORION—open helmet, without beaver or visor but with a strong comb

PALISADE—line of defence, consisting of large wooden stakes

PLACE OF ARMS—besiegers' trench, built at right angles to their lines of approach to the defenders' fortification, for the defence of those lines and for assembling troops; early form of parallel

RAMPIRE—rampart, mound of earth raised for the defence of a place

RAVELIN—a small triangular work beyond the main line of fortification

RETIRADE—retrenchment made behind the main line; any new fortification behind an old work

SCALADO—escalade; the scaling of a fortified place, using ladders

SENTINELS PERDUE—sentries or scouts placed in a forward and concealed position

TARGET—a light round shield or buckler

TRAVERSE—parapets of earth raised at intervals across the covered way of a fortress to prevent its being enfiladed

Index

Page numbers printed in bold type refer to Appendix I, Biographical Notes, in the case of persons, or Appendix II, Glossary, in the case of military terms.

Girard, lieutenant to Prevost d'Hôtel, 204

Gohas, Monsieur de, 216, 219, 220, 221, 222–3

Gondrin, Monsieur de, 215

Gonzaga, Signor Carlo, 114

Gouffier, Claude, Sieur de Boisy, 91

Gourgues, General de, 213

Gramont, Antoine d' Aure, Sieur de, 221, 222–3

Gramont, Jean II, Baron de, 39, 40, 42, 44, 45, 52, 54

Granuchin, merchant of Barge, 71–6, 78–9

Gravelines, battle of (1558), 29, 236

Grenade (Gascony), 203

Grisons, 49

Gruyériens, at Cérisoles, 93, 109, 110, 111, 113

Guasco, Christophe, 61, 69

Guienne, 7, 8, 24; growth of Huguenotism in, 201, 202, 203, 204, 209–10, 212

Guillet, the King's receiver, 210

Guines (near Boulogne), 175

Guise family and interest, 1, 5, 6, 8, 195, 202, 234, 236, 237; Duke of, see Lorraine, François de

Guitart, Pierre, Sieur de Taurines, 99

Hardelot (near Boulogne), 131

Henry VIII, King of England, 2, 4, 48, 127; allies with Emperor, 90, 91, 96, 116, 117–18; before Boulogne (1544), 4, 28, 117, 118; leaves Boulogne 118; surrenders Boulogne, 131; death of, 28, 131

Henry II, King of France, 10, 13, 136, 147, 153, 164, 166, 170, 173, 186, 193, 213, 225, 228, 234, 237; when Dauphin, favours Monluc, 5, 132; at interview between Monluc and Francis I, 91–4, 96; at Boulogne, 118, 120, 121, 125–7; accession of,

131, 132; incites revolt in Siena, 132; chooses governor of Siena, 134–5; defends Monluc, 136–8; criticism of, 167; sends Monluc to Metz, 175–6; commends Monluc on capture of Thionville, 194–5; reviews army at Pierrepont, 195, 196, 197–98; death of, 6, 29, 199, 219, 234

Henry III, King of France, 9, 11, 223, 237; accession of, 29

Henry IV, King of France (Henry of Navarre), 13, 70, 234, 235, 238

Huguenotism, 15, 17, 175, 225, 230, 237; growth of, 6, 23, 29, 199, 200, 201; at La Plume, 201; at Marmande, 203; and Colloquy of Poissy, 204; in Guienne, 209–10; at La Rochelle, 8, 17, 210, 213–14; in Rouen, 235; in Orléans, 237; suppression of, 7–8, 20, 236; massacres of, 203; execution at St Mézard, 206–8; in Béarn, 219

Ivrée (Piedmont), 93, 116

Janin, Corporal, 76, 77, 79

Janot, of Bazordan, 79

Jarnac, Baron de, 211

Jarnac, battle of (1569), 29

Jean Philippe, Count of Rheingau, 120, 121

John William, Duke of Saxony, 195, 196, 197, 198

Labardac, Captain, 83

La Bastide, Captain, 53, 54, 220

La Barrelle, Huguenot minister, 205–6

La Barthe, Paul de, Sieur de Thermes, 94, 156, **236**; joined by Monluc in Piedmont (1543), 71–4, 76, 84, 85, 87–8, 91; in command of cavalry at Cérisoles, 101, 103,